Drawing on detailed legal evidence, highly readable personal case studies and a range of research, Sonia Allan has produced a compelling account of the need for donor conception to shed its stigma and secrecy by opening up its records to the thousands of donor offspring already born and yet to be born.

– Dr Marilyn Crawshaw, Honorary Fellow (formerly Senior Lecturer)
University of York, UK

Sonia Allan has written an important book that sensitively – and globally – approaches the secrecy surrounding donor conception. Based on a thorough discussion of the social, legal, ethical, and moral issues around donor anonymity, *Donor Conception* persuasively argues for the need to give donor-conceived children the right to access information about their biological origins.

– Professor Naomi Cahn, Harold H. Greene
Chair, GWU Law School

Donor Conception and the Search for Information

This book examines donor conception and the search for information by donor-conceived people. It details differing regulatory approaches across the globe, including those that provide for 'open-identity' or anonymous donation, or that take a 'dual-track' approach. In doing so, it identifies models regarding the recording and release of information about donors that may assist in the further development of the law, policy and associated practices. Arguments for and against donor anonymity are considered, and specifically critiqued. The study highlights contrasting reasoning and emphasis upon various interests and factors that may underpin secrecy, anonymity or openness. The book will be of value to academics, students and legal practitioners involved with this area. It is also relevant to policy makers, health practitioners and anyone with an interest in the subject.

Sonia Allan is Associate Professor of health law at Macquarie University, and Head of Department of Health Systems and Populations. She has been a legal academic for over a decade, and has worked in both legal and health contexts. Sonia has published nationally and internationally. She was a Melbourne University Research Scholarship recipient for the duration of her PhD; a 2011 Churchill Fellow for her contribution to Australian society through her international and comparative research into donor conception; a 2011 'Global Health Law Fellow' at Georgetown University Law Center, Washington DC; and received an AMP Tomorrow Fund Grant in 2014. Sonia has, throughout her career, also been active in community outreach and influential in law reform. She has participated in numerous Australian state and federal inquiries on assisted reproduction, as well as inquiries abroad. She has been cited extensively in resulting reports; instrumental in changing laws related to access to information by donor conceived people; and continues to be called upon to consult or comment on issues related to the development of the law.

Biomedical Law and Ethics Library
Series Editor: Sheila A.M. McLean

Scientific and clinical advances, social and political developments and the impact of health care on our lives raise profound ethical and legal questions. Medical law and ethics have become central to our understanding of these problems and are important tools for the analysis and resolution of problems – real or imagined.

In this series, scholars at the forefront of biomedical law and ethics contribute to the debates in this area, with accessible, thought-provoking and sometimes controversial ideas. Each book in the series develops an independent hypothesis and argues cogently for a particular position. One of the major contributions of this series is the extent to which both law and ethics are utilized in the content of the books, and the shape of the series itself.

The books in this series are analytical, with a key target audience of lawyers, doctors, nurses and the intelligent lay public.

Available titles:

The Ethical and Legal Consequences of Posthumous Reproduction
Arrogance, Avarice and Anguish
Browne Lewis

Forthcoming titles include:

The Umbilical Cord Blood Controversies in Medical Law
Karen Devine

Revisiting Landmark Cases in Medical Law
Shaun D. Pattinson

Medical Law-Making and the Role of the Scientific Expert
The Case of ART in Comparative Perspective
Simone Penasa

About the Series Editor
Professor Sheila A.M. McLean is Professor Emerita of Law and Ethics in Medicine, School of Law, University of Glasgow, UK.

Donor Conception and the Search for Information

From secrecy and anonymity to openness

Sonia Allan

Routledge
Taylor & Francis Group
LONDON AND NEW YORK

First published 2017
by Routledge

2 Park Square, Milton Park, Abingdon, Oxfordshire OX14 4RN
711 Third Avenue, New York, NY 10017

Routledge is an imprint of the Taylor & Francis Group, an informa business

First issued in paperback 2018

British Library Cataloguing in Publication Data
A catalogue record for this book is available from the British Library

Library of Congress Cataloging-in-Publication Data
A catalog record for this title has been requested

ISBN: 978-1-4094-4639-2 (hbk)
ISBN: 978-1-138-36349-6 (pbk)

Typeset in Galliard
by Apex CoVantage, LLC

The family the soul wants is a felt network of relationship, an evocation of a certain kind of interconnection that grounds, roots, and nestles.

– Thomas Moore, 1994

This book is dedicated to Mahalia Rose and Gabriel Jackson,
may you be enriched by knowledge and experiences,
and follow in the footsteps of people who do good things!
And
to all the people who have made this book possible,
I thank you.

Contents

Preface

In 2003, I met a young donor-conceived girl, called Narelle Grech, who was searching for information about her donor. I was working at the time for the Victorian Law Reform Commission, on a reference on *access* to assisted reproduction, surrogacy, legal parentage and adoption. The reference's focus was primarily on the adults who wanted treatment, and not particularly on the children born as a result, like Narelle. The reference did, however, consider some aspects of the search by donor-conceived people for information, and did lead to a significant change of the law requiring that donor-conceived people be notified via an addendum to their birth certificates about their status. It was a sign of things to come in that state which has always led the way in terms of recognizing the rights of donor-conceived people to access information about their heritage.

Over the following years, I watched as Narelle, and others like her, pleaded for information. They appeared in newspapers, they spoke to politicians, and they joined and led the growing number of donor-conceived voices around the world calling for information. They knocked on the doors of the doctors who created them – often only to be turned away. I also found that others came forward to ask me for help – my students, my friends, other people I met, they too were donor conceived. I realized that we are all touched by donor conception, whether or not we realize we are.

I asked questions, I conducted research, I listened and over time I came to understand the reasons for their search. I also came to see a great injustice and felt compelled to help. I examined laws, regulations and practices that support donors, recipient parents and donor-conceived people in exchanging information and compared them to regimes that maintain anonymity. I watched as donors came forward, meetings occurred and joy was found. I also witnessed continued searching, loss and death through hereditable diseases that could have been prevented if only information had been known.

This book provides all of the information I have learned over more than a decade of research, writing and advocacy. It delves into the history of donor conception, explains the reasons people search, examines the arguments for and against information release, considers regulatory systems and practices and tells the story of those who search. I hope it will inform people and ultimately assist in ending donor anonymity.

To that end, I have no qualms in stating strongly that this is my view. Being in touch now with hundreds of donor-conceived people, donors and recipients, all of whom call for information release around the world, I am convinced that practices that maintain donor anonymity and therefore deny people fundamental rights of knowledge about their genetic heritage, about who they are and where they come from must end. Likewise, the law should not support, or perpetuate, inequity amongst people who have a right to such information. The rights and interests of people born because of donor conception must be paramount. The time has come for significant change.

–Sonia Allan

Acknowledgements

I acknowledge all of the donor-conceived people, recipient parents and donors who have shared their stories with me over time. I pay particular thanks to Damian Adams, Lauren Burns, Kim Buck, Sarah Dingle, Narelle Grech, Ross Hunter, Caroline Lorbach, Ian Smith, Ray Tonna, Kimberley Turner, Myfanwy Walker and Michael Williams, all of whom have played integral roles in the development of my understanding of the issues that surround donor conception. I also thank the people and organizations who have supported my work and my research. In particular, I thank the Churchill Trust for awarding me a fellowship which enabled me to travel to all countries that release information to donor-conceived people and to closely study their laws and practices. I am grateful to all of the people who met with me on that trip and have spoken or corresponded with me since in this regard.

I am also grateful to Melbourne University Law School, Deakin University School of Law, Georgetown Law and Macquarie University, all of which have been my academic homes while conducting this work. The numerous reviewers that have provided useful comments on my work over time, and other professionals (of which there are too many to individually name) who have provided insight into their work and knowledge, also clearly deserve my thanks.

Finally, but not least, this ongoing journey has been enriched by the presence of my children, Mahalia Rose and Gabriel Jackson, who have travelled all over with me meeting people who do really good things, and who have watched, as they themselves have grown, the inspirational actions of others that can lead, and have led, to positive change.

Foreword

In the course of contemplating what he so evocatively called the 'genes of the soul', Amin Maalouf wrote: 'A person's identity is like a pattern drawn on a tightly stretched parchment. Touch just one part of it, just one allegiance, and the whole person will react, the whole drum will sound.'[1]

Who we are and who we feel ourselves to be are fragile products of a number of factors, including our perceptions of the relationship we have with our forebears and others to whom we are related. The parchment of each one of us is tightly stretched and can easily be damaged. In short, genetic relatedness matters in many ways. Distress and image-confusion frequently attend the discovery of donor-conceived status; this outcome can be exacerbated by an inability to gain access to knowledge about the identity of the donor or donors. A profound sense of decontextualization and not belonging can afflict those who for one reason or another cannot be informed of matters such as their genetic heritage and whether they have siblings. We have long been aware of this phenomenon in relation to those who have been adopted or otherwise displaced from those to whom they are biologically related. As Justice Frankel in *Pratten v. British Columbia (Attorney General)* (2012) 357 DLR (4th) 660 observed of Olivia Pratten: she 'knows almost nothing about her biological father and feels that part of her identity is missing'. Whether the issue is usefully termed 'genealogical bewilderment'[2] or it is helpful to pathologize it by referring to a term such as 'AID child syndrome', analogizing from Kirschner's dubious 'Adopted Child Syndrome'[3], is not important. What is of consequence is the existential gap that is left for many donor-conceived people by the absence of knowledge about their donor parent(s).

As Allan chronicles in these pages, the reasons for secrecy in respect of donor identity have arisen from a variety of sources, including religion, culture and social stigma. The association of donor insemination with eugenics and infertility,

1 Amin Maalouf, *On Identity* (Random House, New York, 2011), p 3.

2 See Kimberly Leighton, 'Geneticizing the Right to Know' in Francoise Baylis and Carolyn McLeod (eds), *Family-Making: Contemporary Ethical Challenges* (OUP, New York, 2014), p 257.

3 See D. Kirschner, 'The Adopted Child Syndrome' (1990) 8(3) *Psychotherapy in Private Practice* 90.

the latter all too readily experienced as the fault of those unable to bear children, has had a significant influence on unpreparedness to lift the veil on assisted reproductive techniques and to enable children born because of them to learn of their biological heritage. Penetrating this veil of silence has proved challenging in many countries.

In addition, there has been a desire to avoid deterring donors from assisting in reproductive technologies by guaranteeing that they would not be harassed by the fruits of their altruism. This argument is frequently advanced in favour of donor anonymity, partly by reference to entitlement to donor choice but also lest donors be deterred and a reduction in supply ensue and, amongst other things, threaten a substantial commercial interest.

Allan's view is that opposition to removal of donor anonymity in the present environment has its origins in outdated fears of the past, ongoing stigma surrounding infertility, a lack of prioritizing of children's rights, concern expressed by the fertility industry about the impact on supply and demand and fear of deleterious financial ramifications if anonymity is removed. She argues that such reasons do not justify maintaining secrecy or anonymity, and that it is the right of donor-conceived people to choose whether they wish to access information about their donor. Allan states that this choice should not be foreclosed by recipients, donors or the fertility industry. She further argues that donors and recipients should be supported in their experiences, rather than condemned to secrecy, stigma and shame.

Fears and concerns advanced in the past about donor conception are generally not regarded today as having much weight. The 1958 House of Lords debates about artificial insemination were characterized by emotive rhetoric about lies and deception. Lord Denning's principal focus was worry about the stability and security of family life. However, the reality is that assisted reproductive technologies have proliferated in the succeeding six decades and become an orthodox means of conception for many couples.

In times past it must be conceded, though, that some doctors' conduct was cavalier and irresponsible – such as in using the sperm from small numbers of donors for many recipients and even inseminating women with mixtures of donors' semen, meaning that some donors fathered large, albeit unknown numbers of children, and in other instances paternity was not even known. Understandably, this has raised the spectre of persons entering inadvertently into consanguineous relationships. A new element was added to the mix with the introduction of donor eggs in Melbourne, Australia, in 1983 and in more recent years the phenomenon of reproductive tourism has further complicated the dynamics of the debate about identity and donor anonymity; in many jurisdictions regulation, as well as arrangements about donor record keeping and registration are informal at best and in some wholly absent.

It is clearly important that we not foist genetic inheritance knowledge on those who do not want it. However, this is not a good reason for failing to make available such information to those who do want it. This aspect of the donor information question is one of autonomy – those who wish to remain in ignorance should be permitted to do so. Those who want information should be permitted it, at least to some degree.

The issue can usefully be viewed through the lens of therapeutic jurisprudence: the challenge is to construct laws and practices that minimize counter-therapeutic outcomes for children born of ART and also for those who are donors, both male and female. This challenge involves identifying what such persons want and need – what is pro-therapeutic and what is counter-therapeutic. A lesson that therapeutic jurisprudence has taught us is that mendacity, deception, coercion and secrecy are frequently damaging as they can engender feelings of confusion, worthlessness, shame, paranoia and anxiety. Why can't they tell me? Why are they hiding things? Is my genetic past so shameful or so dangerous that I should not know about it? What does this mean about who I am? What ramifications might it have for my children?

In addition, a human rights perspective on the issue can make a useful contribution to the debate. As the English High Court found in *Rose v. Secretary of State for Health and Human Fertilisation and Embryology Authority* [2002] EWHC 1593 at [46] (Admin), the right to privacy is at least engaged when a donor-conceived person seeks information about his or her donor. Justice Baker observed that:

> It is to my mind entirely understandable that AID children should wish to know about their origins and in particular to learn what they can about their biological father or, in the case of egg donation, their biological mother. The extent to which this matters will vary from individual to individual. In some instances, as in the case of the Claimant Joanna Rose, the information will be of massive importance. I do not find this at all surprising bearing in mind the lessons that have been learnt from adoption. A human being is a human being whatever the circumstances of his conception and an AID child is entitled to establish a picture of his identity as much as anyone else. We live in a much more open society than even 20 years ago. Secrecy nowadays has to be justified where previously it did not.
>
> (at [47])

The European Court of Human Rights had gone further in some respects in the earlier decision of *Gaskin v. United Kingdom* (1990) 12 EHHR 36 at [48] when it held that people have a 'vital interest' protected by human rights law in 'receiving the information necessary to know and to understand their childhood and early development'. As occurs so often in international law and in human rights law, the question is one of balance because donors also have been held to have a right to privacy. However, it may well be that evolving jurisprudence, especially in light of provisions in the Convention on the Rights of the Child, will give priority to the best interests of children in acquiring at least some knowledge about their genealogical provenance.

Allan does a significant service in chronicling the evolution of and attenuation in donor anonymity laws, the newest development coming from Victoria,

Australia, in early 2017, which will enable (not mandate) further donor-child contact. What is particularly apparent is the diversity of international approach, as of the date of publication of this book, although the general orientation of law reform in the area is toward donor-conceived persons being given a right of access to information about their donors. As Allan identifies, the debate is moving toward what constitutes the best, most sensitive models for information release. Argentina, Croatia, Ireland and Victoria, Australia, have led the way with information about the method of conception on their birth registers. Choice registers of the kind found in Canada, Denmark, Iceland and Hungary provide for the dual track of both open-identity and anonymous gamete donation. Some countries have facilitated information provision by legislation; others, like the United States, have done so more informally.

The associated debate is whether donor-information legislation should operate prospectively or retrospectively. Views of legal purists, as against those with strong opinions on what is just, fair or therapeutic, differ on this contentious issue.

Developing knowledge about genetically inherited diseases and illness vulnerabilities has added a new and important aspect to the debate about donor anonymity. It will be an increasingly potent factor as medico-scientific knowledge extends further and further in terms what can be learned in advance about vulnerabilities to disease and what can be done prospectively to address such vulnerabilities. Medical genetics is one of the most vibrant areas of contemporary research. Increasingly fundamental for any given patient is knowledge about direct genetic forebears. To preclude such knowledge for a patient has the potential to impact materially upon the person's health status and, arguably, upon the person's right to health.

As observed previously, information about one's parents, about one's genetic inheritance and about one's siblings goes fundamentally to a person's sense of his or her place in the world. Our genetic provenance is not easily set aside. Salman Rushdie captured something of its inescapability, the triumph of genes over experience, in *East, West*: '. . . you still think you can escape from your father. You aren't listening to his voice speaking through your mouth, you don't see how your gestures already mirror his; you don't see him in the way you hold your body, in the way you sign your name. You don't hear his whisper in your blood.'[4]

If the law is to shift toward greater access to information for those born because of ART, skilled support services for all affected must be made available and carefully constructed processes set in place. Sensitive, informed, professional assistance is required to reduce the foreseeable potential for distress and confusion when information is provided to a donor or a recipient about the other.

As Allan argues, like in many areas on the intersection of law and medicine, the issues in this area transcend national boundaries. Ongoing reform to law and practice in relation to provision of information to and from donors seems

4 S. Rushdie, *East, West* (Random House, London, 2012), p 201.

inevitable. However, for it to have salutary outcomes, it needs to jettison the secrecy and dissimulation of the past. It should be characterized by cultivation of openness, honesty, compassion and responsiveness to donors, donor-conceived people, half-siblings and their extended families. The quest should be for a balance that keeps consequences that are counter-therapeutic to a minimum and which maximizes the potential for enhanced information to be beneficial for all concerned. Allan's presentation of the voices of persons affected is an important contribution to the debate, as is her painstaking chronicling of the direction of thinking and reform in this important area.

Ian Freckelton QC
Crockett Chambers,
Professorial Fellow of Law and Psychiatry, University of Melbourne,
Adjunct Professor of Law and Forensic Medicine, Monash University,
May 2016

Introduction

The quest to understand and/or cure infertility has existed, across cultures, for centuries. Early Egyptians appear to have logged the first recorded diagnosis for infertility on papyri scribed between 2200 and 1500 BC.[1] There are multiple references to 'barren' women in the bible and their quest for children.[2] The Qua'ran contains two main accounts of infertility[3] and also makes reference to a woman, Aysa, who remained childless due to her husband's impotency.[4] References to artificial insemination in humans are found in Talmudic documents, written more than three centuries ago, which record rabbis discussing the status of a woman hypothetically impregnated by semen previously deposited in bathwater.[5] Early reference may also be found to King Henry IV of Seville – often referred to as 'le-impotente' – regarding attempts to impregnate his wife in the 1400s using artificial insemination with his sperm.[6] However, 'cures' for infertility eluded people for thousands of years, and often continue to do so.

1 Ronit Haimov-Kochman, Yael Sciaky-Tamir and Arye Hurwitz, 'Reproduction Çoncepts and Practices in Ancient Egypt Mirrored by Modern Medicine' (2005) 123(1) *European Journal of Obstetrics and Gynecology* 3–8; P. Morice, P. Josset and J.B. Dubuisson, 'History of Sterility in Ancient Times: I. Sterility in Egypt: Diagnostic Recipes for Sterility and Pregnancy in Ancient Egypt' (June 1995) 23(6) *Contracept Fertil Sex* 423–427. [Article in French] (For example, see the Kahun papyrus which is a gynecological text that described the ancient Egyptian concept of human reproduction.)

2 See for example the Bible stories of Abraham and Sarah (Genesis 15–21); Isaac and Rebekah (Genesis 25:21); Rachel and Jacob (Genesis 29, 30); Manoah and his wife (Judges 13); Hannah and Elkanah (1 Samuel 1); the Shunammite woman and her old husband (2 Kings 4:8–17); and Elisabeth and Zacharia (Luke 1). (In the bible infertility was variously cured by prayer, sacrifice or the use of a handmaid as a surrogate.)

3 Two main accounts of infertility may be found in the Qua'ran in the stories of Ibrihim and Sarah (11:71–73; 51:28–30) and Zakariya pbuh (and his wife Ishba) (Qua'ran 3:38–40; 19:2–4; 21:89–90).

4 Qua'ran (66:11).

5 S. Kordimon, 'Artificial Insemination in the Talmud' (1942–1943) *Harofe Haivrc*; Hebrew, 62; English translation p 164 cited in John K. Critser 'Therapeutic Insemination by Donor: A Review of Its Efficacy' (1995) 4(1) *Reproductive Medicine Review* 9–17.

6 Tim R. Birkhead and Robert Montgomerie, 'Three Centuries of Sperm Research' in T.R. Birkhead, D.J. Hosken and S. Pitnik (eds), *Sperm Biology an Evolutionary Perspective* (2009), p 11. (Nb. The use of a 'donor' was not indicated in such stories.)

To this day, infertility and/or childlessness may cause great despair. Some people will long for a child, unable to conceive via sexual intercourse or unable to carry a child to full term. For some, there is continuing stigma associated with not bearing children. Having a family, inclusive of children, may also be seen as important for social or cultural reasons. Some people have a strong desire for a family grouping, want multidirectional familial comfort and care and/or seek the opportunity to share experiences, knowledge and/or wealth with children they love and care for. Some families may also place importance on continuing genetic lines and/or passing on the family name. These, of course, are but some of the multitude of reasons for which people may seek to become parents.

There are a number of alternatives people may consider to build a family. Some may turn to adoption or foster care; others may care for children of extended family members or within close social or cultural networks or groups. For others, the modern era of assisted reproduction using artificial insemination, in vitro fertilization or a number of other techniques to achieve pregnancy and birth has opened up new avenues for building a family. For some, these options have meant using assisted reproduction to have biologically related offspring using the sperm and eggs or embryo of the people who will parent the child (this option may involve predominantly heterosexual couples, but may also involve some 'shared parenting' arrangements). Other people have turned to donor conception, which is the use of donated sperm, eggs or embryos.

Donor conception is the focus of this book.

Although the introduction briefly presents the history, desire and reasons people may wish to build a family, and some of the methods that they may use, this book is concerned primarily with issues regarding the people who are born because of the use of donor conception. In particular, the focus is on the ethical, social and legal issues surrounding

1. telling donor-conceived people of their donor-conceived status,
2. providing them with information about the person (or people) who provided sperm and/or ova used in their conception, and/or genetically related siblings and
3. supporting them in building relationships with donors and/or siblings if all parties seek them.

Also relevant to this discussion is the disclosure of information to recipient parent(s) and donor(s) who may seek such information, and supporting all parties in moving toward a more open society regarding donor conception practices.

To this end, while donor conception is accessible to varying degrees in many jurisdictions across the globe, it is important to recognize that its progress throughout history has been both celebrated and derided. Donor conception is a practice that has enabled people to have children who otherwise may not have been able to – and, therefore, has been rejoiced – yet, at the same time, it is a practice that has a history veiled in secrecy. Anonymity of the donor has also been emphasized, with the donor's identity remaining unknown in many parts of the world to this day. The emphasis on 'protecting' the parties involved often reflected little or no consideration that such secrecy and lack of information may have had a negative impact on some donor-conceived people. In fact, in some jurisdictions, recipients of donor sperm, for example, were encouraged not to tell their children of the method of their conception and both recipients and donors were told that the donor should remain anonymous. If children were considered, it may have been assumed that it was in their best interest not to know the circumstances surrounding their conception and birth.

In recent times, in many jurisdictions across the world, little has changed. Although an increasing number of jurisdictions have passed laws that prohibit anonymous donations, and provide access to information for some donor-conceived people, for many others, donor conception is still a clandestine practice. Parents often do not disclose the method of conception to children, and donors remain anonymous. For those who do not have access to information, but seek it, calls to lift the veil of secrecy and to disclose information, have been steadily increasing.[7] What is the basis for such calls? What are the psychosocial, ethical and legal arguments for and against the release of information? Is there a human right to information about one's genetic heritage? Does the call for information give rise to 'competing' interests? If so, how may competing interests be balanced? In all cases, if the call for information is heeded, how should the release of information take place? What can we learn from jurisdictions that mandate the release of information to donor-conceived people? What can we do in the future? These are some of the questions considered in this book.

Part I of this book examines the history of secrecy and anonymity in donor conception, and the increasing search for information over time. Chapter 1 sets the scene by looking more closely at the history of artificial insemination (AI) and highlighting early reactions to assisted reproductive technologies (ART) that reinforced it being very much a clandestine practice. It illustrates how acceptance of AI has changed over time and that its use has increased exponentially. It highlights that as the practice has become more widespread, and in many parts of the world the taboo has lessened, secrecy and donor anonymity have nevertheless remained. Chapter 2 contrasts such secrecy and anonymity with the rising call by donor-conceived people, many of whom are now in their twenties, thirties and older, for information. It examines the call for information in light of the reasons and arguments raised for release. In addition, calls by recipient parents, and donors themselves, are acknowledged. Chapter 3 describes the search for information that donor-conceived people, recipient parents and donors undertake.

7 See for example, *Pratten v. British Columbia (Attorney-General)*, 2011 BCSC 565 (19 May 2011); Senate Legal and Constitutional Affairs References Committee, *Donor Conception Practices in Australia* (2011); Victorian Law Reform Committee, *Inquiry into Access by Donor Conceived People to Information about the Donors* (March 2012); S. Allan, 'Psychosocial, Ethical and Legal Arguments for and Against the Retrospective Release of Information about Donors to Donor Conceived Individuals in Australia' (2011) 19(1) *Journal of Law and Medicine* 354.

Personal accounts of searching are included in this chapter and illustrate that the path to understanding is found in the stories of donor-conceived people, recipients, and donors – all who search for information.

Part II details how different nations approach the release of information about a donor-conceived person's status, and about their donor and siblings. It examines laws, guidelines and practices, and shows that some countries enshrine the 'right' of donor-conceived people to information, while others continue to support anonymous donations and secrecy. It provides a compendium for examining laws and practices around the globe that govern anonymous or non-anonymous donations, information release and support. It is detailed in nature, as it is only through such details that one comes to understand what is being done in various jurisdictions in relation to recognizing and acting upon the right of donor-conceived people to information, or maintaining secrecy and anonymity.

The information presented in Part II concerning laws and practices related to information release has been collected by the author employing methods that include extensive searches of government websites and repositories for legal documents; library database searches for international literature regarding the regulation of assisted reproduction and donor conception; searching the World Wide Web for translation of materials; detailed searching of the *International Digest of Health Law* published by the World Health Organization and fieldwork conducted by the author in which she travelled to jurisdictions that provide information release and investigated not only the laws concerning donor conception but also the systems in place and practices within those jurisdictions, as well as reflections by those people directly involved.[8] Part II illustrates that the development of laws and practices is clearly shaped by whose interests are emphasized. These interests include not only those of donor-conceived people, donors and recipients but also that of the modern-day multi-billion-dollar fertility industry.

Chapter 4 details the inquiries, and subsequent laws, in a number of jurisdictions that require non-anonymous donations. The systems and implementation of laws in each jurisdiction are examined, as are the practical realities of those who search for information within the respective regimes. Judicial decisions that support information release in some countries are also considered. Chapter 5 examines the approach taken in countries that allow prospective recipient parents to choose between open identity and anonymous donors. Chapter 6 details those countries that require anonymous donations. While the chapters in this section are divided into three broad areas – releasing identifying information; options between 'open-identity' and anonymous donors; and anonymous donation – it will become apparent that the nuances within jurisdictions make such divisions less clear.

8 S. Allan, *A Cross-Jurisdictional Study of Regulatory Requirements and Practice Regarding the Recording of Donor Information and Its Release to Donor Conceived People* 2012. Report prepared for the Winston Churchill Memorial Trust.

Part III moves to consider arguments for and against anonymity in more detail, as well as considering model approaches to the release of information. In Chapter 7, arguments that have been made in favour of maintaining anonymity are examined, it being argued that ultimately none of the arguments put forward justify the continuance of such practices. Chapter 8 moves further to consider the issues under a human rights lens, identifying the human rights that may be engaged and engaging in a substantive human rights analysis in which the accepted approach of balancing rights to resolve conflicts between competing rights holders is applied. It argues that a human rights approach supports prospective prohibitions on anonymity, and lends itself to support a model for retrospective release of information that balances a right to information with the right to privacy. Chapter 9 considers further the issue of the release of information to *all* donor-conceived people in light of the fact that calls for information are made by those already in existence. It demonstrates that such release would be lawful. It highlights that an analogous model for release may be found in the context of adoption, and that fears about terrible consequences of releasing information in that context have not been realized. Arguments that have been raised in protest of opening records from the past in relation to donor conception are considered and responded to. Alternatives to full retrospective release of information are noted. Consideration is also given to the preservation of records and the kinds of support services that might be needed.

Part IV concludes the book. It sums up the arguments put forward and examines the path forward, both in encouraging parents to disclose donor-conceived status to their children, in educating and supporting parents to do so, and in considering the role regulation may play in facilitating release and access to information.

Part I

Donor conception, secrecy and anonymity

1 A brief history of donor conception, secrecy and anonymity

From the microscope to artificial insemination: seventeenth to nineteenth centuries

The introduction notes that the quest to understand and/or cure infertility has existed, across cultures, for centuries. However, although people lamented infertility for centuries – and there were many rituals, practices and prayers to gods of fertility aimed to increase the chances of becoming pregnant – little was understood about how conception and reproduction occurred. Little progress was made in finding a 'cure' until the latter part of the seventeenth century, when Dutch scientist Antonie van Leeuwenhoek was able to observe spermatozoa for the first time under a microscope. Leeuwenhoek's groundbreaking observations in 1677 were followed by further experimentation and speculation about human reproduction, signaling a significant development in both understanding infertility and creating technologies that could assist conception.

By the eighteenth century, Lazzaro Spallanzani (an Italian physiologist and priest) discovered and described mammalian reproduction, showing that both semen and ovum were required. In 1784, he performed an artificial insemination using a dog. He was also the first person to perform in vitro fertilization with frogs.[1] This experimentation was closely followed by the first known and reported instance of successful human artificial insemination, which involved a wife being inseminated with her husband's sperm. The insemination was conducted by the husband, following instructions given by Dr John Hunter, and was reported following Hunter's death in 1799 by his executor Sir Everard Home.[2]

In France, a successful human artificial insemination, performed by Dr Girault, was reported to have occurred on 5 June 1838. Dr Girault's patient, a young

1 For a brief history of artificial insemination in animals, reflecting research all over the world, see R.H. Foote, 'A History of Artificial Insemination: Selected Notes and Notables' (2002) *American Society of Animal Science*, available at https://www.asas.org/docs/publications/footehist.pdf?sfvrsn=0, accessed 6 November 2014.

2 F.N.L. Poynter, 'Hunter, Spallanzani, and the History of Artificial Insemination' in Lloyd G. Stevenson and Robert P. Multhauf (eds), *Medicine, Science and Culture: Historical Essays in Honor of Owsei Temkin* (Johns Hopkins Press, Baltimore, 1968), pp 97, 99–100.

countess, gave birth to a son on 1 March 1839, the case being the first in a series of twelve, which were reported in a paper published in 1868.[3] In 1866, Dr James Marion Sims similarly reported using artificial insemination to impregnate a wife with her husband's sperm.[4]

Further research, predominantly conducted on animals in the second half of the nineteenth century, led to practical techniques for applying artificial insemination that still remain today.[5] A number of reports were also published during this time of human artificial insemination in France, England, Germany and the United States.[6] It was during these times that secrecy surrounding the practice of artificial insemination of humans appears also to have been established. Strong disapproval met the reports of impregnating a woman with her husband's sperm using 'instrumental insemination'.[7] The practice was publically condemned as 'offensive to natural law'.[8]

In 1998, Simone Bateman Novaes[9] noted that 'the historical origins of assisted conception were clearly tainted by doubts about the morality of the acts involved [including masturbation and instrumental substitution for sexual intercourse] and their legitimacy as medical treatment'.[10] It was said that assisted conception 'could constitute a real social peril' and that 'it was of import to the dignity of marriage that such procedures not be transferred from the domain of Science to the domain of Practice'.[11]

3 L'Abeille Medicale, volume 25, pp 409–417 cited in Poynter above n 2, 1968.

4 James Marion Sims is often referred to as the father of gynecology. Note that Sims, 'a member of a wealthy slave-owning family in the antebellum South [of the United States] controversially honed his expertise in gynecological surgery on slave women. He then moved north and established a women's hospital in New York City and his reported cases of artificial insemination involved free white patients, both charity and private patients.': Kara W. Swanson, 'Adultery by Doctor: Artificial Insemination: 1890–1945' (2012) 87(2) *Chicago-Kent Law Review* 591, 596–597, citing Deborah Kuhn Mcgregor, *Sexual Surgery and the Origins of Gynecology: J. Marion Sims, His Hospital, and His Patients* (Garland Publishing, 1990) 1–2, 257–258, 273–274; Randi Hutter Epstein, *Get Me Out: A History of Childbirth from the Garden of Eden to the Sperm Bank* (2010), 35–48. See also generally, J. Marion Sims, *The Story of My Life* (1884) (Reprinted, Da Capo Press, Cambridge, MA, 1968).

5 See for example the work of Ilya Ivanov, a Russian researcher who developed practical methods for artificial insemination in 1899.

6 Poynter, above n 2.

7 In particular the work of John Hunter, in the United Kingdom, and M.A. Thouret, in France.

8 Tribunal de Bordeaux, 1880, Affaire Lejâtre cited in Simone Bateman Noveaus, 'The Medical Management of Donor Insemination' in K. Daniels and E. Haimes (eds), *Donor Insemination: International Social Science Perspectives* (Cambridge University Press, Cambridge, U.K., 1998), p 109.

9 A Senior Researcher in sociology at the Centre de Recherche Sens, Ethique, Société (CERSES), a centre affiliated to the Centre National de la Recherche Scientifique (CNRS) and to the Université Paris Descartes in Paris, France.

10 Novaes, 'The Medical Management of Donor Insemination' in Daniels and Haimes, n 8, p 110.

11 Ibid.

The previously mentioned Dr Sims went on to conduct fifty-five inseminations on six women using their husband's sperm; however, illustrative of the controversy surrounding the practice during the time, he subsequently was said to have repudiated his own work as immoral.[12]

Given the disapproval of artificial insemination with the sperm of a woman's husband, it is not surprising that the early use of ***donor*** sperm[13] also met with great disapproval. Donor inseminations were predominantly conducted in secret and were not reported for many years. For example, in one of the earliest reported cases of donor insemination (1884), a U.S. physician, Professor William Pancoast, used the sperm of one of his 'best-looking' medical students to impregnate the wife of a sterile Quaker merchant.[14] The woman was anaesthetized with chloroform and not informed of the procedure, although reportedly the husband was told. It was not until 1909, some twenty-five years later, after Dr Pancoast's death, that one of the medical students who had been present revealed the story.[15] Similarly, treatments using donor sperm conducted in the 1880s by Dr Robert Latou Dickinson[16] were not reported until the early twentieth century – some forty years later.

The early twentieth century

The early twentieth century saw increasing openness about artificial insemination as a medical practice, but simultaneously condemnation, secrecy and anonymity concerning donor conception remained.[17] As the newly elected president of the American Gynecological Society, Dr Robert Dickinson reported his own decades of experience with artificial insemination in 1920.[18] He urged gynecologists to study and pool their experience with 'artificial impregnation',[19] and his reports led to slightly more openness among medical practitioners to the practice of artificial insemination as a medical practice. Throughout the 1920s and 1930s,

12 A.D. Weinberger, 'Partial Solution to Legitimacy Problems Arising from the Use of Artificial Insemination' (1959–1960) 35 *Indiana Law Journal* 144.

13 Sperm obtained from a male to whom the woman is not married to or in a relationship with.

14 A.T. Gregoire and R.C. Mayer, 'The Impregnators' (1965) 16 *Fertility and Sterility* 130–134.

15 A letter by Addison Davis Hard appeared in the U.S. journal *Medical World:* Margaret Eichler, 'Of Desperation Born: The Struggle for Children at any Cost', in Joan Turner (ed), *Living the Changes* (University of Manitoba Press, Canada, 1990), p 230.

16 The first successful use of donor semen in the United States is attributed to Dr Robert L. Dickinson who was a pioneer in birth control, sex education and marriage counselling.

17 Hermann Rohleder, *Test Tube Babies: A History of the Artificial Impregnation of Human Beings* (Panurge Press, New York, 1934), pp 139–162 (detailing opposition to any form of artificial insemination based on religion, nature, medical ethics, and morality).

18 Robert L. Dickinson, 'Artificial Impregnation: Essays in Tubal Insemination' (1920) 45 *Transactions of the American Gynecological Society* 141–148.

19 Robert L. Dickinson, 'Suggestions for a Program for American Gynecology' (1920) 45 *Transactions of the American Gynecological Society* 6–7.

one or more papers per year were published on the topic.[20] However, the aspect of whether donor sperm had been used in many such procedures was 'glossed over' and little to no mention of donor conception occurred in published papers during this time.[21] In a review of medical practices and views concerning artificial insemination between 1890 and 1945, leading legal historian Kara Swanson noted that 'if some doctors were "skeptical" about artificial insemination, many were outright hostile to the idea of donor insemination'.[22] The secrecy surrounding such practices even amongst the medical profession was therefore profound.

Religious condemnation dating from around 1897 was also found. For example, the Vatican (the central Catholic religious authority) condemned such practices as being gravely immoral. The view espoused was that donor conception 'infringe[d] the child's right to be born of a father and mother known to him and bound to each other by marriage' and 'betray[ed] the spouses' right to become a father and a mother only through each other'.[23]

In addition to objections regarding masturbation and instrumental substitution for sexual intercourse, there were also religious, ethical, social and legal objections concerning adultery. To this end, Novaes observes the significance of the intermediary role played by medical practitioners during this time when using fresh sperm:

> The conditions under which the three principal participants of [donor insemination] (the woman to be inseminated, the man providing the semen, and the physician) were being brought together, emphasized the moral premises of this arrangement: even if the offer of treatment might ultimately be justifiable in terms of its positive results [i.e. a child], it was nevertheless not perceived as morally appropriate or legally expedient for the infertile couple to be acquainted with the semen provider. The physician therefore, beyond his/her technical role as inseminator, had to intervene as a mediator: someone who makes it possible for semen transfer to take place, without requiring the two parties to meet.[24]

The medical practitioner's intermediary role, which kept the recipient parents and the donor apart and unknown to each other, therefore served as an attempt to lessen the view that donor conception was adulterous. Recipients were often

20 See Ernest Henry Breuer, *Artificial Insemination: A Selected Bibliography of the Medical, Legal, Religious and Moral Aspects of Artificial Human Insemination* (New York State Library, 1948), pp 18–20.

21 Kara W. Swanson, 'Adultery by Doctor: Artificial Insemination: 1890–1945' (2012) 87(2) *Chicago-Kent Law Review* 591, 602.

22 Ibid., 602–603.

23 The earliest statements reflecting this view by the Vatican were made at the *Sacred Congregation of the Holy Office* in 1897, and were reiterated in *Pius XII*, 1949, *Donum Vitae*, 1987 and *Evangelium Vitae*, 1995.

24 Novaes, 'The Medical Management of Donor Insemination', in Daniels and Haimes, n 8, pp 110–111.

told to go away following insemination, to have sexual intercourse, and not to think about the use of third-party sperm. The emphasis on forgetting (or pretending that donor insemination simply had not occurred), reinforced the view that secrecy and anonymity were needed. Novaes further notes the 'secrecy surrounding the procedure and the anonymity of the semen provider became [one of] the primary organizing principles of the practice, and in a certain sense served as the most obvious justification for physician's presence in this situation'.[25]

During this period, what appears to be the only reported judicial opinion on the subject in the Anglo-American world, illustrates the legal view taken toward such actions. In *Orford v. Orford*,[26] a Canadian case heard in 1921, the court was presented with a couple that had married in 1913 and had separated three months later, without having consummated the marriage. Some six years later, Mrs Orford claimed alimony from Mr Orford, stating she had conceived a child using artificial insemination by a donor (without her husband's knowledge or consent). The court did not believe that she had conceived using artificial insemination, and held that she had committed adultery. However, it went on to state that even if she had used artificial insemination by a donor, she would have committed adultery by way of the introduction 'of the seed of a man other than her husband', risking the introduction 'into the family of the man of a false strain of blood'.[27] As a consequence, the child would have been considered illegitimate.

Notably, however, views bound up in morality, religion and natural law that criticized artificial insemination, and moreover the kind that involved using donated sperm, did not stop research or practice. By the 1930s, the practice of artificial insemination by donor was increasingly discussed in the popular press, particularly in the context of a growing movement in eugenics. For example, in an article published in 1934 in *Scientific American* (a popular magazine aimed at bringing science to the public), it was stated:

> Babies of extra-marital paternity are now being born of women who have sterile husbands, by artificial insemination with the life-giving germ from selected men. This is one of the most significant eugenic developments in the history of man.[28]

In the article, it was estimated that between 50 and 150 babies were being born using donor insemination each year.[29]

In a subsequent newspaper article from the same year about a woman who had conceived twins using artificial insemination, her doctor, Dr Frances Seymour (the Medical Director at the National Research Foundation for the Eugenic

25 Ibid., p 111.
26 *Orford v. Orford*, 58 DLR 251 (1921).
27 Ibid.
28 John Harvey Caldwell, 'Babies by Scientific Selection' (1934) 150 *Scientific American* 124, cited in Swanson, above n 21, p 606.
29 Ibid.

Alleviation of Sterility Inc.), disclosed that she had also assisted two unmarried businesswomen in the prior year to conceive using sperm chosen from a local blood donor list. The men were referred to in the article as 'ghost fathers'.[30] The story ran in newspapers across the United States,[31] and led to both increased controversy and increased requests for such treatment.

The mid-twentieth century

Over the next ten years, a group of doctors founded the American Society for the Study of Fertility and Sterility and established the journal *Fertility and Sterility.* However, donor insemination continued to be controversial, including amongst doctors. A survey conducted in 1947 revealed that 10 per cent of the society's members refused to carry out donor insemination, and while the other 90 per cent were not opposed in principle, only half (45 per cent) actually performed the technique.[32] The technique was also far from perfected, and medicine not having yet realized the issue of timing for ovulation, failure often resulted despite multiple attempts.

Outside of the United States, the history of donor insemination was also significantly tainted by the eugenics movement during World War II, when doctors in Nazi Germany performed donor-insemination experiments on Jews, gypsies and concentration camp prisoners.[33] Such experimentation highlighted the potential for misuse of donor insemination – a fear that is still prevalent today.[34]

30 'Ghost' Fathers: Children Provided for the Childless, *Newsweek*, 12 May 1934, 16 cited in Swanson, above n 21, p 607.

31 'Synthetic' Babies Born to 12 mothers, *New York Times*, 1 May 1934; 13 Babies in N.Y. Have Test Tube as Father, *Chicago Daily Tribune*, 1 May 1934; Parents of 'Test Tube' Twins Reveal Eugenic Baby Practice, *Washington Post*, 1 May 1934; Laboratory Twins Born to Couple on Long Island, *Los Angeles Times*, 1 May 1934; Birth of 'Test tube' Twins Reveals 'Lab Baby' Technique, *Billings Gazette*, 1 May 1934, cited in Swanson above n 21, fn 90.

32 Alan F. Guttmacher, John O. Haman and John MacLeod, 'The Use of Donors for Artificial Insemination: A Survey of Current Practices' (1950) 1 *Fertility & Sterility* 264, 266.

33 Baruch C. Cohen, 'The Ethics of Using Medical Data from Nazi Experiments' (Copyright 2012, The American-Israeli Cooperative Enterprise), available at http://www.jewishvirtuallibrary.org/jsource/Judaism/naziexp.html, accessed 22 February, 2012. Note the statements cited in Cohen of Doctor Jay Katz, Yale Law School, who described the Nazi experiments with one phrase 'They're of no scientific value'; similarly, Brigadier General Telford Taylor, Chief Counsel for the prosecution at Nuremberg, described Nazi experimentations as 'a ghastly failure as well as a hideous crime . . . [that] revealed nothing which civilized medicine can use'; and Lord Immanuel Jakobovits, Chief Rabbi of the British Commonwealth of Nations and the pioneer of Jewish Medical Ethics, said that 'using the Nazi data offers not a shred of meaning to 6,000,000 deaths. In fact, use of the data would serve to dishonor them even more so'.

34 D. King, 'Preimplantation Genetic Diagnosis and the "New" Eugenics' (1999) 25 *Journal of Medical Ethics* 176–182. NB. For discussion of the use of the word 'eugenics' in relation to PGD see S. Wilkinson, '"Eugenics Talk" and the Language of Bioethics' (2008) 34(6) *Journal of Medical Ethics* 467–471.

Attitudes toward donor insemination remained negative for the decades that followed.

Post–World War II

The post–World War II era saw increasing acceptance of artificial insemination using a husband's sperm, but not in the case of donor insemination. For example, in the United Kingdom, the Archbishop of Canterbury stated that while artificial insemination by a husband may be justified, artificial insemination by a donor was wrong and against Christian standards. In a report by a commission appointed by the archbishop, it was stated that 'early consideration should be given to framing of legislation to make the practice a criminal offence'.[35] However, legislation prohibiting donor insemination was not subsequently enacted.

In fact, post–World War II scientific advances,[36] first with animals and then with humans, marked the entry of donor insemination into even greater public realms in the United Kingdom, the United States and beyond. In 1949, Christopher Polge, a British doctoral student, developed improved methods of freezing and thawing sperm in chickens and then in cattle.[37] In 1950, Cornell University scientists discovered that antibiotics could be added to the sperm solution in AI processes to protect against possible contamination.[38] In 1953, the first successful pregnancy resulting from the use of frozen and thawed donor sperm was reported.[39] These results were seen as significant discoveries and subsequently changed the face of human infertility treatment involving donor sperm, as the capacity to freeze sperm meant that it was no longer necessary for the 'donor' in donor conception to be present.

Nevertheless, although practical obstacles were slowly being addressed, the moral and legal debates about such procedures continued. These discussions continued to focus on issues of adultery, illegitimacy, paternity and the rights of legal inheritance of the child from the donor and/or husband/non-biological father.[40] Conflicting views continued to be seen.

35 A report of a Commission appointed by His Grace the Archbishop of Canterbury, Author Unknown, *Artificial Human Insemination*, 1948, S.P.C.K. For a brief critique of this report written at the time of its publication see 'Artificial Human Insemination' (1948) 162(4124) *Nature* 790.

36 Such advances were not related in any way to the experiments conducted by the Nazis in World War II.

37 C. Polge, A.U. Smith and A.S. Parkes, 'Revival of Spermatozoa after Vitrification and Dehydration at Low Temperatures' (1949) 164(4172) *Nature* 666.

38 R.H. Bratton and R.W. Bratton, 'The Fertility of Bovine Semen in Extenders Containing Sulfanilamide, Penicillin, Streptomycin, and Polymyxin' (1950) 33 *Journal of Dairy Science* 544–547.

39 R.G. Bunge, W.C. Keettel and J.K. Sherman, 'Clinical Use of Frozen Semen: Report of Four Cases' (1954) 5(6) *Fertility and Sterility* 520–529.

40 For example see John L. Spiegel, 'Seed of Doubt' (1955–1956) 17 *University of Pittsburgh Law Review* 659–673; Unknown, 'Child Conceived through Artificial Insemination by a Third-Party Donor Is Illegitimate–Gursky v. Gursky, A [legislation]' (November 1964)

For example, in the United States, the 1948 New York case of *Strnad v. Strnad* held that a child conceived by donor insemination was the legitimate child of the husband who consented to the procedure, as it viewed the situation of donor conception during marriage as 'no different than that pertaining in the case of a child born out of wedlock who by law is made legitimate upon the marriage of the interested parties'.[41] However, in *Doornbos v. Doornbos*,[42] divorce proceedings heard in 1954 in the Cook County Illinois Superior Court, Judge Gorman ruled that a child conceived during the marriage using donor insemination (with or without the husband's consent) was illegitimate.[43] Judge Gorman stated that donor insemination was 'contrary to public policy and good morals, and considered adulterous on the mother's part' and that 'a child so conceived was born out of wedlock and therefore illegitimate. As such, it is the child of the mother, and the father has no rights or interest in the said child'.[44] *Doornbos* was hailed by one commentator who said:

> It should be recorded in the annals of our times as an excellent reflection of the natural law on a touchy and morally involved question – a question which encompasses legal, medical, moral, psychological, and social problems. . . . And although bills dealing with artificial insemination and the legitimacy of the children born of this practice have been introduced in the legislatures of six states [of America], none as yet has been passed. The legal solution to the problem of artificial insemination by donor lies not in a complex statute declaring this undesirable and unnatural practice legal and providing for all of its complicated legal ramifications, but rather in the passing of a simple law declaring it illegal as against public policy and good morals. This is the only possible natural law solution to the problem.[45]

Almost ten years later, in 1963, a New York Court in the case of *Gursky v. Gursky*,[46] chose to follow *Doornbos* holding that a child conceived by means of an artificial donor, again with the husband's consent, was not the legitimate issue of the husband. The court distinguished the case from *Strnad* on the basis that *Strnad* had involved the question of the husband's right to visitation.[47] However, in the following year, Georgia became the first state to

---

63(1) *Michigan Law Review* 160–167; John R. Valeri, 'Donor Insemination – No Clear Legal Future in Prospect' (Spring 1968) 3(2) *Portia Law Journal* 235–244.

41 *Strnad v. Strnad*, 78 NY.2d 390 (NY Sup Ct 1948) at 391.

42 *Doornbos v. Doornbos*, 23 U.S.L.W. 2308 (Superior Court, Cook County, Ill., 13 December 1954).

43 Ibid.

44 Ibid.

45 Albert Sidney Johnson III, 'Natural Law and Artificial Insemination' (1955) 5(2) *Catholic University Review* 189, 191.

46 *Gursky v. Gursky*, 242 NY 2d 406 (NY Sup Ct 1963).

47 Ibid., 410.

pass a statute legitimizing children conceived by donor insemination, on the condition that both the husband and wife consented in advance in writing to the procedure.

In the United Kingdom, similar conflicting views were seen during the post–World War II period. It was during this period that the now infamous Barton Clinic operated in London. The Barton Clinic was run by Austrian scientist Bertold Wiesner and his wife, Dr Mary Barton, and between 1940 and 1960, an estimated 1,500 children were conceived because of donor insemination – illustrating a demand. The clinic was highly controversial, not only because it used donor sperm but because it marketed its services to middle- and upper-class women, on the basis that the donor sperm came from a small number of specially selected, 'highly intelligent' men. Dr Barton had been quoted as saying: 'I matched race, colouring and stature and all donors were drawn from intelligent stock.' She added: 'I wouldn't take a donor unless he was, if anything, a little above average. If you are going to do it [(i.e. create a child)] deliberately, you have to put the standards rather higher than normal.'[48] One man, a neurochemist named Derek Richter, was later found to have fathered more than 100 children at the clinic, while it has been estimated that Bertold Wiesner may have been the biological father to anywhere between 300 and 1,000 children.[49] Mary Barton later destroyed many of the medical records, and it is assumed that most of those conceived at the clinic are not aware of the circumstances of their conception or their genetic history.

Postwar British parliamentary considerations

In 1958, the House of Lords debated the issue of artificial insemination of married women.[50] Lord Blackford, who moved to have the practice of donor insemination deemed as adultery, also emphasized the extensive nature of the 'deception' and 'lies' involved, and condemned the procedure in terms of it being the work of 'Beelzebub'. He stated:

> It has been brought out by the noble Lord, Lord Denning that it involves for its so-called success, as even its advocates admit, deliberate and prolonged deception, and perjury at one point or another, and this may or may not be

48 Sara C Nelson, 'Bertold Wiesner, British Man, Fathered Between 600–1000 Children at His Own Clinic', *Huffington Post UK*, 4 September 2012, available at http://www.huffingtonpost.co.uk/2012/04/09/bertold-wiesner-british-man-fathered-between-600–1000-children-at-own-clinic_n_1411758.html, accessed 16 March 2016.

49 The figures were calculated based on DNA tests carried out in 2007 on eighteen people conceived at the clinic between 1943 and 1962, which revealed two thirds of the group were Dr Wiesner's children. The range is thus wide, as the true number is not known, and given that records were destroyed, actual tracking and determination of how many other offspring exist is almost impossible.

50 *Artificial Insemination of Married Women*, HL Deb 26 February 1958 vol 207 cc926–1016.

> successful. A lie, indeed, is of its very essence, which is not surprising as it appears to come from the Father of Lies. It opens the door to possibilities still more loathsome than itself. We must, and I believe this country will, reject with horror this brain-wave of Beelzebub.[51]

In the same debate, the Lord Archbishop of Canterbury ultimately condemned the medical profession for allowing some of its members to perpetuate a 'conspiracy of secrecy':

> My Lords, may I ask the noble Lord a question? He said that this practice might be driven underground. But is it not a fact that it is now underground, and that the doctor, donor, husband and wife do this in secrecy – which is what I understand by the term "under-ground"? . . . I am sure that that could be decided at once. But every couple who, after a period of childlessness, have a child will have to bear the suspicion of their neighbours that the child has been born by [artificial insemination by donor]. I would repeat what I said nine years ago, and it is still true: that many nervous, adolescent children will have a haunting fear from time to time, as they do now, one which can never be resolved, that they do not belong to their supposed parents. If a child asks his father, to end the whole atmosphere of doubt, the father will have to reply with the truth or a lie; and I cannot think that the father will lie to his own supposed son. The strange thing in the whole of this matter, to my mind, is that the medical profession should have been content that some of its members, on their own individual authority, should take the law out of the hands of Church and State into their own hands and should act in a conspiracy of secrecy in a matter of such far-reaching spiritual, moral, legal and social import.[52]

Similarly, other Lords expressed deep concern about the secrecy and deception involved in the practice.[53] Lord Denning closed his speech by saying:

> So much for the legal considerations. Just one word on its social significance. It seems to me that if this practice became widespread it would strike at the stability and security of family life; it would strike at the roots of our civilisation. I would say to the doctors "Where by your science are you leading us? Seek to relieve suffering by all means, but do not do it by secrecy and deception. 'For what is a man profited, if he shall gain the whole world, and lose his own soul?' "[54]

51 Ibid., 955–956.

52 Ibid., 974, 999–1000.

53 See Ibid., per Lord Denning, 944–946; The Lord Bishop of Norwich, 965; Lord Merrimen, 985–986; and the Lord Bishop of Exeter, 992–993.

54 Ibid., 947.

Lord Merriman suggested the setting up of safeguards, including a compulsory register containing 'a full statement of the facts, the name of the donor, and the rest of it. . . .'[55] The Lord Bishop of Exeter said:

> [T]he result of all this secrecy is that the whole life of the family is, and must be, based upon fraud and deception. Parents will continually speak of the child as "our child" and will continually speak to the child as its father and mother. The whole life of the family and its very centre will therefore rest upon and be vitiated by a living deception. I cannot believe but that it would be much better to get rid of all this secrecy and, with the secrecy, of that unmistakable element of furtiveness which at present surrounds the whole of this business.[56]

In closing, Lord Blackford moved to withdraw his motion that artificial insemination by donor be made illegal due to it being adulterous as he was satisfied that some views had changed in this regard. He added that his second objective, which was to use the motion 'as a peg on which to hang a full debate on [artificial insemination by donor]', had been achieved.[57]

In that same year, the case of *MacLennan v. MacLennan* saw a Scottish court determine that 'artificial insemination by donor without the consent of the husband is not adultery' because the definition of adultery required two parties physically present to engage in a sexual act.[58] However, while it seemed that some people had shifted toward accepting that the practice occurred, this shift did not resolve the secrecy that surrounded the practice, sustained by continued negative views about it.

Professor Ken Daniels, an expert in social work and commentator on donor conception, noted that:

> [L]ittle had changed by 1960 when a UK interdepartmental committee, chaired by Lord Feversham determined that donor insemination was 'undesirable' and should not be practiced. . . . Donation itself was also viewed with deep suspicion, with the personal motivation of donors being called into question. The committee decided that donation 'is an activity which might be expected to attract more than the usual proportion of psychopaths'.[59]

55 Ibid., per Merrimen, 986.

56 Ibid., per the Lord Bishop of Exeter, 992–993.

57 Ibid., per Lord Blackford, 1016.

58 *MacLennan v. MacLennan*, 1958 S.C. 105; 1958 S.L.T. 12 (Outer House, Court of Session, Scotland).

59 K. Daniels and K. Taylor, 'Secrecy and Openness in Donor Insemination' (1993) 12(2) *Politics and Life Sciences* 155, 156.

The public response to the Feversham committee inquiry was said to have been similarly negative, ranging from disapproval to abhorrence, with little to no support for donor insemination given other than by the practitioners themselves.[60]

However, over time, attitudes were changing. In 1968, the then U.K. Minister for Health announced that donor conception would be available through the United Kingdom's public health system (the NHS), if recommended on medical grounds.

The 1970s

By the 1970s, sperm-freezing techniques had improved, sperm banks had developed, instrumental insemination had become commercialized in many countries and there was significant call for its use. Technological advances further increased the occurrence of donor conception worldwide with the first in vitro fertilization (IVF) baby born in the United Kingdom in 1978.[61] Since then, numerous assisted reproductive technologies (ART) have been developed.

It was during the 1970s and following years that laws in some jurisdictions were passed to provide legal certainty regarding the status of children (and that of their parents) who were born as a result of using ART, including where donor gametes (ova or sperm) were used. In such instances, the donor of sperm was declared not to be a parent (thereby having no rights or responsibilities), and the husband of the woman who underwent the procedure, subject to his consent, was declared the father.[62] With the passing of such legislation, many fears surrounding illegitimacy or questions of legal parentage, responsibility for the child and inheritance were resolved; however, secrecy remained the guiding principle for many of those involved.

Laws concerning legal parentage around the world, however, differed, and many, to this day, leave issues of legal parentage unresolved.

60 J. Blizzard, *Blizzard and the Holy Ghost* (Peter Owen, London, 1977) cited in Daniels and Taylor, n 59, p 156.

61 S. Shivaji, 'The Journey of R.G. Edwards: From a Single Cell to Louise Joy Brown' (2011) 100(4) *Current Science* 489. NB She was not donor conceived.

62 In Australia see: *Artificial Conception Act 1985* (WA); *Family Relationships Act 1975*(SA); *Parentage Act 2004* (ACT); *Status of Children Act 1996* (NSW); *Status of Children Act* (NT); *Status of Children Act 1974* (Tas); *Status of Children Act 1978*; and *Status of Children Act 1974* (Vic). In the United Kingdom see: *Human Fertilisation and Embryology Act 1990* (UK) s 28. In the United States in 1973, the Commissioners on Uniform State Laws approved the *Uniform Parentage Act* model legislation that provides that if a wife is artificially inseminated with donor semen under a physician's supervision, and with her husband's consent, the husband is legally considered the natural father of the donor inseminated child. That law was followed by similar legislation in many states. See for example, Ala Code § 26–17–21(a); Alaska Stat § 25.202.045; Col Rev Stat § 19.4.106; Ill Ann Stat Ch 750.40/3(a); Mass Gen Laws § 46.4B; MCLS §333.2824; Minn Stat § 257.56; Mont Code Ann § 40.6.106; NC Gen Stat § 49A–1. NJ Stat Ann § 9.17.44; NY Domestic Relations Law (Consol) § 73; NM Stat Ann § 40.11.6; Ohio Rev Code Ann § 3111.30 to 3111.38; Wis Stat Ann § 891.40(1); Wyo Stat § 14.2.103.

Professor Daniels described the situation in the 1970s (and well into the 1980s) as one in which doctors continued to tell families not to mention the child's origins to anyone, including the child. The few studies that looked at families who were using donor insemination reported that parents had no intention of telling their child(ren), and as donors were matched as closely to the legal father as possible and no notation was made on the birth certificate, secrecy was enshrined.[63]

Mr Damian Adams and Ms Caroline Lorbach[64] further note in relation to this period that it was 'not unusual in the past for doctors to use sperm from more than one man to confuse paternity thereby placing a further barrier to identification of a child's biological parent' and that the general belief was that anyone involved in the conception (donor, recipient or donor conceived) 'could not and should not seek information about each other'.[65] Some academic scholarship argued that the relationship between father and child, as well as the psychological health of the child, would be jeopardized if information about the donor-insemination treatment was revealed to the child.[66] It appears that secrecy and anonymity during this time was viewed as a practice that fell within 'private' family realms. Going well beyond considerations of just confidentiality or privacy, such secrecy and anonymity would remain well entrenched for decades to come.

On the other hand, some families chose not to keep the secret and the children conceived by donors during the 1970s as well as those to come (into the 1980s and beyond) would grow up to be some of the strongest proponents for removal of anonymity and an end to secrecy. However, as will be seen, that was still a long time to come.

The late-twentieth century

In 1978, Louise Brown, the world's first child conceived via in vitro fertilization (IVF) (a procedure where fertilization of an egg occurs outside of the body and the embryo then implanted) was born in Oldham, Britain.[67] Into the 1980s and the late-twentieth century, assisted reproduction, including donor conception,

63 Daniels and Taylor, n 59, p 156.

64 A donor-conceived person and recipient parent respectively, as well as experienced advocates for the release of information to donor-conceived families, and leaders of donor conception support groups.

65 D. Adams and C. Lorbach, 'Accessing Donor conception Information in Australia: A Call for Retrospective Access' (2012) 19(4) *Journal of Law and Medicine* 704, 709.

66 R. Cook, S. Golombok, A. Bish et al., 'Disclosure of Donor Insemination: Parental Attitudes' (1995) 65(4) *American Journal of Orthopsychiatry* 540–559; F. Shenfield, 'Privacy Versus Disclosure in Gamete Donation: A Clash of Interest, of Duties or an Exercise in Responsibility' (1997) 14(7) *Journal of Assisted Reproduction Genetics* 371–373; F. Shenfield and S.J. Steele, 'What Are the Effects of Anonymity and Secrecy on the Welfare of the Child in Gamete Donation?' (1997) 12(2) *Human Reproduction* 392–395.

67 S. Shivaji. 'The Journey of R.G. Edwards: From a Single Cell to Louise Joy Brown' (2011) 100(4) *Current Science* 488–490.

became widespread. The technology advanced rapidly and egg donation also became a reality. The world's first child conceived via egg donation at the Monash IVF Clinic was born in Victoria, Australia, in 1984.[68] In July 1983, a Southern California clinic also reported a successful pregnancy, and subsequent birth on 3 February 1984, resulting from the use of a donor egg that was fertilized with the recipient husband's sperm and then transferred into the wife's uterus.[69] During this period, some jurisdictions engaged in further political inquiries to consider whether assisted reproduction needed to be regulated and if so how. Many such inquiries included consideration of donor conception and the rights of donor-conceived people to information. Across the globe, there was acknowledgment of donor-conceived people's possible interest in, and/or rights to, information about their genetic heritage. However, there was also variance in whether such interest was seen to prevail over the practice of secrecy and anonymity.

In some jurisdictions such as Sweden, some states of Australia and Austria, reports recommended that donor-conceived offspring had a right to identifying and or non-identifying information about their donors. Yet, in other jurisdictions, despite acknowledgement of the issue, support remained for not disclosing a donor-conceived person's status and the donor of gametes remaining anonymous. Table 1.1 lists numerous inquiries across the Western World that explored issues of donor conception and the release of information during this time period. The list is not exhaustive, but illustrates a significant rise in inquiries and reports during the period, and therefore an increase in public discussion of the practices and issues raised by donor conception.

Interestingly, Table 1.1 not only illustrates the differing ethical, social and legal positions taken in relation to information released during the 1980s, but also gives indication that over time, some jurisdictions changed their position and moved to require information release. The positions taken by the respective jurisdictions are further explored in Part II of this book, which discusses laws and practices regarding information released in the modern day. Suffice to note here that it is clear that while some jurisdictions continued practicing secrecy and anonymity, others, particularly in Europe and Australia, showed growing recognition, as donor conception became more widespread, that children conceived using donor gametes may seek, and had a right to know, information about their donor. Some jurisdictions passed laws early to recognize this right (see for example Sweden, Austria and Victoria), while others would take some time. Nevertheless, for some, the culture of secrecy and anonymity surrounding sperm and egg

68 Reported on Monash IVF clinic's website: "In 1983, the team achieved and delivered the world's first human frozen embryo IVF pregnancy and birth, and in 1984, the first donor egg IVF pregnancy," available at http://monashivf.com/the-history-of-ivf-a-chronology, accessed 16 March 2016.

69 D. Greenfield and S. Caruso-Klock, 'Assisted Reproductive Technology and the Impact on Children' in Sharon N. Covington and Linda Hammer Burns (eds), *Infertility Counselling: A Comprehensive Handbook for Clinicians* (Cambridge University Press, 2006), p 478.

Table 1.1 Committee inquiries and reports on donor conception and subsequent laws (if any) during the 1980s and late twentieth century

Year	*Jurisdiction*	*Committee/Report*	*Supported release of information/ Subsequent laws (Nb. Laws may have subsequently changed – See Part II)*
1983	Sweden	Swedish Committee on Insemination Statens offentliga utredningar (SOU) (Swedish Government Official Reports) 1983:42	Yes, recommended anonymity should be prohibited. From 1985 laws commenced: information about donor held in special hospital records; donor-conceived children can access when 'sufficiently mature'.
1982–1984	Victoria	Committee to Consider the Social, Ethical and Legal Issues Arising from In Vitro Fertilization: 1 Interim Report (Waller, September 1982) 2 Issues Paper on Donor Gametes (Waller, April 1983) 3 Report on Donor Gametes and In Vitro Fertilization (Waller, April 1983) 4 Report on the Disposition of Embryos Produced by In Vitro Fertilization (Waller, April 1984)	Yes. A Central Register for information was set up via the *Infertility (Medical Procedures) Act* 1984. The law originally provided that donor-conceived people born with sperm donated after 1988 could access non-identifying information once they reached 18, while information that identified any person may only be released with the consent of the person about whom it relates. (Subsequent laws that came into force in 1995 prohibited anonymity, and required donor consent to release of information. Victorian laws have continued to broaden access over time, see Part II).
1984	South Australia	Report of the Working Party on In Vitro Fertilization and Artificial Insemination by Donor (January 1984)	No. Anonymity required. (Note – guidelines were later introduced in Australia in 2004 supporting information release and requiring all donors to consent to release of information; laws in South Australia changed in 2010 that adopted such guidelines as requirements for registration.)
1984	Queensland, Australia	Report of the Special Committee Appointed by the Queensland Government to Enquire into the Laws Relating to Artificial Insemination, In Vitro Fertilization and Other Related Matters (Demack, 1984)	Yes. The committee recommended oversight of ART and donor conception, however legislation in Queensland was never enacted. (Qld follows guidelines introduced in 2004 which support non-anonymous donation and information release, see Part II).

(*Continued*)

Table 1.1 (Continued)

Year	*Jurisdiction*	*Committee/Report*	*Supported release of information/ Subsequent laws (Nb. Laws may have subsequently changed – See Part II)*
1984	United Kingdom	Council for Science and Society (United Kingdom), Working Party, Human Procreation: Ethical Aspects of the New Techniques (May 1984)	No. Anonymity supported.
		Department of Health and Social Security, Report of the Committee of Inquiry into Human Fertilisation and Embryology (Warnock, July 1984)	No. Anonymity supported. Subsequent laws enacted in 1991 provided for recording of donor information, but not release of identifying information. Changes to the law removing anonymity would not occur until 2005, see Part II.
1984–1985	Tasmania, Australia	Committee to Investigate Artificial Conception and Related Matters 1 Interim Report (1984) 2 Final Report (1985)	Yes. Agreed that recipients and children of donor sperm should have access to non-identifying information about the donor. Recommended consent by donor before identifying information should be released. Urged proper recordkeeping at the institutional level. No laws were passed. (Tasmania follows guidelines introduced in 2004 which support non-anonymous donation and information release, see Part II).
1985	Ontario, Canada	Law Reform Commission, Report on Human Artificial Reproduction and Related Matters (1985)	No. The report supported the provision of false information on birth certificates and the anonymity of the gamete donor.
1984–1985	Australia (Federal)	Family Law Council 1 Interim Report (1984) 2 Creating Children: A Uniform Approach to the Law and Practice of Reproductive Technology in Australia (July 1985)	Yes, however, no national laws exist. (At a national level National Health and Medical Research Council Guidelines introduced in 2004 support non-anonymous donation and information release, see Part II).

1985	Germany	Minister for Research and Technology and Justice Minister, Working Group, In Vitro Fertilization, Genome Analysis, and Gene Therapy (Benda, German Federal Republic, 1985)	Yes. The Benda Report recommended that a child conceived by donor insemination should have free access to the details of his or her parentage, stating that the personal details of the donor be recorded and made available to the child produced when he or she turns 16. Similar recommendations were made in a 1986 report by the national legal association. Subsequent Court judgements have upheld this right.
1986	Spain	Congress of Deputies, General Secretariat, Special Commission for the Study of Human In Vitro Fertilization and Artificial Insemination, Report (1986)	No. Laws introduced in 1988 enshrined anonymity and secrecy in the law. The view of the committee was that anonymity protects both the donor and the child.
1986	United States	American Fertility Society, Ethics Committee, Ethical Considerations of the New Reproductive Technologies (September 1986)	Yes. No laws were introduced during this period to prohibit anonymity. U.S. states vary in practices. See Part II.
1984–1986	Western Australia	Committee to Enquire into the Social, Legal and Ethical Issues Relating to In Vitro Fertilization and Its Supervision 1 Interim Report (1984) 2 Report (1986)	No. Initial support for anonymity would later give way to a system that requires non-anonymous donation. Record keeping occurred from 1991, however laws would not be introduced until 2004 – See Part II.
1984–1986	Netherlands	Health Council, Committee on In Vitro Fertilization and Artificial Insemination by Donor 1 Interim Report on In Vitro Fertilization (1984) 2 Report on Artificial Reproduction, with Special Reference to In Vitro Fertilization, Artificial Insemination with Donor Sperm, and Surrogate Motherhood (1986)	No. Although subsequent inquiries and laws were introduced in 2004 to enable information release. See part II.
1986	New South Wales, Australia	New South Wales Law Reform Commission, Report 49 (1986) – Artificial Conception: Human Artificial Insemination	No. Recommended legislation be enacted to protect the anonymity of the donor. Such legislation was never enacted. (Laws enacted in 2010 provided for information recording and release).

donation was slowly being replaced by acceptance of the rights and interests of donor-conceived offspring to know about their donor.

Into the modern era of assisted reproduction

The availability of donor conception in the twenty-first century has risen exponentially. In the modern day, donor conception may involve the use of donated sperm or eggs or both, or a donated embryo. It may involve a woman using donor sperm if her husband (or male partner) is infertile or unable to use his own sperm (for example, due to a risk of passing on a genetic disorder) or if she does not have a male partner (i.e. she is single or in a lesbian relationship). It may involve the use of donor eggs; for example, in cases in which there has been ovarian failure, where there is the risk of passing on a genetic condition or increasingly if a woman is of a more mature age (often past 40). When donor eggs are used, they may be fertilized with the male partner's sperm, or donor sperm may be used if, for example, the woman does not have a male partner. Donated gametes or embryos may also now be used in some jurisdictions in surrogacy situations, in which a woman bears a child with the intention of handing it over to another person or couple to rear. Donor sperm may be used in such arrangements by either artificially inseminating the surrogate mother, known as 'traditional surrogacy', or by implanting in a surrogate mother embryo(s) which have been created by using donor sperm together with eggs from the 'commissioning woman' or donor eggs, known as 'gestational surrogacy'. Spare embryos from all of the previously described processes may also be donated to other women or surrogates.

Depending upon the jurisdiction, a sperm donor may donate sperm privately or at a hospital clinic, sperm bank, sperm agency or other brokerage arrangement (or any combination of, or all, of these). Private donor arrangements are also known to occur in which recipients may choose self-insemination or 'natural insemination' (i.e. via sexual intercourse). Egg and embryo donation, being more technical and invasive, take place in hospitals or clinics, and are less readily available.

In the modern day, laws vary across jurisdictions in relation to who may access donor conception (at least via a formal setting), what may be accessed and the legal ramifications (for example, concerning legal parentage of children) that result from using donor conception. For example, sperm, egg and/or embryo donation are not permitted everywhere, or are only permitted in certain circumstances.

The law still also varies concerning anonymous or non-anonymous donations. That is, in some jurisdictions sperm donation may only be permitted if requirements are met that the donation must be non-anonymous (i.e. allows for identity release). In other jurisdictions the law remains that sperm donation is anonymous. Payment may be permitted or prohibited; some countries may not permit or practice it at all.

Similarly, egg donation may fall under the following categories:

- illegal (e.g. Italy, Germany and Austria)
- legal only if anonymous and altruistic (without any compensation for the egg donor) (e.g. France)

- legal only if *non*-anonymous and altruistic (e.g. Australia, Canada – noting Australia allows reimbursement for 'reasonable expenses')
- legal only if anonymous, but egg donors may be reimbursed for inconvenience and/or expenses (e.g. Spain, Czech Republic and South Africa)
- legal only if *non*-anonymous, but egg donors may be compensated a limited sum for inconvenience and effort (e.g. the United Kingdom)
- legal whether or not it is anonymous, and egg donors may be compensated (e.g. the United States)
- unregulated (e.g. where no laws or other guidelines, exist)

In some countries, religion may influence what is or is not permitted.[70] For example, Christians may accept IVF provided that a husband and wife use their own sperm and eggs and no fertilized embryos are destroyed or discarded; Sunni Muslims may engage with fertility treatments that do not involve third-party donation of gametes; Shi'ite Muslims in some countries (but not others) may accept egg donations; in some Jewish communities donation may be accepted, but there is a question as to whether the donor needs also to be Jewish. It is important to note, however, that such practices (even if permitted) may still prove controversial within particular religions or sects.

In the twenty-first century, it is also important to note that an industry has developed in which people increasingly travel abroad to access reproductive services using donated gametes and/or surrogate mothers in some circumstances. This practice may occur because they cannot access such services in their home country, because they intentionally wish to use gametes/embryos that are anonymous or for other reasons such as cost or the safety and quality of services. This situation adds another complexity to the issue of whether, and if so how, information should be made available to children.

With the above in mind, there is no doubt that in the modern day, ART using donated eggs, sperm or embryos, as well as in some circumstances surrogacy, is a growth industry. In 2013, a study estimated that there had been over 5 million children born as a result of the use of assisted reproductive treatment since 1978.[71] The numbers of donor-conceived people remain unknown. However, it may be confidently assumed that donor conception touches the lives of several million people including donors, donor-conceived people, those accessing ART (recipients), siblings of donor-conceived people (biological and non-biological) and extended families. A number of places around the world also recognize different family forms including single, de-facto, GLBTI or married parent families, and recognize the children within them. However, many have not come to the point

70 S. Arabsalehi Nasrabadi, 'Shia and Sunni Attitudes Towards Egg Donation' (2014) 11 *Journal of Jahrom University of Medical Sciences* 81; Bagher Larijani and Farzaneh Zahedi, 'Ethical and Religious Aspects of Gamete and Embryo Donation and Legislation in Iran' (2007) 46(3) *Journal of Religious Health* 399–408.

71 G.D. Adamson, M. Tabangin, M. Macaluso & J. de Mouson. 'The number of babies born globally after treatment with the assisted reproductive technologies (ART) 100(3) *Fertility and Sterility*, S42.

of recognizing that children, or the adults they become, may have an interest in information about their conception, and about their donors and/or surrogate mothers. The following chapters explore the call for such information, and the search that some donor-conceived people, recipients and donors engage in to obtain the information they seek.

2 The call for information

Donor-conceived people, recipients and donors

Introduction

The history of donor conception illustrates that the secrecy surrounding the practice and decisions made concerning donor anonymity were focused primarily on sex, marriage, morality, adultery, masturbation, the presence of a doctor who would perform the insemination, inheritance, legal parentage and stigma concerning male infertility. As illustrated in Chapter 1, secrecy and anonymity were, and continue to be, influenced by moral, religious and/or legal views that primarily (if not solely) focus on the adults involved in the process.

Of course, moral, religious, social, cultural and legal views do often deeply, and reasonably, influence what a person, couple, community or even country accepts, permits or prohibits. However, once people engage in the process of assisted reproduction using a donor or surrogate, the matter becomes more complex. The process is not just about the adults engaged in the donor conception – the recipient(s), donor(s), brokers and doctors – it results in a child, and so therefore arguably, the child's future rights and interests must also be considered.

Decisions to maintain secrecy and anonymity do not appear to have been ill intended or meant to cause harm or distress to the resultant donor-conceived person. However, the interests and/or needs that some donor-conceived people have in knowing about their conception and/or genetic heritage have been largely ignored.

In the present day, while a number of jurisdictions recognize that donor-conceived people have an 'interest' or a 'right' to information, not all donor-conceived people who seek information have access to such records. Secrecy surrounding donor conception practices and the maintenance of anonymity of donors remain. There are significant inequities for donor-conceived people seeking information, depending on when and where they were born. Some will be able to access information, while others will not.

Throughout the late twentieth century and into the twenty-first century, as donor-conceived people have grown, reached maturity or even started their own families, there has been a clear increase in public demand for access to identifying and non-identifying information. This chapter therefore delves further into such calls, by examining the ethical and psychosocial arguments put forth as reasons for wanting information released. For some donor-conceived people, searching for information about their donor reflects a quest for identity, is seen as relevant to their sense of self, and involves the desire to know more about their genetic heritage. There is also the desire to know familial medical history, particularly where there may be a serious heritable illness. Some donor-conceived people discuss the risk and fear of forming consanguineous relationships, that is, partnering with someone that is a half-sibling or donor. Others just want to know their donor's name, they may want to thank the donor, and they may wish to know why the donor donated.[1]

Cutting through all of the arguments or reasons for acknowledging that some donor-conceived people desire information, and do search, is the position that if, as a society, we accept such practices, then we should not be perpetuating a system that actively deceives people about their origins, or denies them information most other people have.[2] Openness and honesty, and a right to choose for themselves, therefore also underpin the call. A fight for equality is prevalent.

Each of these arguments is further examined in this chapter, along with the recognition that recipient parents and donors have also increasingly expressed, and emphasized, the need for, and/or willingness to exchange information. But first, to place the call for information in a broader context, it is recognized that genealogical tracing is something that many other people do in the modern day, and that while discussion of information release for donor-conceived people often focuses on the *reasons* that they search (and either supports or discounts them), it is also important to keep in mind that sometimes those who seek information do not actually need to have a special *reason* at all. It is here that discussions of equity come into play.

Searching for information – genealogy understanding

What is it that donor-conceived people seek when, after being told the method of their conception, they decide they want to know more? Most often, they wish to know who their donor was; information about him or her, and possibly further information about their genetic heritage, and possible siblings. In some senses, their search for information may be seen as reflective of the practice of genealogy,[3] which is the tracing of a line of descent continuously from an ancestor.[4] However, often it is much more – for some, as stated previously, it is about identity, having a full picture of one's self and an understanding of how one came into being. Nevertheless, genealogical tracing is a good starting point to understand what

1 S. Allan, 'Psychosocial, Ethical and Legal Arguments for and Against the Retrospective Release of Information about Donors to Donor Conceived Individuals in Australia' (2011) 19(1) *Journal of Law and Medicine* 354.

2 R. Chisholm, 'Information Rights and Donor Conception: Lessons from Adoption?' (2012) 19(4) *Journal of Law and Medicine* 722.

3 From Greek: *genea*, 'race' or 'generation'; and *logos*, 'knowledge'.

4 *Oxford Dictionary of English* 3rd edition (Oxford University Press, Oxford, U.K. 2010).

searching entails and the importance that understanding one's history holds for many people and cultures.

Genealogy illustrates that a quest to identify the people to whom an individual shares connections, the quest to trace lineage, family, history and kinship, is almost as old as human history itself. It is also at least as old as the quest to cure infertility! When conducted by individuals or families, genealogy has been said to be a narrative of how outside forces shape an individual; a journey to build the story of one's own becoming.[5] Early evidence of this practice may be seen in historical cave paintings, tombstone art, petroglyphs and pictographs.[6] The value of genealogical information to a variety of cultures is also displayed throughout the ages, in the importance of family tracing to ancient Egyptians,[7] Assyrian record keeping (which was of significant genealogical value),[8] early Greek attempts to trace ancestry back to their gods,[9] and the Ancient Romans who practiced genealogy to 'distinguish between the patrician class (those with noble ancestry) and plebeians (commoners)'.[10] There are also biblical references found in the chapters of the begats. The first eight chapters of the book of the Chronicles give genealogies from Adam down through Abraham and other Old Testament patriarchs, and the New Testament gives varying accounts of the genealogy of Jesus Christ.[11] There was careful documentation of the names of emperors and other rulers in successive Chinese dynasties, and a number of Chinese religions promote active ancestor worship.[12] Genealogy has been integral to Japanese society[13] which utilizes the term *keifu* to designate not only blood ties but also other bonds that strengthen the family unit. Genealogical tracing has also been the custom of Incas, Maoris, North American Indians and the Haida people in Canada.[14]

From the Middle Ages, genealogy became important in Europe for the passing on of fiefdoms. Then, from around the sixteenth century, the United Kingdom, Germany and Scandinavian countries began to comprehensively record christenings, baptisms, marriages and burials. The recording of births, deaths,

5 Ronald Bishop, 'In the Grand Scheme of Things: An Exploration of Genealogical Research' (2008) 41 *The Journal of Popular Culture* 393, 394 citing Martin Saar, 'Genealogy and Subjectivity' (2002) 10(2) *European Journal of Philosophy* 231–245.
6 Donna Potter-Philips, 'History of Genealogy' (1999) *Family Chronicle*, available at http://www.familychronicle.com/HistoryOfGenealogy.html, accessed 9 February 2013.
7 Douglas J. Brewer and Emily Teeter, *Egypt and the Egyptians* (Cambridge University Press, 2001), p 95.
8 Potter-Philips, above n 6.
9 Ibid.
10 Ibid.
11 Ibid.
12 Ibid.
13 Extensive genealogical records can be found as far back as the Heian period (794–1185), in Japan as evidence by the publication of the *Shinsen Shōjiroku* in AD 814 which compiled the genealogies of 1182 families.
14 Potter-Philips, above n 6.

and marriages eventually became enshrined in the law – both reinforcing the importance placed on recording such information, and enabling better tracing of connections via paper-based records. In the 1820s in the United States, John Farmer, a historian and genealogist, 'succeeded in persuading [his] fellow citizens that genealogy was central to their understanding of American family, local, and national history'.[15] In 1845, the first genealogical society was founded and known as the New England Historical and Genealogy Society (NGS).[16]

While not without controversy – as genealogy, like donor conception, was in some parts influenced by the eugenics movement[17] – genealogy eventually became a pursuit that involved 'commoners' as well as 'noblemen', and modern-day scholars and researchers are interested in tracing lines of descent, mapping 'family trees', and investigating human connections.[18] In the United States, the importance many people place on genealogy led to the introduction of a resolution to designate the month of October as Family History Month.[19] Vast increases in the availability of family history resources have been seen with the advent of the Internet, which has also enabled cooperation on a global scale among researchers. Market research conducted in 2012 found 84 million people had spent money over the Internet to conduct genealogical research.[20]

With the possibility of DNA testing, this trend has only increased. In 2015, 700,000 to 1 million people were reported to have undergone DNA testing for genealogical reasons using the major DNA testing companies.[21] In 2016, it was

15 François Weil, 'John Farmer and the Making of American Genealogy' (September 2007) 80(3) *The New England Quarterly* 408–434.

16 Known as 'the New England Historical and Genealogical Society'.

17 Elizabeth Shown Mills notes that 'Genealogy became a tool of ideologies and prejudices rooted in concepts of blood, heredity, race, and stock. Genealogical organizations, including NGS, echoed those ideas. The first issue of the NGS Quarterly praised the (Northern European) "Blood that Made the Sturdy Races of New Netherland." That same year, the society's head, a physician, focused his presidential address on "The Problems That Now Confront Us" – specifically, the "degeneracy and decay of modern society" and the "negative" influence of immigrants. He argued that solutions to these "problems" lay in wise reproductive choices made possible by the new "sciences" of genealogy and eugenics.' Similar comments appeared in other genealogical journals.

18 See E.S. Mills, 'Genealogy in the "Information Age": History's New Frontier?' (December 2003) 91 *National Genealogical Society Quarterly* 260–277.

19 First established pursuant to United States Senate, Resolution 160 of the 107th Congress, 1st Session, 2001, and United States Senate, Resolution 330 of the 107th Congress, 2nd Session, 2002.

20 Global Industry Analysts Inc., *Genealogical Products and Services* 2012, cited in Bruce Falkner, Ancestry.com's Genealogical Juggernaught, *Bloombergs Business Week*, September 2012; See also PR Web, Online Researchers Spur Growth of Genealogy Industry, According to a New Report by Global Industry Analysts, Inc., 2012, available at http://www.prweb.com/releases/genealogy_research/ancestors_archives/prweb9092131.htm, accessed 16 March 2016.

21 International Society of Genetic Genealogy (ISOGG), Genetic Genealogy 2015, available at http://www.isogg.org/wiki/Timeline:Genetic_genealogy_2015, accessed 16 March 2016.

reported that over 3 million people had already used direct-to-consumer genetic testing to find information about their ancestry.[22]

In modern times, people researching their genealogy describe their motivations to include the desire to carve out a place for one's family in the larger historical picture, a sense of responsibility to preserve the past for future generations and a sense of self-satisfaction in accurate storytelling.[23] Genealogy has thus become a form of scholarship, a certain type of history tracing and building that appeals to a large number of people across cultures and time. People, seek information to not only understand their personal origins but also to have a sense of place within human history.

Donor-conceived people and their call for information

Donor-conceived people's quest for information may therefore be reflective of an intrinsic human desire to map one's familial ancestors; a desire that exists in many cultures and communities across the globe. However, the circumstances of their own genealogical 'becoming' can be somewhat more complicated. They may begin to build their family tree based upon those who parent them, as this is a very important part of their story. Some also want information about their *genetic* relatives, their donor, siblings, and other genetic relatives.[24] They may be interested in knowing about their genetic ancestors and extended biological family just as many other people in the general population are interested in knowing such information.

However, beyond this, for certain donor-conceived people, there are deeper motivations for searching for genetic relatives. Some report that their quest involves a search for identity, self-understanding, the need for medical history, a fear of forming consanguineous relationships with first-degree relatives and an important fight for equality and truth. It is to these issues that the discussion now turns.

22 Joyce C. Harper, Debbie Kennett, and Dan Reisel, 'The End of Donor Anonymity: How Genetic Testing Is Likely to Drive Anonymous Gamete Donation out of Business' (2016) *Human Reproduction*. Published online, 16 April 2016, doi:10.1093/humrep/dew065, available at http://humrep.oxfordjournals.org/content/early/2016/04/08/humrep.dew065.full, accessed 16 May 2016.

23 Ronald Bishop, 'In the Grand Scheme of Things: An Exploration of Genealogical Research' (2008) 41 *The Journal of Popular Culture* 393–412.

24 The majority of offspring when surveyed also wish to know the identity of any half-siblings; J.E. Scheib, M. Riordan and S. Rubin, 'Adolescents with Open Identity Sperm Donors: Reports from 12–17 Year Olds' (2005) 20(1) *Human Reproduction* 239 (89%); V. Jadva, T. Freeman, W. Kramer and S. Golombok, 'Experiences of Offspring Searching for and Contacting Their Donor Siblings and Donor' (2010) 20(4) *Reproductive Biomedicine Online* 523 (78%).

A sense of identity

Despite a child's development being shaped by social and biological factors, for some, knowledge of their immediate genetic heritage is considered as being integral to their self-identity. As such, it has been reported that when donor-conceived individuals discover they are not biologically related to their parent(s), some have reported feeling a sense of 'lost identity' and a corresponding desire to know more about their donor.[25]

In studies conducted to evaluate the consequences of non-disclosure on an individual's sense of identity, some respondents described feeling as though they were 'freaks' or 'products of experiments' or that they were in some way 'incomplete'. McNair writes, '[T]hese sentiments suggest that identity is related to genetic inheritance in some way, and a fuller sense of identity for a donor-conceived person may only be achieved through access to details about their donor.'[26] Such sentiments are illustrated, for example, by Lauren Burns who found out that she was donor conceived at age 21. She said:

> You know, I'd look in the mirror and just have so many questions and so few answers. And it was almost like a splinter in my brain: it was just something that continuously bothered me that I thought about.

Lauren engaged in an extensive search for the man who had donated sperm to assist in her conception, and saw this information as an integral part of her identity.[27]

Such sentiments are not only seen in donor-conceived people who find out late about their status as donor conceived, they may also exist for donor-conceived people who have known about their status all along. For example, Damian Adams, a donor-conceived person born in 1973, whose parents had always been open with him about his having been donor conceived, said:

> While I started off searching for non-identifying information (as I at one time agreed with anonymity), I have now changed my perspective, and I wish to know who this person is. This view changed after the birth of my daughter. It was a moment not too dissimilar to the moment that parents often report experiencing when they hold their child for the first time and stare into their baby's eyes. It was an acceptance and knowledge of a biological connection.

25 A. Turner and A. Coyle, 'What Does It Mean to Be Donor Offspring? The Identity Experience of Adults Conceived by Donor Insemination and the Implications for Counselling and Therapy' (2000) 15(9) *Human Reproduction* 2041; Jadva, Freeman, Kramer and Golombok, above n 24, at 524.

26 Dr Ruth McNair, *Outcomes for Children Born of A.R.T. in a Diverse Range of Families* (Victorian Law Reform Commission, Victoria, Australia 2004), p 43.

27 Lauren Burns, Searching for C11, *Australian Story*, 11 August 2014, available at http://www.abc.net.au/austory/content/2014/s4065081.htm, accessed 16 March 2016.

That no matter what might happen in the world, we would always be father and daughter. No one or no thing would ever be able to change this. This biological connection made me think about how I would feel if my daughter grew up not knowing who I was. I need to complete the picture of who I am not only for myself but also for my children. My search is just as much for them as it is for me. The implications of being donor conceived do not end with me but continue on into the following generations.[28]

For Damian, his quest for information about his donor extends beyond himself as he desires to pass this information about who he is, and who his social and biological ancestors were, on to his children and future generations.

Genealogical bewilderment

In some instances, the term 'genealogical bewilderment',[29] has been used to describe the sense of insecurity and/or confusion that donor-conceived people may feel when wondering about their genetic heritage, who their donor is or their own self-identity. The term refers to a notion first developed in the 1950s and 1960s to explain what psychologists Erich Wellisch and H. J. Sants considered the cause of poor outcomes for some of their adopted patients. Sants said that a 'genealogically bewildered child is one who either has no knowledge of his natural parents, or only uncertain knowledge of them . . .' and that such lack of knowledge 'fundamentally undermine[s] his security and therefore affects his mental health'.[30] In the donor conception (or surrogacy) context, it has been used to describe the issues some donor-conceived people express as the result of being donor conceived and denied information about their genetic heritage.

However, one must note that while examples abound of people who describe insecurity, doubt, and feelings of loss of identity when told of their donor-conceived status, examples also abound of people who do not seem to have suffered any fracturing in self-identity or feelings of bewilderment, but who may still wish to find information. Thus, there is an array of feelings donor-conceived people have about their families, their identity and their sense of self.

Some donor-conceived people describe a family setting in which there was a lack of bonding and self-doubt – knowing that there was a secret but not knowing what that secret was – and feelings of relief and anger on finding out. For

28 Questions for Damian Adams, 'Donor Conceived Adult' (2 October 2008) *The New Atlantis: A Journal of Technology and Society*, available at http://www.thenewatlantis.com/blog/conceptions/questions-for-damian-adams-donor conceived-adult, accessed 16 March 2016.

29 Turner and Coyle, above n 26; E. Wellisch, 'Children Without Genealogy: A Problem with Adoption' (1952) 13(1) *Mental Health* 41–42; H. Sants, 'Genealogical Bewilderment in Children with Substitute Parents' (1964) 37(2) *British Journal of Medical Psychology* 133–141.

30 Sants, above n 29, p 133.

example, one donor-conceived person described her feelings on finding out that she was donor conceived (at age 41) as follows:

> I had finally got to the bottom of this enormous secret and everything suddenly made sense. But then I felt angry. I should have grown up knowing this key information about me and where I come from. At the age of six, I was left to grieve a man I believed to be my father, when actually my father was alive and living 80 miles away. And I grew up thinking that the reason my mother couldn't seem to bond with me must be that I was worthless.[31]

The same donor-conceived person described her sense of relief and self after having discovered her biological father:

> I'm a different person because of it. I've read my father's autobiography . . . and discovered huge similarities. I'm happier and calmer for knowing about him and ultimately who I am.[32]

Another donor-conceived person suggests that his donor conception created remoteness from his social father, and alludes that keeping a child's donor conception a secret is ultimately destructive in some way:

> It certainly helped explain things like my father's remoteness . . . this large, empty space opened up in my life and I became determined to fill it by finding out about my biological father. Now that I have found out who he was, there is no doubt I do identify with him. It hasn't weakened my sense of family – the one that I was brought up in, I mean. In fact, I believe that knowing what I do now while I was growing up might have made my relationship with my social father, now dead, closer. Any big secret sits in the middle of a family like a landmine – you have to watch what you say because any bit of conversation might lead to that secret. That is certainly the way we lived.[33]

For others, the concept of genetic bewilderment does not adequately describe their situation as it indicates a level of distress, harm or dysfunction that has not existed for them. For many, the desire to know more about their donor often co-exists with the love and affection they feel for and from their non-biological parent(s); in many cases, these relationships have been reported to be strong and positive.[34] For some, discovering that they were donor conceived produces an

31 Christine Whipp, United Kingdom, 2011. In Kate Hilpern, 'Donor Conception, I'd Got to the Bottom of a Secret,' *The Guardian*, 5 November 2011.

32 Ibid.

33 Barry Stevens, United Kingdom, 2011. In Kate Hilpern, 'Donor Conception, I'd Got to the Bottom of a Secret' *The Guardian*, 5 November 2011.

34 P.P. Mahlstedt, K. LaBounty and W.T. Kennedy, 'The Views of Adult Offspring of Sperm Donation: Essential Feedback for the Development of Ethical Guidelines within the Practice

acute awareness of how much they were wanted by parents who endured fertility treatment in order to give birth to them.[35] Nevertheless, such positive feelings about the family within which the donor-conceived person lives, and the relationships he or she has, can, and do, coexist with a desire to know about one's donor (and other relatives) and the features and characteristics they may share.[36] Feelings of frustration, and even anger, at being denied information about their donor-conceived status may again exist simultaneously:

> I don't understand how you couldn't feel resentment about being lied to about something like this. That certainly doesn't mean you can't feel grateful for how much they did to get you. I personally feel both. It's tough being lied to by your parents about something so integral to your understanding of yourself. At the same time, I love my parents and am grateful for how much they wanted me. My point is, it's mainly the lie that causes resentment. Not the fact that I am a donor child.[37]
>
> (*Dan: donor conceived* 1/08)

In contrast, however, it must be noted that for other donor-conceived people, neither genealogical bewilderment nor loss of identity nor a desire to have information about or to know their donor is experienced. This view is clearly illustrated in the following statement by an adult donor-conceived person:

> I was conceived through sperm donation, and my mother was adopted, so the nature and meaning of genetic relationships is something that has long been thought about and felt deeply in my family. I have never met my donor "father", and I have no desire to do so. I do not see this lack of contact with my biological father as something missing in my life, and I have no hurt at the fact of my creation. . . . This is a pervasive and cruel cultural myth, this idea that you cannot know who you are unless you know your biological parent. My whole life I have been subjected to the shocked responses of people who – on learning that I don't know my donor – could not understand how

of Assisted Reproductive Technology in the United States' (2010) 93(7) *Fertility and Sterility* 2236.

35 Mahlstedt, LaBounty and Kennedy, above n 34; S. Golombook, A. Brewaeys, A. Bish et al., 'Families Created by New Reproductive Technologies: Quality of Parenting and Social and Emotional Development of Children' (1995) 66 *Child Development* 285.

36 Turner and Coyle, above n 25; Jadva, Freeman, Kramer and Golombok, above n 24, p 524; Michelle Dennison, 'Revealing Your Sources: The Case for Non-Anonymous Gamete Donation' (2008) 21(1) *Journal of Law and Health* 1, 13; Vardit Ravitsky, 'Knowing Where You Come from: The Rights of Donor Conceived Individuals and the Meaning of Genetic Relatedness' (2010) 11(2) *Minnesota Journal of Law, Science & Technology* 655, 670.

37 Donor Sibling Registery, *Voices of the Donor Conceived, Donors and Parents, Stories, and Thoughts from Donor Families* (2008), available at https://www.donorsiblingregistry.com/sites/default/files/files/voices%20of%20the%20donor%20conceived.pdf, accessed 16 March 2016.

> I could be comfortable with this and believed I must be harbouring hurt about it. . . . The reality is you – the things that make you really you – are not your genes.[38]

The previous quote illustrates that there are a variety of feelings about donor-conceived status and identity (both of self and within a family) and that not all people's feelings may be likened to genealogical bewilderment (as defined by Sants or as generally adopted to refer to confusion about identity). There are varying degrees of wanting information, differences between people who were lied to about their status and those that were not, people who feel hurt and those who do not, those who suffer deep psychological impact from not knowing who their donor was and those who do not, and those who for a multitude of other reasons do or do not want information (whether feeling harmed in some way, or not).

Perhaps what is key here is that those who do not want information are not affected by not having it, and if it were available could simply choose not to access it. However, for those for whom knowledge about genetic heritage *is* important for reasons of self-identity and/or those described as follows, it appears unreasonable to deny them. It is also unreasonable to discount such feelings or the call for information about genetic heritage, when there was a value placed on at least some genetic connection with their rearing parents in the first instance. That is, donor conception most often takes place using artificial insemination of the mother's egg or egg donation using the father's sperm. It may be confusing (or even bewildering!) for some to know that a genetic connection mattered to the parents to this extent, but at the same time to be told that the genetic link to their 'donor' and half-siblings does or should not matter to them.

Access to medical information

The importance of having access to information about a biological parent's medical history is undeniable.[39] There is now significant understanding that it is useful to know whether there is a familial history of heart disease, diabetes, cancer, mental health issues and/or other heritable diseases. There are advantages for diagnoses, prognosis, screening, prevention and treatment.

Donor-conceived individuals who are denied access to familial medical histories may be placed at an increased risk of suffering from a preventable disease because of not having access to information about their genetic heritage. For example, a donor, who donated in the 1970s or 1980s, when donor conception

38 Amy Corderoy, Submission DCP77, 26 October 2011, Law Reform Committee, *Inquiry into Access by Donor Conceived People to Information about Donors*, available at http://www.parliament.vic.gov.au/images/stories/committees/lawrefrom/iadcpiad/submissions/DCP77_-_Amy_Corderoy.pdf, accessed 16 March 2016.

39 Centers for Disease Control and Prevention (CDC), 'Awareness of Family Health History as a Risk Factor for Disease' (2004) 53(44) *MMWR Morbidity and Mortality Weekly Report* 1044–1047.

was shrouded in secrecy, may not until more recently have become aware that they are a carrier of certain diseases. Similarly, a donor-conceived individual may become aware of a heritable condition, but has no way presently to notify his or her donor(s) or half-siblings conceived using the same donor gametes. As there is often no linkage between the donor and the donor-conceived person, or vice versa, or to donor-conceived siblings in many parts of the world, alerting relevant parties to health information is problematic. This secrecy may have ramifications not just for the person unaware of such information, but for generations to come.

Two modern-day examples of the ramifications of donor anonymity on health outcomes clearly illustrate the significant consequences that denial of information can produce.

Narelle Grech

The first example is that of Narelle Grech, a donor-conceived woman who died on 26 March 2013 following a two-year battle with bowel cancer. The following extract is from a submission she made to her state government in 2011 concerning her condition, lack of knowledge about her donor, the impact it had on her, and her fear that her eight other (unknown) donor-conceived siblings were at risk:

> My name is Narelle Grech. I am 28 years old, donor conceived and on May 2nd this year [2011] I was diagnosed with stage 4 bowel cancer. My life has been turned upside down since my diagnosis. I have never been ill in my life, there is no history of cancer on my maternal side of the family and there were no real warning signs that this illness would strike at such a young age. It is believed that a person who is diagnosed with stage 4 (medically deemed to be "incurable") bowel cancer has likely inherited it through their genes.
>
> When I was first told about this diagnosis by my surgeons following emergency surgery (to remove the large tumour which had caused my large bowel to rupture) he said it was most likely related to a genetic factor. At this point I cried, not only for the fact that I was now terminally ill, but also as I most likely inherited this disease from my paternal family and my anonymous sperm donor T5.
>
> Never having a complete medical history was never a concern to me, until this year. And now I see why it is vital that not only donor conceived people have access to their genetic information, but they are also given full access to their medical histories and where possible this is updated every 5 years or so. Had I known that cancer is in my family I could have been scanned and tested for this years ago. The choice to be tested would have been mine and this is the most frustrating thing in all of this. The system that has helped to create me has also left me powerless to know basic information regarding my identity and more importantly my own health. If I had this knowledge upon finding out at 15 years of age I would been able to make the decision to be tested for this type of cancer. The cancer may also not have grown by

> this point, or at least not be metastasized (having spread extensively to my liver and lungs) deeming me incurable. Maybe it could have been caught early, giving me the opportunity to beat it, but as it stands the prognosis is grim. My oncologist told me that on average people who present as I do can expect to live for approximately 5 years at most. I am not ready to die and have started chemotherapy, but this is to "increase my life expectancy" and it is a terrible experience to have to go through. I cannot work or enjoy the life that I once knew. I feel like my youth has been taken away from me and I am furious to think that this could have been prevented. I cannot explain what it's like to have to face such questions about mortality at the age of 28.
>
> I am also concerned that my 8 half siblings, who were conceived by the same donor, may be walking about and carrying this possible disease without knowing it. Not only may they have no idea that they are donor conceived they may also be terminally ill. They may have passed this illness onto any children they have. This diagnosis does not only affect me, it possibly affects so many other people and they should be made aware if this is the case.
>
> In seeking to access my records and information about my biological father (sperm donor T5) I am not wishing to impede on his privacy or cause him any undue effects. What I want is something that most people take for granted, the choice to know their ancestry, their identity and their complete medical history. I never realised how great an impediment answering "unknown" to the question of paternal medical history on my medical forms would be. Now I am facing dying before I know who my father is, who my paternal family is, who I am. I am beyond angry. I am beyond frustrated and I am tired of waiting for the legislation to change so that ALL donor conceived people are treated with the dignity and respect that every other Victorian is awarded – that they are provided with THEIR TRUTH. . . .[40]

In Narelle's case, the then Premier of the state in which she lived (Victoria, Australia), stepped in and granted access to her files. She met with her donor father only months before her death. He said of Narelle's fifteen-year search for information, that if he had been contacted earlier, he would have come forward. Her eight siblings have yet to be found or notified – noting that some may not even know they are donor conceived and an active search does not appear to be under way. Narelle's biological father (as she referred to him) continues to campaign for the release of information to donor-conceived people.[41]

40 Narelle Grech, Inquiry Submission to Victorian Law Reform Committee: Inquiry into Access by Donor Conceived People to Information about Donors, August 2011, 5/09/2011mhtml:file://S:\Law Reform http://www.parliament.vic.gov.au/images/stories/committees/lawrefrom/iadcpiad/submissions/DCP67_-_Narelle_Grech.pdf, accessed 16 March 2016.

41 See for example news media stories regarding the reunion of Narelle Grech and Ray Tonna, and her subsequent death: Farrah Tomazin, 'Suddenly She's There': Daughter and Donor Dad United, *The Age*, 17 March 2013, available at http://www.theage.com.au/victoria/

Sperm donor 7042

The second case example is that of an anonymous Danish sperm donor (number 7042) from Nordic Cryobank ApS. The man transmitted the nerve disorder neurofibromatosis type I (NF1) to a number of donor-conceived offspring worldwide.[42] Effects of neurofibromatosis can range from hearing loss, learning impairment, and heart and blood vessel (cardiovascular) complications to severe disability due to nerve compression by tumors, loss of vision and severe pain. The condition may lead to a shortened life expectancy by an average of fifteen years.

The total number of donor-conceived offspring of donor 7042 remains unknown.[43] In September 2012 the Danish National Board of Health, the Danish Broadcasting Corporation and DR TV reported forty-three children conceived in Danish fertility clinics of which twenty-five are Danish citizens and eighteen are citizens in Norway and Sweden.[44] Donor specimens have also reportedly been used in the United States, Canada, Belgium, Ireland, Georgia, Greece, Spain and Thailand.[45] Annette Hagerup and Cecilie Pederson, from the Centre for Rare Diseases Department of Pediatrics, Aarhus University, report that '[a]ccording to the world's largest sperm bank, Cryos International – Denmark ApS, who exports to more than 70 countries, one single donor could possibly father more than 200 children globally' (5, 6). In relation to donor 7042, there were reports in 2015 that there were ninety-nine donor-conceived people across the world conceived using the sperm of donor 7042, although this number has been contested by the Danish sperm bank.

It appears that, thus far, eighteen affected donor-conceived children have been identified – eleven from Denmark, Sweden and Norway; five from the United States; and two in Belgium. Again, due to the widespread use of the sperm, and the donor anonymity, the actual number of offspring affected remains unknown.

Broader arguments have been made in relation to this incident (and others in which autosomal dominant diseases have been diagnosed in offspring of sperm donors).[46] The first is that the number of pregnancies permitted from one sperm

suddenly-shes-there-daughter-and-donor-dad-united-20130316–2g7mv.html, accessed 16 March 2016; Farrah Tomazin, Sperm Donor Daughter Dies After Reunion, *The Age*, 7 April 2013, available at http://www.theage.com.au/victoria/sperm-donor-daughter-dies-after-reunion-20130406–2hdvd.html, accessed 16 March 2016.

42 Anders Hanson, 'Danish Sperm Donor Passes Neurofibromatosis on to Five Children' (2012) 345 *British Medical Journal* e6570.

43 Annette Hagerup and Cecilie Pederson, 'Re: Danish Sperm Donor Passes Neurofibromatosis on to Five Children: Response' (2012) 345 *British Medical Journal* e6570.

44 Ibid.

45 Ibid.

46 There have been other reports of incidents in which sperm donation has led to offspring inheriting diseases including, for example, hypertrophic cardiomyopathy, Marfan syndrome and polycystic kidney disease. See B.J. Maron, J.R. Lesser, N.B. Schiller, K.M. Harris, C. Brown and H.L. Rehm, 'Implications of Hypertrophic Cardiomyopathy Transmitted by Sperm Donation' (21 October 2009) 302(15) *Journal of American Medical Association*

donor should be limited. In fact, the Danish law regarding artificial conception recently underwent revision with the Danish Board of Health recommending restricting the earlier permitted number of twenty-five to twelve pregnancies per sperm donor. The second brings forth the argument that there is an urgent need for international legislation and regulation as the donor industry ships sperm and eggs worldwide. The primary goal of these first two measures would be to avoid a greater number of affected offspring from a disease gene-carrying sperm donor than could have occurred from natural conception.

Other suggestions regard the practice of screening, and also the ongoing exchange of information among donors, recipients and donor-conceived people. In an article published in the journal *Human Reproduction* in 2012, Callum et al. recommended that documentation and communication of health information must continue after the collection and distribution of gametes. They recommend a systematic, confidential system for the collection and investigation of reports of birth defects and the long-term health of donors, donor-conceived persons and their biological relatives; assessment of the information reported and interpretation of the relevant risks for other biologically related individuals by knowledgeable healthcare professionals; an established structure for communicating health updates and risk information to individuals to whom it may be relevant; and complete traceability of gamete distribution records, or preferably, accurate documentation of birth records and periodically updated client contact information.[47] Such measures clearly rely on being able to identify and locate donors, recipients and donor-conceived offspring.

Fear and risk of forming consanguineous relationships

Yet another reason given for the call for open disclosure about donor-conceived status and removal of anonymity is that some donor-conceived individuals report the fear of unknowingly forming relationships with siblings or possibly their unknown donor.[48] While the actual occurrence of such relationships is unknown (as the actual number of donor-conceived individuals is unknown) such a risk may be higher in jurisdictions with small populations and a significant number of donor-conceived individuals in existence.

While it has been claimed in international reports that one way to avoid half-siblings forming relationships is through the restriction of a donor to one donation, it is clear that this is not and has not been the approach to donor conception

1681–1684; (12) The Donor Sibling Register. Medical Issues, available at https://www.donorsiblingregistry.com/resource-library/medical-issues, accessed 16 March 2016.

47 P. Callum, L.M. Messiaen, P.V. Bower, F. Skovby, J. Iger, S. Timshel, C.A. Sims and R.E. Falk, 'Gonosomal Mosaicism for an NF1 Deletion in a Sperm Donor: Evidence of the Need for Coordinated, Long-Term Communication of Health Information Among Relevant Parties' (2012) *Human Reproduction* 1–4, doi:10.1093/humrep/des01.

48 Marilyn Crawshaw, *Submission 156*, 7 to the Australian Senate Legal and Constitutional Affairs Reference Committee Inquiry into Donor Conception Practices in Australia (2010).

anywhere.[49] In many clinics and doctors' surgeries, donors are likely to have donated multiple times. Some donors may also have donated at multiple clinics, and across jurisdictions. The risk of siblings (and/or donors) forming relationships with related individuals may be more acute in states and territories with small populations, where donor conception has been practiced with inadequate record keeping or where information is retained but unavailable.[50]

Entering consanguineous relationships may also have legal ramifications. For example, in Australia, the Commonwealth Marriage Act makes unlawful marriages between an individual and their parent or an individual and their half-sibling.[51] The effect of this provision is to invalidate the marriage because such relationships fall under a prohibited category within the act.[52] In that jurisdiction, state criminal law also makes incest between individuals and their parents and half-siblings a punishable offence.[53] While such an offence requires knowledge of blood relations, if half-siblings were unwilling to separate upon discovering their biological connection, this places them in an uncertain position regarding the legality of their relationship. However, beyond the legal difficulties, there is also the chance that such relationships would bear children, leading to genetic or chromosomal difficulties in those children due to having genetically related parents.[54]

49 In Victoria, the maximum number of families is 10, *Assisted Reproductive Treatment Act (2008)* (Vic) s 29. In New South Wales, the number is 5, *Assisted Reproductive Technology Act (2007)* (NSW) s 27(1). In Western Australia, the number is 5 *Human Reproductive Technology Act 1991* (WA) (see 'Paragraph 8.1, Human Reproductive Technology Directions (WA), Western Australian Government Gazette, 30 November 2004, p 5434). In Queensland, South Australia, Tasmania, the Northern Territory and the Australian Capital Territory, the NHMRC guidelines cover the issue and provide that 'clinics must take all reasonable steps to reduce the numbers of genetic relatives created through donor gamete programs' to protect donor conceived people, and donors, from having too many genetic siblings or too many offspring, respectively': NHMRC Guideline 6.3. A number of submissions to the Senate Committee noted concern that despite limiting numbers, inconsistent registration of donors between states prevents accurately knowing the amount of families a donor has assisted: Senate Legal and Constitutional Affairs Reference Committee, *Donor Conception Practices in Australia* (2011), p 73, [5.16].

50 New South Wales Law Reform Commission, *Artificial Conception: Human Artificial Insemination*, Discussion Paper 11 (1984).

51 *Marriages Act 1961* (Cth) s 23(1)(b) makes marriages involving 'prohibited relationships' void. Section 23(2)(a)-(b) states that marriages 'between an individual and their parent and an individual and their sibling, including half-siblings' are 'prohibited relationships'.

52 Ibid.

53 See for example, *Crimes Act 1958* (Vic) ss 44 (2) & (4).

54 Robin L. Bennett, Arno G. Motulsky, Alan Bittles, Louanne Hudgins, Stefanie Uhrich, Debra Lochner Doyle, Kerry Silvey, C. Ronald Scott, Edith Cheng, Barbara McGillivray et al., 'Genetic Counseling and Screening of Consanguineous Couples and Their Offspring: Recommendations of the National Society of Genetic Counselors' (2002) 11(2) *Journal of Genetic Counseling* 97–119. (Note this article in recognizing the risk associated with forming consanguineous relationships makes recommendations for genetic counselling and screening for consanguineous couples and their offspring. Donor conceived individuals unaware

Moreover, the more significant and perhaps impactful situation for some donor-conceived people is that *the fear* of this occurring causes great distress.[55] Psychosocial and ethical dilemmas regarding the *threat* arising from consanguinity risks may in fact pose the greater risk to the emotional and social well-being of some donor-conceived individuals. For example, Crawshaw[56] describes how some donor-conceived individuals question 'whether their attraction to someone may be "genetic sexual attraction", and that an otherwise innocent statement such as "you look just like so-and-so" carries a very different significance to those personally affected by donor conception'.[57] She makes the point that 'the living experience with regard to consanguinity does not necessarily reflect the statistical risk'.[58] In other words, regardless of the actual statistical likelihood, or the legal ramifications, it is the lived experience that may have the biggest (negative) impact on a person who lacks information about his or her donor and/or half-siblings and therefore fears forming a relationship with a genetic relative.

Analogy with adoption

There are also similarities between donor-conceived people and adoptees. Psychologists have drawn many parallels between their experiences. In particular, donor-conceived and adopted people may share common feelings concerning being denied information about their status, being denied access to information about their biological parent(s) and/or siblings, and about the secrecy that has shrouded both practices.[59]

It is unsurprising, therefore, that like adoption, some donor-conceived people who are told (or discover) the truth about their status will seek further information about their genetic heritage. However, like adoptees, reactions will vary. For some, access to information may become an all-consuming issue, while others may be less affected or involved, perhaps only mildly interested or even uninterested.[60] Some may want contact with donors, half-siblings or other genetic relatives, while others will want to learn the facts, but not necessarily make contact. Some may seek information to share with their own children (for example, an accurate medical history) and for some, genetic information may be significant

---

of their relatedness to others would not have the opportunity to undergo such counselling/screening.)

55 Commonwealth, Senate Committee Hansard, 3 November 2010, oral evidence of donor-conceived individuals.

56 Honorary Fellow in Social Work, University of York; Chair of PROGAR (Project Group on Assisted Reproduction); expert social worker in matters related to donor conception and assisted reproduction.

57 Marilyn Crawshaw, *Submission 156*, 7 to the Senate Legal and Constitutional Affairs Reference Committee Inquiry into Donor conception Practices in Australia (2010).

58 Ibid.

59 Turner and Coyle, above n 25.

60 Chisholm, above n 2, citing NSW Law Reform Commission, Report 69 (1992) *Review of the Adoption Information Act 1990*, at 5.72–5.109.

not only to the donor-conceived person but to others, including descendants. For others, information will not be sought at all.

The issue becomes whether it is the donor-conceived person who is given the choice rather than that choice having been made for him or her prior to conception. Donor-conceived people (or adoptees) never agreed to being deceived or denied information by others.

It is also important to note a fundamental difference between donor conception and adoption. Professor Richard Chisholm, former Justice of the Australian Family Court, pointed out that '[t]he adoption process is intended to find a permanent home for an existing child, in circumstances where the birth parents are unavailable or are considered unable or unwilling to bring up the child[;] the donor conception process is intended to *produce* a child'.[61] If there had been no adoption, we would have a baby needing a home. If there had been no donor conception, we would have no baby.[62] This fundamental difference is important when considering the experiences of, and calls for information by, both groups. As a consequence of this difference, Chisholm argued that 'the case for information rights for donor offspring is at least as strong as the case for adoptees, and arguably even stronger' as they are intentionally created to meet the needs of others.[63]

Parents of donor-conceived individuals

Parents unable to provide information to their children

Laws in jurisdictions that do not provide for information release, also affect the parents of donor-conceived people. These parents are prevented from providing their children with information that many actually desire to impart. For example, during the Senate Committee Inquiry, the Victorian Infertility Counsellors Group submitted:

> Up until the [Assisted Reproductive Treatment Act 2008 (Vic)], fertile women had to travel interstate to seek treatment and did therefore not come under Victorian legislation [which provides for information recording and release]. These women and their children therefore do not have the same access to information about their donor origins as do donor-conceived offspring in the rest of the Victorian community. These women find it particularly difficult not to be able to provide their children with up to date and accurate information about their donor, often only having a few lines of

61 Chisholm, above n 2, p 736.
62 Ibid.
63 Ibid., p 739.

> information to share with their child. A retrospective national register would assist in rectifying this inequality.[64]

Issues of equity are again apparent. Parental interests and a desire to be open and able to provide their child with information about that child's genetic heritage are clearly denied. Parents are also affected in other ways. They may 'wish to thank the donor for helping them become a family and/or may wonder what they are like and what their child has inherited'.[65] They may also wish to refer to the donor by a name when telling their children about the method of conception, rather than referring to the person as 'donor'. Without laws mandating the retrospective release of information, parents are unable to share information within their families.

Parental curiosity about donor-conceived siblings and donors

In 2009, researchers from the United Kingdom's Cambridge University Centre for Family Research recruited 791 parents via the Donor Sibling Registry[66] to study why parents seek information about their donor-conceived children's donor-conceived siblings and donors.[67] The study found that the principal motivation of parents for searching for their child's donor siblings was curiosity. In relation to their search for their donor, their primary reason was to enhance their child's sense of identity.[68] Eleven per cent of parents who had found their child's donor siblings had found ten or more, with one parent finding fifty-five.

An overwhelming majority of parents reported positive experiences when contacting and meeting their child's donor siblings and donor. Few negative experiences were reported: 2 per cent reported negative experiences of contacting their child's donor siblings for themselves and 1 per cent of parents reported negative experiences for their child.[69] Parents frequently described feeling excited and happy on their child's behalf when they found donor siblings. They viewed the addition of such relationships to their children's lives as 'enriching', 'wonderful'

64 Senate Legal and Constitutional Affairs Reference Committee, *Donor Conception Practices in Australia* (2011), p 46 at [3.58].

65 Victorian Assisted Reproductive Treatment Authority, *Time to Consent?* Information Pamphlet, 2008.

66 The Donor Sibling Registry is a U.S.-based international registry that facilitates contact between donor conception families who share the same donor.

67 T. Freeman, V. Jadva, W. Kramer and S. Golombok, 'Gamete Donation: Parents' Experiences of Searching for their Child's Donor Siblings and Donor' (2009) 24(3) *Human Reproduction* 505–516. The parents consisted of 39 per cent lone mothers, 35 per cent lesbian couples and 21 per cent heterosexual couples. Also 91 per cent (717) of parents lived in the United States, 5 per cent (37) in Canada and 1 per cent (8) in the UK; other countries of residence included Austria, Germany, Ireland, Spain, Sweden, Australia, New Zealand and Israel.

68 Ibid.

69 Ibid., 511.

and 'fun'.[70] Most parents reported that the impact of searching for both their child's donor siblings and their child's donor had a 'neutral' or 'positive' influence their relationship with their child.[71] The study concluded that having access to information about a child's donor origins is important for some parents and has potentially positive consequences.[72]

Although based upon a 'self-selecting' group of parents – participants who were already engaged in seeking information (they had signed up to the register) – such results support the release of information. In particular, they show that 'kinship relationships are based on both direct and indirect genetic connections and shared understandings and experiences, out of which new concepts of the family are being defined and negotiated'.[73] As the world shifts to recognize and embrace diversity, and to support varying family types, it should also allow for extended family connections that are being newly defined in relation to donor conception.

Parental fear of telling

Some parents, however, may fear disclosing that their child was donor conceived. Some may have kept the secret for a long time, and feel they are now unable to tell for fear of rejection or the possibility of losing the child (or adult) they love.[74] Many parents received treatment when the culture of secrecy was strong, and may genuinely feel that they are protecting their children and their families by remaining silent or are ashamed of their battle with infertility.[75] Daniels stated that 'confidence is required in order to resist potential stigma and view donor conception as a way to build families in a positive manner'.[76]

Although the Cambridge University study illustrates that many of these fears may not become reality, some parents who conceived in the time when secrecy was emphasized, may need significant support in telling their children, and in accepting their offspring's desire for information. Nonetheless, when parents find the courage to tell, many describe feeling a sense of relief in telling their children, and in that they have been able to 'pass the baton' to the donor-conceived individual, recognizing that the information rightly belongs to them.[77]

70 Ibid.

71 Ibid., 509.

72 Ibid.

73 Dr Tabitha Freeman, research associate at the Centre for Family Research, University of Cambridge, available at http://www.disabled-world.com/news/research/donor-conceived-children.php, accessed 9 May 2011.

74 Ken Daniels, 'Donor Gametes: Anonymous or Identified' (2007) 21(1) *Best Practice and Research Clinical Obstetrics and Gynaecology* 113–128.

75 Ibid.

76 Ibid.

77 Public Communications by Parents and Donor conceived Individuals at the Victorian Reproductive Treatment Authority, 'Time to Tell Seminar', 7 May 2011, Victoria.

Donors

Donors do not necessarily wish to remain anonymous

It is not necessarily the case that past donors wish to remain anonymous.[78] In its submission to the Australian Senate Committee Inquiry in 2010, the Donor Conception Support Group quoted a former sperm donor who stated:

> I was a sperm donor during 1997–1998. [M]y donations were during the period when [d]onors had to sign away any future contact. This was a condition of participation and I only wanted to help people – but at the back of my mind was the hope that the rules would change to allow the resultant children to trace their donor fathers, if they wished to do so.[79]

Similarly, the Victorian Assisted Reproductive Treatment Authority (VARTA) stated that the belief that secrecy was paramount to protect all parties to the arrangement was based on myths 'that donors would not want to be contacted, that parents would not want to know more about their donor, and that donor-conceived individuals would not want information about their donor if they really loved their parents'.[80] VARTA stated that 'donors do not forget they have donated and often wonder about the people they helped to create. Who are they? Are they healthy? Are they happy? Are they loved?'[81]

At a seminar held in Victoria, Australia, aimed at educating parents about how to tell their children they were donor conceived, one donor stated:

> At the time of my donations, made in the early [19]80s, I don't think I understood what I was doing. I don't think I gave truly informed consent, as I was simply asked to sign a form, and had a brief discussion with the people who worked at the clinic about what had to be done from there. I don't believe I had a contract with anyone. I think I was told that it was anonymous, but this wasn't explained, and having seen an ad in the paper, and having known an infertile couple, I just wanted to help people. It was not until I had my own children that it began to dawn on me. I then one day received a letter from the ITA [infertility treatment authority], stating I had helped to conceive seven (7) other children. They are out there somewhere, they might not know, I have so many questions, and fear I will never know, they will never know.[82]

78 Rainbow Families Council, *Submission 73*, 2; DCSG, *Submission 122*, 139 to the Senate Legal and Constitutional Affairs Reference Committee Inquiry into Donor Conception Practices in Australia (2010).

79 DCSG, *Submission 122*, 74 to the Senate Legal and Constitutional Affairs Reference Committee Inquiry into Donor Conception Practices in Australia (2010).

80 Victorian Assisted Reproductive Treatment Authority, *Time to Consent?* Information Pamphlet, 2008.

81 Ibid.

82 Donor, Victorian Reproductive Treatment Authority, 'Time to Tell Seminar', 7 May 2011, Victoria.

Studies have also shown that donors who may once have wished for anonymity may at a later date wish to meet the donor-conceived individuals, that their thoughts on the matter may change over time.[83] Some studies have also indicated that the majority of donors agree to the release of medical records;[84] however, there is yet to be a system put into place that ensures these records are updated and that vital information is disseminated to offspring and recipient parents. There does not seem to be a blanket refusal to share information.

As seen in the following chapters, arguments made against the release of information about donors often center on the right to maintain privacy or the promise for anonymity that was made. However, because anonymity was mandated by the medical profession at the time of donation, one may question the perpetuation of secrecy and denial of information in an age where entitlement to information has been established.

In reviewing the release of information, we must not assume that donors wish to remain anonymous. For many donors, particularly in jurisdictions where there were no registers and no legislation, they were not given any choice. Legislation providing for the release of information could provide an 'opt out' for donors who do not wish to be contacted by allowing contact vetoes or preference statements similar to those described in the prior adoption analogy. This scenario is further discussed in Chapter 4, which illustrates that Victoria, Australia, has adopted this system, and in Chapter 8 and Chapter 9, which further explore issues pertaining to information release.

Arguing for openness and honesty

There are additional reasons that drive some donor-conceived people to search for information. Some report simply wanting to know a name for their donor; others wish to say thank you; while others want to know whether they have any half-siblings. Whether the reason is to address a harm that has been suffered, to prevent future harm or simply to search for information about one's biological heritage (donor conceived or not), it is clear that underpinning this search is a strong desire for openness and honesty. Simply put, they call for an end to secrecy and anonymity, and an opportunity to choose for themselves.

Professor Richard Chisholm, a former Family Court Judge and Law Commissioner, highlights general support for openness and honesty – or in the negative

83 M.A. Crawshaw, E.D. Blyth and K.D. Daniels, 'Past Semen Donors' Views about the Use of a Voluntary Contact Register' (2007) 14(4) *Reproductive Biomedicine Online* 411–417; K. Daniels, E. Blyth, M. Crawshaw and R. Curson, 'Short Communication: Previous Semen Donors and Their Views Regarding the Sharing of Information with Offspring' (2005) 20(6) *Human Reproduction* 1670–1675.

84 J.N. Robinson, R.G. Forman, A.M. Clark, D.M. Egan, M.G. Chapman and D.H. Barlow, 'Attitudes of Donors and Recipients to Gamete Donation' (1991) 6(2) *Human Reproduction* 307–309; P.P. Mahlstedt and K.A. Probasco, 'Sperm Donors: Their Attitudes Toward Providing Medical and Psychosocial Information for Recipient Couples and Donor Offspring' (1991) 56(4) *Fertility and Sterility* 747–753.

sense, 'a concern about any system that depends on deception or concealment' – in the legal system for 'not only background commentaries but in explicit form in some adoption legislation'.[85] He notes that support for openness and honesty 'is also reflected in numerous legal decisions in Australia and elsewhere'.[86] In the context of donor conception, he quotes the Canadian Royal Commission on New Reproduction Technologies:[87]

> Commission research showed that maintaining secrecy about the means of conception can be contrary to the best interest of the child. . . . Adults born through DI reported that the decision to keep DI a secret was very damaging – they felt deceived and said they had always sensed that something was "wrong" in the family. Some told the Commission that they found out about the method of conception at a time of family crisis, such as a divorce or death in the family. . . . Discovering the truth in this way is doubly traumatic; the shock of discovery during an already stressful period is coupled with the realization that your parents had lied to you all your life.

One might conclude that the starting point for donor conception should not be secrecy and shame, but rather openness and honesty. Such a position would enable donor-conceived people to choose whether they wished to have information about their genetic relatives. However, without knowledge, there appears a significant risk of unnecessary damage, which for some people can be devastating. Compounded with the angst for those who choose to search and find a trail of contradictions, dead ends and/or closed doors, there is good reason that an increasing number of jurisdictions have moved to releasing information to donor-conceived people. The search is discussed in the Chapter 3 and in Part II, which examines laws around the world governing information release (or anonymity).

85 See for example *Brianna v. Brianna* (2010) 43 Fam LR 309; (2010) FLC ¶93-437; [2010] FamCAFC 97, discussed in R. Chisholm, 'Parentage: Some Testing Problems' (2010) 24 *Australian Journal of Family Law* 242. Earlier decisions to similar effect include *S v. McC (orse S); W v. W* [1972] AC 24 (Lord Hodson); *G v. H* (1994) 181 CLR 387 at 391 (Brennan and McHugh JJ); 124 ALR 353; *G v. H* (1993) 16 Fam LR 525; (1993) 113 FLR 440; (1993) FLC 92-380 at 79,942 (Fogarty J); *Taylor v. Burgess* (2002) 29 Fam LR 167; (2002) FLC 93-120; *W and G (No 1)* (2004) 35 Fam LR 417; (2005) FLC ¶93-247. See also *Re D (Paternity)* [2007] 2 FLR 26 (Hedley J), discussed by C.J. Bryant in *Brianna*, below, at [23], and by C. Smart, 'Law and the Regulation of Family Secrets' (2010) 24(3) *International Journal of Law, Policy and the Family* 397–413 cited in Chisholm, n 2, p 734.

86 Ibid.

87 Ibid., quoting *Pratten v. British Columbia (Attorney-General)*, 2011 BCSC 565 (19 May 2011) at 38.

3 The search

Introduction

Chapter 2 illustrated how the call for information about donors and genetic siblings by donor-conceived people may be placed in the context of broader human and cultural interests in genealogy. The chapter also moved beyond consideration of the popular enterprise of tracing one's ancestors to considering the deeper psychosocial and ethical reasons some donor-conceived people search for information about their donors and siblings. This chapter considers in more detail what searching for such information entails for donor-conceived people, recipient parents and donors. It begins by briefly detailing the avenues for finding information, and then includes some personal stories by people who have conducted searches successfully, as well as those who are still searching for information.

Can one start with the birth certificate?

Significantly, although most genealogists begin a search with a birth certificate that names the genetic mother and father, the birth certificate of a donor-conceived person will not provide the name of the sperm, egg or embryo donor(s). That is, while birth certificates were once a method of documenting genetic lineage, these documents now support the secrecy and anonymity surrounding donor conception. The law in all jurisdictions generally permits the recording of the 'legal parent(s)' and neither the donor-conceived person's status nor genetic progenitors appear on the birth certificate.

Only a few jurisdictions in the world provide for notification of donor-conceived status,[1] and notably such laws are only recent, meaning that those people who may be notified of their status are either in their infancy or not yet born. Thus, on being told of their conception, most donor-conceived people will look for contextual information (i.e. what donor conception actually is), and then proceed to finding out if laws exist that will enable them to access information, and the methods by which such information is released.

1 See discussion in Chapter 4 regarding Victoria, Australia, Ireland, Argentina and Croatia.

Jurisdictions that require information release by law

In some jurisdictions, including the Australian states of New South Wales,[2] Victoria,[3] Western Australia[4] and South Australia[5]; Austria;[6] Croatia;[7] the Netherlands;[8] Norway;[9] Finland;[10] New Zealand;[11] Sweden;[12] Switzerland;[13] the United Kingdom;[14] Uruguay;[15] Argentina;[16] and Ireland,[17] information is available to the donor-conceived person as a result of anonymous donations being prohibited or access to information being available on approval. In these jurisdictions, donor-conceived people who know they were donor conceived and wish to obtain information about their donor(s) may turn to a special register, to the clinic or hospital that assisted in their conception or apply for judicial approval to access identifying and/or non-identifying information about their donor(s), and possibly donor siblings. Donors and recipient parents in some jurisdictions may also be able to obtain some non-identifying information under these laws.

The laws and practices surrounding the recording of information and its release in these jurisdictions are further detailed in Part II. However, even where laws exist, there is no guarantee that identifying information can always be obtained. More success exists in jurisdictions that maintain central registers, rather than clinic- or hospital-based files.[18] In some countries that permit access to information, but did not centralize data, clinical records may have been destroyed. Furthermore, information in countries that have passed laws is generally only

2 *Assisted Reproductive Technology Act 2007* (NSW).
3 *Infertility (Medical Procedures) Act 1984* (Vic); Infertility Treatment Act 1995; Infertility Treatment Regulations 1997; *Assisted Reproductive Treatment Act 2008* (Vic).
4 *Human Reproductive Technology Act 1991* (WA).
5 *Assisted Reproductive Treatment Act 1988* (SA), s 16; *Assisted Reproductive Treatment Regulations 2010* (SA), reg 8.4(c).
6 Fortpflanzungsmedizingesetz. 275 Bundesgesetz, 1992.
7 *Zakon O Medicinski Pomognutoj Oplodnji (Law on Medically Assisted Reproduction*, 12 July 2012) (Croatia), No: 71–05–03 / 1–12–2, Article 15(2).
8 Wet donorgegevens kunstmatige bevruchting, 2002.
9 Act on Biotechnology 2003.
10 Act on Assisted Fertility Treatments (1237/2006).
11 Human Assisted Reproductive Technology (HART) Act 2004.
12 Lag om insemination (Law on Insemination) 1984 (replaced by Genetic Integrity Act 2006).
13 Federal Act on Medically Assisted Procreation of 18 December 1998 – FF 1996 III, 197 (LPMA).
14 Human Fertilisation and Embryology Authority (Disclosure of Donor Information) Regulations 2004.
15 Law Regulating Human Assisted Reproductive Techniques (22/11/2013 No 19.167).
16 Código civil y comercial de la nación (Civil and Commercial Code of the Nation), Title V, Ch2, approved by Law 26,994.
17 Children and Family Relationships Act 2015 Act No. 9 of 2015.
18 S. Allan, A Cross-Jurisdictional Study of Regulatory Requirements and Practice Regarding the Recording of Donor Information and Its Release to Donor Conceived People 2012. Report prepared for the Winston Churchill Memorial Trust.

accessible to donor-conceived people born after the law was enacted, as most laws operate from that date forward.[19] Therefore, those born prior to the enactment of laws are unable to access their records.

Some donor-conceived people, recipient parents and donors will thus continue to search via other avenues in the hope of finding the information they seek.

Other paths that people take

Ask the doctor, clinic or hospital

Donor-conceived people who cannot access information via a register will often proceed to locating and seeking answers from the doctor, clinic or hospital where the insemination took place.[20] For others, they may find that the doctor has since passed away, and they will need to find where the doctor's records are now kept (if they haven't been destroyed), before having to ask whether the current holder of such records will give them information.

For some, doctors provide non-identifying information about the donor(s), but many are unwilling to provide information at all. For example, Cushing quotes a response to a donor-conceived person by the obstetrician involved in his conception:

> He was completely unwilling to give any information citing the fact that this was done in total secrecy as was quite common back then and that everyone was sworn to secrecy and the donor had wanted it that way as well.[21]

Adams and Lorbach, in detailing the search for information in Australia, highlight the frustrations that information seekers may meet when approaching the clinics involved in their conception.[22] They report that clinics may not respond, or if they do, applicants may be given different information at different times. There also exists no standardized consensus among clinics in the same jurisdiction,

19 Note in Switzerland a retrospective clause was enacted which technically provided that all donor-conceived people could access information. Those conceived prior to the establishment of the Swiss register, however, are required to approach clinics. In practice, the gaining of information is difficult if not impossible, as laws that permit the destruction of medical records after ten years mean that clinic-based information may no longer exist. In Victoria, laws will come into force in 2017 that allow access to information by all donor-conceived people who inquire about their donor regardless of when a person was born. At present, such access may be granted subject to the consent of the donor. See further in Chapter 4.

20 A.L. Cushing, '"I Just Want More Information About Who I Am": The Search Experience of Sperm-Donor Offspring, Searching for Information About Their Donors and Genetic Heritage' (2010) 15(2) *Information Research*, available at http://informationr.net/ir/15-2/paper428.html, accessed 16 March 2016.

21 Ibid., quoting 'Paul'.

22 D. Adams and C. Lorbach, 'Accessing Donor conception Information in Australia: A Call for Retrospective Access' (2012) 19(4) *Journal of Law and Medicine* 704, pp 709–710.

or across the world, as to the amount of personal and non-identifying information that is collected or released.[23]

Search the yearbooks of local colleges and universities

Although some simply give up their search after contacting the doctor or clinic that assisted in their conception, others may turn to searching school yearbooks for potential lookalikes. Some focus particularly on medical school yearbooks based on the knowledge that many donors in the 1970s or 1980s were medical students.[24] In one example in the United States, a young donor-conceived woman used a college's medical student yearbooks to send out letters to more than 600 men.[25] Despite not finding her biological father, she did receive more than 250 responses, 40 of which proclaimed to be donors and subsequently undertook 16 paternity DNA tests.

Others have noted that accessing yearbooks may be difficult and expensive. Such yearbooks are also more common in the United States, and may not exist in other jurisdictions.

Put your name on a voluntary register . . . and hope for a match

Others turn to voluntary registers in which people place their information and donor codes, in the hope that their donor or genetic siblings also register and they find a match. There are a variety of such registers around the world, including but not limited to:

1 The United States Donor Sibling Registry, which was founded in 2000 by Wendy Kramer, a mother who conceived her son by donor insemination.[26] The Donor Sibling Registry states that it has 47,081 registrants, including donors, parents and donor-conceived people, and that it has made over 13,000 matches between half-siblings and/or donors. A yearly membership fee of $75, or a one-time payment for permanent membership of $175, is charged.[27]
2 The Donor Conceived Register in the United Kingdom,[28] which is available throughout the United Kingdom and is intended for anyone who donated in a United Kingdom clinic or was conceived following treatment in a United

23 Ibid., p 710.
24 Cushing, above n 20.
25 K. LaBounty, *My Story*, 13 November 2008, available at http://childofastranger.blogspot.com.au/2008/11/my-story.html, accessed 16 March 2016.
26 Donor Sibling Registry, available at https://www.donorsiblingregistry.com/, accessed 16 March 2016.
27 Ibid.
28 Donor Conceived Register, available at http://donorconceivedregister.org.uk/, accessed 16 March 2016.

Kingdom clinic before August 1991. Noting that because of storage and distribution practices it is possible that donor-conceived people born before December 1992 could find donor-conceived half-siblings or their donor on the register. (Note – Post 1991 information is held on a central register operated by the Human Fertilisation and Embryology Authority).

3 The AMFOR Donor Offspring Register,[29] which is a free worldwide register that has approximately 2,500 registered parents, donor-conceived people and donors (predominantly from the United States).

4 There are government-based voluntary registers in some Australian jurisdictions (including Victoria, New South Wales and Western Australia).

5 The FIOM voluntary DNA register in the Netherlands which works in collaboration with Canisius-Wilhelmina Hospital (CWZ), Nijmegen, and maintains a dedicated DNA database for those conceived or donating prior to 2004 (post-2004 are permitted access to information by law).

6 The 'registers' or discussion groups operated by sperm banks. For example, Fairfax Cryobank in the United States operates a Donor Conceived Connections forum where adults (18+) that were conceived via donor sperm can discuss various topics and possibly connect with half-siblings.[30]

However, voluntary registers rely on all parties placing their names on the register, and then being able to match with each other. Although the U.S. Donor Sibling Registry appears to have had significant success, many voluntary registers around the world do not adequately resolve the quest for information. Some have described it as 'a lottery' in which the success of some leads to empty or unsatisfied hope by others who sometimes have been waiting for years without a result. Many people do not find matches due to other parties not placing their information in the same voluntary register. There have also been reports of some people who were a match, and were both on the same voluntary register, but failed being matched on the register.

Place an advertisement in the newspaper and/or engage with the media

Many donor-conceived people, recipient parents and donors have also gone public with their search, placing advertisements in newspapers, being interviewed for news or talk show programs and/or participating in documentaries about their lives and search. Many who do so tell the most personal aspects of their stories and discuss their feelings and experiences publically in the hope to not only find information for themselves but also to drive change regarding information

29 AMFOR Donor Registry, available at http://www.amfor.net/, accessed 16 March 2016.

30 Fairfax CryoBank Family Forums, available at http://blogandforum.fairfaxcryobank.com/forum/index.php, accessed 16 March 2016.

release. Many not only participate in interviews but have written articles, created blogs and/or contributed to discussion forums.

The growing media attention, public debate and personal stories that have become known via all of the varied media have in some instances led to connections between donor-conceived people and their donors and/or genetically related siblings. For others, they regularly engage with such media to no avail.

Although using public media has not always resulted in finding the person sought, there have been wider implications from the growing media attention. If we reflect on the secrecy outlined in Chapter 2, and the minimal discussion of donor conception that took place in the early to mid-twentieth century, we can see an exponential growth of openness and discussion over time. It is apparent that in the twenty-first century, this topic is at least being openly discussed. Interestingly, within that discussion, despite the calls for information being the loudest from adult offspring and recipient parents and donors who were involved in past practices in which anonymous donation was the norm, some fertility clinicians have placed themselves in the media opposing information release.[31] The secrecy and anonymity that was ingrained in past practices is at times closely guarded by those practitioners who implemented it. Nevertheless, it is also apparent that the voices of the offspring, recipients and donors who seek information are being increasingly represented via public media and that there has been a shift over time in broader societal understanding of the plight of those who search – at least in some jurisdictions.

Employ DNA testing

Donors and donor-conceived people may turn also to using genetic testing in an attempt to find their genetic relatives,[32] which may help establish genetic relatedness between a donor-conceived person and his or her donor(s) and siblings by identifying how much DNA one person has in common with another.[33] Simply put every child inherits half of his or her DNA from each genetic parent. People share 50 per cent of their total DNA with siblings with whom two biological parents are in common, and 25 percent with half-siblings with whom one biological parent is in common. In addition, they share 25 per cent of their DNA with grandparents, uncles and aunt, 12.5 per cent with cousins, 6.25 per cent with first cousins once removed, 3.125 per cent with second cousins and so on. Several types of DNA testing can predict such possible relationships

31 For example, see David Handelsman, Allow Sperm Donors to Maintain Their Past Anonymity (OpEd), *The Age*, 8 May 2013, available at http://www.theage.com.au/comment/allow-sperm-donors-the-right-to-maintain-their-past-anonymity-20130507–2j5o4.html, accessed 16 March 2016.

32 Adams and Lorbach, n 22, p 713–715. M. Klotz 'Wayward Relations—Novel Searches of the Donor-Conceived for Genetic Kinship' (2016) 35 *Medical Anthropology Quarterly* 45–57.

33 Typically, those relationships of third cousins and beyond can become too distant to identify the donor; however, it is not outside the realms of possibility.

with donors and other relatives. Y-DNA testing may assist males to follow their paternal line. X-DNA testing allows sisters of different mothers to determine if they have the same father. Mitochondrial DNA (mtDNA) testing is useful for tracing the maternal line since mitochondrial DNA is inherited from the mother.[34]

Combined DNA index system (CODIS) testing, which is employed by agencies such as the Federal Bureau of Investigation in the United States, has been used – sometimes in conjunction with other tests – to identify possible biological links between people in the UK Donor Conceived Register and FIOM in the Netherlands. This testing is discussed further in Chapter 4 in relation to those jurisdictions. Both bodies run voluntary DNA registers for donors and donor-conceived people who were born prior to laws requiring the recording and release of identifying information about donors in the respective countries.[35] Matches from within both organizations have relied on people voluntarily placing their names on a register and submitting to DNA tests. Matches are made based on probabilities of relatedness.

In addition, once expensive and difficult to obtain, DNA testing is also accessible via ancestry-tracing agencies and direct-to-consumer companies. The group Spenderkinder in Germany, which supports donor-conceived people searching for information, outsources its DNA testing and analysis directly to FamilyTree DNA.[36] FamilyTree DNA[37] has a project group specifically for donor-conceived people and donors. Examples of people finding their donor via direct-to-consumer DNA testing companies show that such tracing has not relied on the gamete donor having had a DNA test himself. It has been reported that the DNA profiles of relatives who may have undertaken testing for genealogy or health interests may be used.[38]

Such tests are increasingly being used by donor-conceived people with more success than they have had lobbying for changes to the law or asking clinics to support them in their searches.[39] However, it is important to note that the results

34 D. Adams and S. Allan, 'Building a Family Tree: Donor Conceived People, DNA Tracing and Donor "Anonymity"' (2013) 7(2) *Australian Journal of Adoption* 1–16.

35 Allan, Churchill Report, above n 18

36 See Spenderkinder website, available at http://www.spenderkinder.de, accessed 16 March 2016.

37 See Family Tree DNA website, available at http://www.familytreedna.com/, accessed 16 March 2016.

38 R. Lehmann-Haupt, Are Sperm Donors Really Anonymous Anymore? DNA Testing Makes Them Easy to Trace, *Slate*, 1 March 2010, available at http://www.slate.com/id/2243743/, accessed 16 March 2016; A. Motluk, 'Anonymous Sperm Donor Traced on Internet' (2005) 2524 *New Scientist* 6; R. Stein, Found on the Web, with DNA: A Boy's Father, *Washington Post*, 13 November 2005, available at http://www.washingtonpost.com/wp-dyn/content/article/2005/11/12/AR2005111200958.html, accessed 16 March 2016.

39 Australian Broadcasting Corporation RN network. Background briefing: the donor detectives. RN Network 2015; 6 December. http://www.abc.net.au/radionational/programs/backgroundbriefing/the-donor-detectives/6996896 (accessed 16 May 2016).

of DNA testing are often just one piece of the puzzle[40] since further paper tracing and investigation such as that described previously (sometimes referred to as 'triangulation') may be necessary before a definitive match can be made in some instances. It must be understood that different DNA tests have varying degrees of accuracy, and DNA testing is only one tool that may combine with other knowledge in the search for information. DNA testing as a search tool – rather than a test to see if two people are linked – is also seen by some as a last resort, as searching for spurious family links on public DNA databases can create false hope, and for others, it is sometimes overwhelming.

In addition, there have been mistaken links from test results that only reflect probabilities, which then must be interpreted.[41] One well-published mistake was that of two women who believed they were sisters based on the results of DNA testing conducted through the former UK DonorLink. It was later proved that they were not related, which led to great disappointment and stress. UK DonorLink subsequently explained that the initial results had been qualified according to the way in which the tests are interpreted – i.e. that they reflect probabilities and should not be taken as definitive.[42]

Nevertheless, there has been increasing recognition that healthcare professionals, potential parents and donors should be informed that anonymity may no longer be protected given the existence and growth of direct-to-consumer DNA testing.[43] It should also be noted that not only may such testing be used actively by those searching for information but that it has the potential to uncover donor-conceived status not previously known.[44]

Lobby governments for changes in the law

Donor-conceived people, recipient parents and donors also continue to actively lobby governments for changes to the law that would support information

40 A. Motluk, 'Anonymous Sperm Donor Traced on Internet' (2005) 2524 *New Scientist* 6; R. Stein, Found on the Web, with DNA: A Boy's Father, *Washington Post*, 13 November 2005, available at http://www.washingtonpost.com/wp-dyn/content/article/2005/11/12/AR2005111200958.html, accessed 16 March 2016.

41 N. Pryer, Despair of the DNA 'Sisters': In a Terrible Mistake That Casts New Doubt on DNA Profiling, It Turns Out They Weren't Related at All, *Mail Online*, 22 February 2010, available at http://www.dailymail.co.uk/femail/article-1252590/Despair-DNA-sisters-In-terrible-mistake-casts-new-doubt-DNA-profiling-turns-werent-related-all.html, accessed 16 March 2016.

42 Ibid.

43 P. Borry, O. Russo, W. Dondorp, G. De Wert, B.M. Knoppers, H.C. Howard, 'Anonymity 2.0: direct-to-consumer genetic testing and donor conception' (2014) 101 Fertil Steril 630-632.

44 Joyce C. Harper, Debbie Kennett, and Dan Reisel, 'The End of Donor Anonymity: How Genetic Testing Is Likely to Drive Anonymous Gamete Donation out of Business' (2016) *Human Reproduction*. Published online, 16 April 2016, doi:10.1093/humrep/dew065, available at http://humrep.oxfordjournals.org/content/early/2016/04/08/humrep.dew065.full, accessed 16 May 2016.

release for all those who search. Some have approached politicians and legislators individually, bringing to the attention of such people their personal stories. Groups that support donor-conceived people and their families have also been instrumental in seeking change. Some people have been active in coordinating actions and giving a voice to those who personally may not be comfortable with being in the media or who need support in navigating governmental and legislative systems.

Both individuals and groups have also been active in writing submissions to governments whenever an inquiry into such matters has been conducted, and in later driving change once the reports from such inquiries are finalized. These activities have included meeting with politicians and legislators who can implement such changes into laws. Examples of such inquiries, their recommendations and changes to the law are further discussed in Chapter 4. Those who search have found that lobbying and engagement with officials have been instrumental in making changes to laws in certain jurisdictions. These laws now support donor-conceived people and put an end to anonymity. For others, information release has not been achieved, but their activeness in this space (for twenty years or more in some instances) has contributed to the growing discussion and movements regarding seeking information and what to do about its release.

Personal stories of searching

Although people employ numerous methods in their search for information, some might have difficulty in understanding what is involved, how people affected by donor conception feel, what they have experienced in searching, what they have found, and what the future holds. The following stories of two donor-conceived people – one who is still searching for his donor, and one who found hers; a recipient family's story; and that of a donor, – provide examples of the experiences of people who search, as well as serving to further illustrate not only what is involved but the deeply felt effects donor conception has had on the lives of the people involved.

Donor-conceived person: Michael Williams, September 2015

My name is Michael (Mike for short), and I was conceived at Dr Lachlan Hardy-Wilson's clinic in Tasmania in 1981. My story follows, in the hope that someone might be able to help me find information – but I want to first stress I am not after anything other than knowledge about my donor and/or potential siblings, in an attempt to have a better picture of how I came about, who helped in that process, and my biological heritage. I don't want to infringe on anyone's privacy, create relationships if they are not wanted, or anything else. I also want to assure you that I am a decent person, honest and trustworthy. I am a lawyer working in Melbourne.

So, a little more about me and my search.

I am now 33 years old. I was told by my mother when I was 21 that my legal father is not my biological father. My mother holds Dr Hardy-Wilson in the highest regard and, of course, I do too given that he is a major reason that I was born. In fact, I understand the reasons my mother underwent assisted reproduction, and the broader issue of couples who have such a strong wish to have children, and truly appreciate that they sought assistance. However, I have been searching for information about my background ever since as the revelation that I was donor conceived also created so many questions in my mind.

I have been searching for information ever since my mother told me. It is so important to me.

Sometimes I am told different things by different people. I am told by some that all records have been destroyed, but I have also received other information that gives me some hope that one day I might find the information.

I am left wondering whether any one knows if the medical records from Tamar Street, Launceston, were retained. On one occasion I was told that no information exists about donors who attended Dr Hardy-Wilson's clinic, but other people, who knew Dr Hardy-Wilson, say that he would never have destroyed his records and that they must be held somewhere.

I have at times put advertisements in the newspaper asking people if they donated sperm in the early 1980s. Sometimes donors have come forward, and have been willing to find out if it was them. I have had DNA tests, but unfortunately it was not the right man. In that I have found that the men who have contacted me also wonder about the offspring they helped to create.

There is a much greater atmosphere of openness today, and I hope that if I can find more of the donors, then perhaps there is hope after all. The not knowing, the searching, the wondering who could be my donor and if I have any other siblings never really leaves me. Sometimes I push it to the back of my mind, but it comes up again. I have been searching now for twelve years.

I am really just trying to understand more about myself. I don't want to impinge upon anyone, or make anyone upset. I would actually love just to have openness and to find the missing pieces of my puzzle so that I can move on with my life without searching and wondering anymore.

I write another letter, put another advertisement in the paper, contact another politician, and write to anyone that I can find that was connected to the clinic or to the doctor that ran the practice. I hope that someone may wish to help me, or know me, or discuss Dr Hardy-Wilson and what he did for me and my mother (giving me life, helping my mother have a family), and any information they might have to help me in my search for information.

I have also watched as legislation has been passed in Victoria giving all donor-conceived people access to information about their donors, where such information exists. I think this needs to happen everywhere. All people have a right to know who they are, and where they came from.

Donor-conceived person: Myfanwy Walker, September 2015

How much will these words on a page tell you about me? I will describe myself as best as I can, but what picture will you have of me as a person, will it be enough? Or do you need to meet me as a real, living, breathing human being with all my facets and frailties in order to truly know me?

My name is Myf, I am 34, a graphic designer, married with two children, ages 6 and 1. I am an atheist and Anglo Saxon. I have a fair complexion and am of medium build, 5 foot 3 inches tall with blue eyes and A+ blood type.

Were it not for the most mundane and yet miraculous happenstance of a man picking up a certain newspaper in a convenience store on a particular day, this is all I would know about my biological father; in 1977 he was 26, a student, married with two children ages 3 and 1 week, not religious and Anglo Saxon. Fair complexion, medium build, 5-foot-8-and-a-a-half inches tall, blue eyes and A+ blood type.

Three years later in 1980 I would be conceived, thanks to this anonymous man's cryogenically frozen sperm. Whilst the facts of my conception were initially withheld from me, I did eventually discover the truth, at age 20, amidst the maelstrom that was my parent's separation and subsequent divorce.

Always a quiet, shy and self-conscious person, never entirely comfortable in my own skin, the revelation that my dad wasn't my biological father simultaneously made perfect sense and utterly destroyed me. I was set adrift in a sea of questions, who is this man? Who am I? What does he look like? What are his interests? Do I have other siblings, who are they? And I grieved. For the loss of a biological connection to my dad and his family, the place that I thought I held within that family heritage and most deeply, my own identity. I felt broken and lost.

On reflection, my immediate resolve to search for answers provided direction and focus in the fog. It was the only empowering and positive route available and so I began. I applied to the Royal Women's Hospital for any information they held about my donor and to request his consent so that I may know his name. I was required to attend a counselling session after which I was given the brief description noted above and his donor code CP. I was also told I had three donor-conceived sisters born to three separate families. A letter was written to CP's last known (24-year-old) address but not unexpectedly no reply was received.

I then requested that the clinic conduct a search, this consisted of a fruitless review of the telephone directories and electoral roll. My last resort was to request that the hospital ethics committee confidentially release his name to an experienced search agency so they could conduct a more extensive search on my behalf, this was denied and I was told there was nothing more that could be done for me.

Whilst the counsellor I saw at the clinic was lovely and I believe did everything she could within her power to help me, in a wider clinical and societal context I felt like an unwanted problem. Fourteen years ago, it was not common for donor-conceived people to be actively and openly searching for their biological parents nor was it accepted that it was something we wanted or even needed to do. I felt like an oddity, largely unsupported and misunderstood.

Fortunately, I had been able to find a support group, based in NSW which helped ease my feelings of isolation to an extent. In November 2001, I had the opportunity to attend a conference for donor-conceived people in Sydney, I jumped at the chance to meet other people like me. To promote the conference and DC-related issues, I participated in a story for The Australian *newspaper, the article ran on the front page with a large photo of me.*

CP aka Michael Linden just happened to buy The Australian *that day, seeing the photo and reading the article he realized that he was in fact the man I was looking for. He made contact with the support group, I received his name and phone number and we were able to meet for the first time some weeks later. Meeting Michael and getting to know him over time enabled me to put a lot of those original questions I had to rest. I was able to develop an understanding of him as a person and my family history and that in turn fostered a deep sense of self-awareness that I don't think I would have otherwise had. That equilibrium has anchored me during times of great stress, change and when presented with difficult choices, the inevitable life experiences that we all face.*

Despite being a reserved and private person, the strength of my need to find out more about myself and my parentage was such that (in the absence of an alternative) I was compelled to expose myself and my situation to the nation in the media. Whilst my action did result in the remarkable outcome of making contact with my donor, I felt considerable anxiety in sharing such intimate details about myself with the world. My family and my dad's infertility was also exposed and I had innumerable personal questions and criticisms to answer from friends and strangers.

My story became the ultimate lure for other donor-conceived people to participate in media in the hope that they might have the same success. But mostly, they have little success. It makes me incredibly angry that donor-conceived people still have to beg, search, plead and tell their stories over and over again to a sometimes ignorant and judgmental public audience, because the medical profession and successive governments have failed to implement policies and legislation to support them and to facilitate the release of fundamentally important information.

And what does the future hold? I still hope that I might one day be able to meet my three unknown half sisters. I think it is most likely they are unaware they are donor-conceived, assuming they are well and alive. But in the meantime, risks and secrecy prevail. Last year one of my naturally conceived sisters (my donor's own daughter) died of metastatic breast cancer at the age of 36. I notified the clinic in the hope that they might pass on that information to my half sisters themselves or at least their families. The clinic was disinclined to do so as they did not regard the death of a half-sibling from breast cancer at a comparable age to my DC half sisters significant enough to warrant contacting the families. Thus my experience of dealing with clinics electing to act as the gatekeepers of vital information that rightly belongs to individuals (who arguably remain in their care) continues.

The relative ease of my journey to self-knowledge and empowerment has also, however, left me feeling obligated and able to advocate for others who are still grappling with a serpentine bureaucracy and inadequate or non-existent assistance. I still see an ART industry that is fraught with conflicting ideologies and ethically questionable practices. The public presentation of ART as a compassionate and laudable response to the need for a child, hides a flipside – profiteering, poor success rates, the exploitation of men and women for their reproductive capacity and precious little regard for the rights and interests of the people created.

I found my donor, serendipitously. But I am left with questions, not answers. . . . If donor-conceived people want to know who their biological parents and half-siblings are, what are we to make of practices that intentionally sever these relationships pre-conception? What are the real consequences for all involved?

Recipient parent: Caroline Lorbach, July 2015

Conceiving our three children in the late 1980s to early 1990s using three different donors at two different clinics was a complicated way to start our family and had ramifications later on. When choosing the donors we were given some basic information about each of them: height/weight range, eye/hair colour, career and, oddly, for one of them his IQ.

At the time this small amount of information seemed okay, our focus, like many others at the time, was in conceiving but we did make one very important decision, we would tell our children the truth about their conception. That was as far as our thoughts went; we had no counselling.

It has been over twenty years since my husband and I first started on our quest for information with which to answer our children's questions and I still don't think that I have come to terms with how difficult getting information was.

Our first approach to the two clinics was to ask them in writing to provide all the information they had on record about each donor. Asking was stressful; there were no protocols to follow. It was also at a time when people like us were starting to question the secret system that medical professionals had put in place. Clinics had made it very clear to the Donor Conception Support Group (of which we were founding members and I was the National Consumer Advocate) that they were happy with the system the way it was, with donors being anonymous and information being limited to scraps of very basic non-identifying information.

What came back was basically what we had been told when selecting our donors bar an added religion for one and some interests for another. There was no mention of medical histories. I called the clinics to ask about medical histories and was told their histories contained "nothing of importance". Nothing about medical histories was ever put in writing. I couldn't understand that when we went to our family GP we often got asked, "Is there a family history of . . ." but the doctors at fertility clinics didn't think that a full medical history was important for our children.

In 1996 we decided to write a letter to each of our children's donors, we wanted to thank them and also to give them a little bit of information about our children, after all we knew something about them and maybe they were curious about the children they had helped to create. We were also concerned about how safe donor records were, there was nothing to stop them being destroyed seven years after the last entry just like any other medical record. We hoped that forming a small link with each of our children's donors may mean that the records might be kept longer.

Even though we were the first couple to approach these two clinics with such a request we thought we had imparted to them how important it was for us to get further information for our children. Both clinics wanted our letters to be open so that they could read what we had written and see that we were not seeking the donor's identity.

The letter to our eldest son's donor was like this:

> *We are writing to you to let you know how grateful we are that because of your donation we were able to have a family, and we wanted to let you know a little bit about Andrew. He was born in 1989, is blonde and has hazel eyes. He is a very bright and curious child who reads just about everything he can get his hands on. He has a very deep interest in dinosaurs and electronics. Andrew thinks deeply about many things and is always full of questions. Andrew has been told about how he was conceived; he had not asked very many questions about it. He did ask once: "Am I bright because of the donor?" Andrew now has a brother and a sister who have two different donors. We would be happy to accept any correspondence from you through the clinic at Bondi and thank you for taking the time to read this letter.*

The clinic at which Andrew was conceived took about a year to respond to our request, but finally the scientist in charge of the sperm bank agreed to contact the donor and ask if he wanted to receive our letter. After a few months we received a phone call from the scientist telling us that he had been unable to contact the donor, he must have moved. It hadn't occurred to us that the clinic wouldn't keep in contact with the donors.

Meanwhile, the second clinic was a little bit quicker to decide whether they would contact the donors on our behalf.

The response was mixed; a scientist told us that they could not contact Callum's donor but Elizabeth's donor had agreed to receive our letter.

A year later, we contacted both clinics again and asked them if they would initiate another search for Andrew's and Callum's donors, perhaps using electoral roles.

Andrew's clinic was now allowing their counsellor to make contact with donors and she found his donor without any problems, he had never moved and was at the same address where he had lived when he was donating. My immediate response was to say to the counsellor over the phone "So, we were lied to." There was no admission that this had happened. We were told that while Andrew's donor did not want contact with us, he had given a lot more information about himself and his family history which the counsellor typed up and sent to us.

The other clinic did manage to contact Callum's donor this time, but the scientist who did the contacting told us that he did not want contact and she had not asked him for any further information.

While all this was happening, my husband and I did a newspaper article about donor conception and the need for legislation. There was a photo of the both of us with Elizabeth who was at the time about 18 months old. In the article, we spoke about telling our children the truth and how little information we had on their donors. We gave an example of the very generic non-identifying information that we had on Elizabeth's donor (which was very similar to the information we had on each of our children's donors). Not long after this article was published I had a phone call from the clinic counsellor to inform me that the clinic was angry with us for publishing donor information and reminded me that we had signed a contract with the clinic to never seek the identity of the donor. I cried for days; it had never been our intention to seek out the identity of the donor. Nothing in the article identified him and if he happened to recognize himself he wasn't obliged to contact us.

I'm not sure, even today that clinics realize the power we perceive them to have. They hold information about our children which is, in effect, like a birth certificate, it is the only link to the other half of their biological heritage. I spoke to the clinic and asked if they would like my husband and I to speak to the staff to explain that we had spoken to the media in order to help other parents with openness in donor conception and to educate the public about how little information we had with which to answer our children's questions. We thought it might be good for the clinic to be able to have a discussion with parents raising donor-conceived children, as we knew that the staff had never had the opportunity to do this. They didn't take us up on our offer.

A while after the article was published we received a letter from the donor (sent via the clinic) saying that he had seen the article and knew it was us (we had given him our first names in the letter we wrote to him). The handwritten letter was lovely giving information about his family and history and saying that if Elizabeth ever had any questions to write to him.

We also now have a contact number and name for Callum's donor. He contacted a member of the Donor Conception Support Group a few years ago looking for our family – to this day we do not know how he knew who we were and that we were part of the Support Group.

He explained that years ago he did not want contact because of his wife but now that his wife had passed away he was happy to have contact. Because Callum was now an adult we told him all of this and left it to him to contact his donor if he wished. So far he hasn't.

Ours is a complex story but so many in donor conception are; it is an example of never giving up and pushing for what you feel is right and necessary for your children, but it is also a story that should never have been needed to be told. Adoptees fought a battle many decades ago to have the right to access information about their birth origins and rightly so; how much longer will it take for donor-conceived people to have that right as well so that stories like our family's can be consigned to history?

Donor: Ian Smith, August 2015

One sperm donor's journey – a personal stocktake: from altruism to activism

My name is Ian. I am the biological father of nine children. Two of my offspring live with me and seven I have never met. This circumstance, one about which I now have deep misgivings, came about because I was a sperm donor at the Prince Henry's Hospital in Melbourne in the mid-1980s.

My becoming a sperm donor – while seemingly a simple action of altruism at the time – has, in the years since, led me into a deep examination of the consequences of my actions. I came to feel that, with the best intentions, but without full understanding at the time, I have given away seven members of my family. I know very little of them and may never know more. I am firmly resolved, however, of the importance of two things. First, it is imperative that I make myself available to my unknown offspring – to whatever degree they wish and to be available for contact when and if they chose to connect with me. Second, I am committed to working for changes which will go some way to rectifying past mistakes – in particular working for changes to legislation and practice which will enable donor-conceived people born from sperm donations in the past to have proper access to knowledge of their biological heritage. That latter is a fundamental human right.

Where it all began – altruism: "I can help"

I became a sperm donor in 1987, at the Prince Henry's Hospital, in response to a media call from Dr Gab Kovacs for more donors. I was then in my early thirties and I saw no prospect of marriage and children at the time. I was acting from altruistic intentions. I was aware of issues of infertility because I had a close friend who was in that circumstance. I wanted to help people who wished to have children but could not do so. I saw that I could help and I felt good about doing so.

I gave a blood sample and details of my hair and eye colour, ancestry, height and weight, level of education and occupation, and some very brief information about personal interests. I signed a consent form – which, interestingly when viewed in retrospect, made no mention of anonymity nor did it place restrictions on contact between me and any offspring. I was given a sterile jar and sent off to produce a semen sample. It seemed very simple then. Only later was I to realize that it was, and is not, simple.

Done and slipping from mind

After completing perhaps ten donations, I ceased attending the clinic and the experience slowly slipped from my mind. Partly this was because anonymity and discretion were emphasized by the clinic, and partly because I was left with a sense that perhaps the sperm donations would not actually be used to create children – maybe just used for research? For whatever reason, it largely went from my mind and I heard nothing more from the clinic – until twelve years later.

Brought back to mind – news of seven offspring!

In 1999 I received a registered letter, redirected from a long-gone residence, from the clinic. The letter informed me, in a matter-of-fact way, that my frozen semen would be "only made available to couples wishing to complete their families". This was a bombshell. I knew that there were children born from my sperm donations – children as much a half of me as are the two children of my marriage and who live with me. I am the biological father of nine children, seven of whom I have never met, and may never meet.

Reflection – what can I do?

The news of my seven unknown offspring set me on a path of long and deep consideration. At times I felt, and still feel, quite anguished that I have seven other children somewhere in the world who carry a part of me and my genetic and family background, but over whose lives I have no direct influence at all. I wonder if they are alive, if they are healthy, happy, well cared for and loved. I hope that they are but all I can do is hope. One day I may meet some of them – maybe all. Who knows? Or maybe I will meet none and will forever wonder about them. It seems to me that the process of being a sperm donor is somewhat akin to giving a child up for adoption with all of these wonderings and anxieties left with the birth parent. Just like birth parents whose children have been adopted I feel that I have given away seven of my children. Given away with good intentions – and without fully realizing the impact of my actions – but given away nonetheless. That thinking can take me to very dark places – but it is the reality that I must accept.

Action – joining the voluntary register

Awareness of my seven donor offspring coincided with activity to publicize the importance of donor-conceived children knowing their biological heritage. In my reflection one thing became very clear for me. That was that the interests and well-being of the children – all of them – are paramount. Regardless of what the legal framework was at the time of my being a sperm donor, I believe that I do have responsibilities to the children born as a result of my sperm donations. At the least, those people have a right to know what my part of their genetic heritage is – more if they want more. So I joined the Voluntary Registry in my state, lodging an open letter to be given to any children who made contact. That letter is a heartfelt expression of my motivations as a donor and my thoughts about my unmet and unknown offspring. I tell them that I think about them often and wonder who and how they are, and what is happening in their lives. The letter also tells of a "jigsaw" experience in my life when, at the age of 27, I met for the first time my maternal grandfather – at once seeing so many familiar elements of appearance and character. In conclusion, the letter invites and welcomes contact – whenever and however they wish it to be.

I have experienced at least the first steps of such contact. The youngest of the people conceived as a result of my sperm donations made contact through the Register. We shared our first names with each other, she has been given the open letter that I wrote, and at her request I provided some genetic, medical, and ancestry information about me and my family. I wait now to see if and when she wants to take this contact any further. I hope that may happen and that we can learn something of each other. However, even if that does not happen I take solace in the fact that at least one of my unknown children does have my letter to them – and thus she knows that I do think of her and I wish for her a healthy and happy life.

Reflection – impact on my family

In all of this complicated matter, there has also been the question of how and when I would tell my children – the ones who live with me – about their other half-siblings. In the end it was quite simple, and they have taken on quite equably – and with a degree of curiosity – the fact that that they have half-siblings whom they may or may not ever meet. Interestingly, when I first discussed this with my daughter – who was 15 at that time – she had been doing a school project on adoption. In that project, she considered the notion of contacting a birth parent – she taking on the role of the adopted child. This allowed an easy analogy to be made in our discussion about people who are genetically my children, and her half-siblings, but of whom we know very little.

Still and all, by my intentioned actions before they were born I have left the children of my marriage with potential complications which they may have to deal with, but which they had no say in creating. The same applies for my partner who may one day have to deal with others coming into my life who are genetically related to me and our children, but with no biological connection to her at all. I am fortunate that my family dealt with this all in a mature and sensible fashion as we wait and watch to see where the story may next go.

Activism for change

At the time of my joining the Registry, I met a donor-conceived person for the first time. We were both fascinated in our perspectives on the two sides of the donor equation. That person was Narelle Grech – a young woman who spent half of her life searching for her biological father – a man whom she knew only as "T5". I shared too with Narelle and others, activism to bring about change in legislation and practice. And then I saw Narelle's joy at finally finding her "other father" only for that to be followed by the cruel blow of Narelle's death just weeks later.

Inspired by Narelle, and other donor-conceived people whom I met, I saw that I could make a difference by bringing forward the voice less heard – that of a former sperm donor – into public discourse. I spoke at seminars, gave media interviews and wrote submissions and opinion pieces for publication.[45] *Subsequently, I was instrumental in bringing together former sperm donors in the MADMen (Melbourne Anonymous Donors) group. In August 2015, I was featured in a documentary* Sperm Donors Anonymous *– described by its producers as a cautionary and inspiring tale about the effects of anonymous sperm donation on donor-conceived children, their families and on the sperm donors themselves.*

How do I feel about all of this?

At a personal level my reflection on the impact of my actions in becoming a sperm donor, creating seven offspring with whom I have no connection and know close to nothing about, has left me deeply motivated to bring about change and to right the wrong of imposed donor anonymity. I hope one day to meet my offspring – if they wish to meet me. However, if I do not I will be happy and satisfied if I can know that I have played some part in enabling other donor-conceived people to meet their biological parents – their donors.

45 Examples: http://www.theage.com.au/victoria/father-figures-20111112-1ncxt.html and http://www.theage.com.au/opinion/society-and-culture/knowing-about-your-biological-origins-is-a-basic-right-20120408-1wj7s.html; and http://www.parliament.vic.gov.au/images/stories/committees/lawrefrom/iadcpiad/submissions/DCP55_-_Ian_Smith.pdf (links supplied by Ian Smith, accessed 16 March 2016).

Clearly, such stories illustrate just what it means to search, as well as to advocate, for the recording and release of information about donors and other genetic relatives. Many other stories abound.

Conclusion

Donor conception is a controversial practice that has a history shrouded in secrecy. Condemned as 'offensive to the natural law', immoral and adulterous, early experiments with assisted reproductive technologies practiced anonymity with the intention of protecting those parties involved. Treatments were provided clandestinely and secrets harbored from society and the resultant child. The anonymity of the donor, in particular, was further reinforced through medical practices such as using sperm from multiple donors to confuse parentage.[46]

The long-held belief has been that all parties involved in donor conception should not seek information about each other, with some academic scholarship even suggesting that the psychological health of the child would be jeopardized if information about his or her donor conception was revealed.[47] While the secrecy and anonymity of the practice originated with the practitioners performing the insemination, it quickly passed into the 'private' family realm, with parents deciding to keep the nature of their child's parentage a secret.

However, the emphasis placed on 'protecting' the parties involved in donor conception has failed to consider the potentially negative impact secrecy and lack of information can have on the resultant child. The influence of moral, religious and/or legal views on the necessity of anonymity have focused primarily (if not exclusively) on protecting the adults involved in the process. Yet, because the process results in a child, the child's future rights and interests must also be considered. As these children have grown and reached adulthood, the stories of their searches have been told. Their stories are joined by those of their parents and their donors, who also have searched.

As such, the path to true understanding is to listen to those who have lived the experience. The previous personal reflections provide examples of all parties (whether it be donor, donor-conceived person or rearing parent(s) of the donor-conceived person), and of how enforced anonymity and restrictions placed on donor information may have (and in some cases have had) significant impact on their lives. In the case of donor-conceived people, learning information about their donor, and perhaps reaching out to them, is an important step for many once the secret of their status has been revealed. Accessing the medical history of their donor is also an important preventative measure for heritable illnesses. A refusal to disclose medical histories of donors may result in donor-conceived people not being able to undergo early screening and/or diagnosis, therefore missing the opportunity for early treatment or preventive measures. The history

46 Adams and Lorbach, above n 23.
47 Ibid.

of deciding prior to conception or birth that sperm, egg or embryo donations would be anonymous leave many feeling deprived of the right to have full knowledge of how they came into being and of their identity.

The secret system of anonymity has also affected donors, who may at a later stage wonder about the children they helped to create. In the era of secrecy, donors may not have even desired anonymity; it was a condition for donation, and any desired connection was denied by the medical profession prior to conception.

However, as time has progressed, children have grown, and donors have thought often about their role in conceiving them. Laws and practices have also continued to evolve, speaking in different ways on this issue around the world. It is to consideration of these laws and practices that this book now turns.

Part II

Regulatory approaches around the world

4 Jurisdictions that have laws granting access to identifying information

Introduction

The call for openness regarding donor conception records has not always gone unheard.[1] In the present day, several countries have legislation that provides access to identifying and non-identifying information about donors to donor-conceived people. In other jurisdictions, the right to access information has been recognized via court judgments or in national guidelines that uphold the right to information about one's genetic heritage.

This chapter details the laws, systems and practices that have developed in such jurisdictions. It illustrates the strengths and weaknesses of each, while recognizing the commitment within these jurisdictions to support people born because of donor conception, their families and the donors themselves. It is purposefully detailed to provide information that is not easily found elsewhere. This level of detail also enables in-depth consideration and comparison of differing approaches around the world.

Focus is on the development of the law, what the law provides, whether donor-conceived people are notified of their status, and any support systems that exist for donor-conceived people, recipient parents and/or donors. Although the jurisdictions discussed in this chapter might have different systems, their recognition of a donor-conceived person's lawful right to access information about their

1 Note the call was made by many beyond donor-conceived people, donors and recipients. For example see George J. Annas, 'Fathers Anonymous: Beyond the Best Interests of the Sperm Donor' (1980–1981) 14 *Family Law Quarterly* 1; L. Waller, *Report on Donor Gametes in IVF* (Melbourne: Committee to Consider the Social, Ethical and Legal Issues Arising from In Vitro Fertilisation, 1983); Katherine O'Donovan, 'A Right to Know One's Parentage?' (1988) 2 *International Journal of Law and the Family* 27; Erica Haimes, 'Secrecy: What Can Artificial Reproduction Learn from Adoption' (1988) 2(1) *International Journal of Law and the Family*, 46–61; Royal Commission on New Reproductive and Genetic Technologies, *Proceed with Care* (Ottawa: Minister of Government Services, 1993); Maclean Sarah and Marvis Maclean, 'Keeping Secrets in Assisted Reproduction – The Tension between Donor Anonymity and the Need of the Child for Information' (1996) 8(3) *Child and Family Law Quarterly*, 243–252; Eric Blyth, 'Donor Assisted Conception and Donor Offspring Rights to Genetic Origins Information' (1998) 6(3) *International Journal of Children's Rights* 237–254.

donors reflects a society that places paramountcy on the best interests of the person born as a result of donor conception, and the importance of donor-conceived people being able to learn about their genetic heritage, familial medical history and kinship if they choose to do so.

Jurisdictions that have legislation requiring non-anonymous donation

Starting in the early 1980s, a number of jurisdictions across the globe have introduced legislation to provide for the recording and release of information to donor-conceived people (and donors/recipients in some jurisdictions). This section details these laws, as well as the practices, support services and other relevant information regarding the recording and release of information to donor-conceived people, their donors and/or recipient parents under such legislative regimes.

Because each jurisdiction's laws are complex and detailed, basic summary information is provided in Table 4.1 before a further detailed discussion. The information in Table 4.1 provides the jurisdiction, law and the year the law was passed in order of enactment, as well as noting whether the laws operate prospectively (i.e. after the date of enactment) or retrospectively (to all people conceived before and after the act), as well as whether information is held in a hospital, clinic or register.

Discussion is generally ordered according to when laws first came into force to enable the reader to not only understand the law and practices in each jurisdiction but also to provide a developing picture of when and where donor-conceived people have been able to access information over time, across the globe. However, because Australia has state laws, it is listed according to the first state that enacted legislation (Victoria, in 1984) and includes the other states within that section of discussion.

Detailed discussion of the respective jurisdictions

Sweden

The law

Sweden was the first country in the world to place a complete ban on donor anonymity. Enacted on 1 March 1985,[2] this law mandates the release of information to donor-conceived people via access to records held in the hospital at which the conception took place.

2 Lag om insemination (Law on Insemination) 1984 (enacted 1985), replaced by Genetic Integrity Act 2006.

Table 4.1 Table of Laws Requiring the Recording and Release of Information

Jurisdiction	*Legislation*	*Date of implementation*	*Access*
Sweden	Lag om insemination (Law on Insemination) 1984 (replaced by Genetic Integrity Act 2006)	18 March 1985	Prospective (hospital/clinic based)
Victoria (Australia)	1 Infertility (Medical Procedures) Act 1984 2 Infertility Treatment Act 1995; Infertility Treatment Regulations 1997 3 Assisted Reproductive Treatment Act 2008	1 1985 (with consent) 2 1 January 1998 3 2010 (new act maintained status quo); amended 2015; 2016	Prospective from 1998; 2015 — Retrospective with consent for those conceived pre-1998 2016 – Full retrospective release for all donor-conceived people, contact veto/ preference system from 1 March 2017 (register based)
Austria	Fortpflanzungsmedizingesetz. 275 Bundesgesetz	1 July 1992	Prospective (clinic based)
Switzerland	Federal Act on Medically Assisted Procreation of 18 December 1998 – FF 1996 III, 197 (LPMA)	1 January 2001	Retrospective (register based post-2001; clinic based pre-2001)
The Netherlands	Wet donorgegevens kunstmatige bevruchting, 2002	1 June 2004	Retrospective with consent (register based)
Norway	Act on Biotechnology 2003	1 January 2005	Prospective (clinic based)
Western Australia	Human Reproductive Technology Act 1991 (WA)	2004	Prospective (register based)
United Kingdom	Human Fertilisation and Embryology Authority (Disclosure of Donor Information) Regulations 2004; and Human Fertilisation and Embryology Act 2008	1 April 2005	Prospective (but donors that donated 1991–2005 can 're-register' to consent to release) (register based)
New Zealand	Human Assisted Reproductive Technology (HART) Act 2004	22 August 2005	Prospective (register based)

(*Continued*)

Table 4.1 (Continued)

Jurisdiction	*Legislation*	*Date of implementation*	*Access*
Finland	Act on Assisted Fertility Treatments (1237/2006)	1 September 2007	Prospective (register based)
New South Wales (Australia)	Assisted Reproductive Technology Act 2007	1 January 2010	Prospective (retrospective with consent recommended, but pending) (register based)
South Australia	Assisted Reproductive Treatment Act 1988 (SA); Assisted Reproductive Treatment Regulations 2010 (SA).	1988– Identifying information cannot be released without consent; amended 1 July 2010 – enshrine NHMRC Guidelines	Clinic based: • Identifying information can be obtained via clinics subject to consent • Consent must have been given post-2004 donations under NHMRC Guidelines NB. Some records not held by clinics and therefore fall outside of the act. (A review of the operation and effectiveness of the act was being conducted in 2016.)
Washington State (United States)	Wash Rev Code Ann §26.26.750	July 2011	Prospective (clinic based) NB. Subject to veto by donor
Croatia	*Zakon O Medicinski Pomognutoj Oplodnji (Law on Medically Assisted Reproduction*, 12 July 2012) (Croatia), No: 71–05–03 / 1–12–2	12 July 2012	Prospective (register based)
Uruguay	Law Regulating Human Assisted Reproductive Techniques (22/11/2013 No 19.167):	22 November 2013	Based on application to the court
Argentina	Código civil y comercial de la nación (Civil and Commercial Code of the Nation), Title V, Ch2, approved by Law 26,994.	1 October 2014	Prospective (birth registration and medical records)
Ireland	Children and Family Relationships Act 2015 Act No. 9 of 2015	6 April 2015	Prospective (register)

The law was introduced following an extensive committee inquiry established in 1983, in which the Swedish Committee on Insemination viewed its primary purpose as safeguarding the needs and interests of children born because of artificial insemination.[3] Drawing analogies between donor conception and the experiences of adopted children, the committee was convinced that it was in the best interests of donor offspring to be told the truth about their genetic origins.[4]

The committee considered arguments concerning whether the importance of biological fatherhood was being overemphasized, whether social relations were the most important and whether the child's relation to the social father would be weakened if the child learned about the identity of the biological father. However, it concluded that not only were some arguments incompatible but all were unfounded. The Swedish Committee drew again upon the experience of adoptees, which demonstrated that while children want to know about their biological origin, they will not necessarily reject their adoptive parents.[5]

The subsequently introduced law was intended to give donor-conceived children the same legal rights and practical possibilities as adopted children in Sweden. It provides that a person conceived through fertilization outside the body using an egg other than the woman's own or sperm from a man who is not the woman's spouse (or live-in partner)[6] has the right to access data concerning the donor, if he or she has reached sufficient maturity.[7] However, 'sufficiently mature' was not defined in the text of the act. In 1987, formal instructions issued from the National Board of Health and Welfare clarified the application of the law and specified the age as 'the upper teens'. Data concerning the donor is recorded in a special journal, which must be kept for at least seventy years.[8] Note, the use of donor gametes can only be performed at a university hospital, and because there are fewer than ten university hospitals in Sweden, there are only that many special journals. In all cases, the donor remains anonymous to the recipient parent(s).

Donor-conceived people born before the law banning anonymity in 1985 could possibly obtain information through their mother's journal, although since donors remain anonymous to recipient parents, this access might prove difficult.

3 In Sweden, before the Government can draw up a legislative proposal, the matter in question must be analyzed and evaluated. The task may be assigned to officials from the ministry concerned, a commission of inquiry or a one-man committee. Inquiry bodies, which operate independently of the Government, may include or co-opt experts, public officials and politicians. The reports setting out their conclusions are published in the Swedish Government Official Reports series (Statens Offentliga Utredningar, SOU).

4 Statens offentliga utredningar (SOU) 1983:42, pp 110–121.

5 B. Ingemar and B. Lindahl, 'Medical Ethics in Sweden' (1988) 9(3) *Theoretical Medicine* 309, 313–316.

6 Nb. Re ART generally, a recipient parent can only use a donated egg *or* donated sperm (not both) because in Sweden you cannot 'adopt an embryo'.

7 *The Genetic Integrity Act [2006:351]* (Sweden), chapter 6, section 5.

8 *The Genetic Integrity Act [2006:351]* (Sweden), chapter 6, section 4.

Notification of donor-conceived status

Application by the donor-conceived person for information relies on a child knowing or suspecting his or her donor-conceived status. In the latter instance, if a person has reason to assume that he or she was conceived using donated gametes, the social welfare committee is obliged, on request, to help this person find out if there are any data recorded in a special journal.

In practice, however, there is no enforcement or guarantee that a child born in Sweden as a result of donor conception will know of his or her status, and although the Board of Health Regulations says that the parents should be informed and supported in how they let their child know, there are no specific services available charged with this duty. Therefore, it is assumed that doctors and hospital staff carry out this function. Current disclosure rates in Sweden are unknown; however, it appears that disclosure rates have increased over time, as illustrated by a number of separate studies.

A study conducted in 2000,[9] which investigated whether parents intended to disclose donor status to their children, concluded that compliance with the law was low (at only 11 per cent actual disclosure). The majority of parents surveyed (89 per cent, or 132 parents) had not informed their children of their status. However, sixty-one parents said they were intending to tell their children later (as the children were on average around 3.5 years of age), while sixteen were not sure, and twenty-eight said they would not tell their children. Interestingly, 59 per cent had informed someone else. Gottlieb et al., therefore, also raised concern that the child may, in the future, find out by someone else, if their parents did not disclose.[10]

In comparison, a study conducted in 2006 by Lalos et al.[11] found that more than half of parents interviewed (61 per cent) had told their children about the method of conception. Almost all parents had told someone else. Most parents told their children early (at approximately 5 years of age for the first child), and did so to 'avoid accidental discovery', a 'desire for openness' and based on a 'person's fundamental right to know his/her genetic origin'.[12] On the other hand, some parents did not tell their children because they considered donor insemination a private matter or they were afraid of other people's attitudes.[13] Despite the number of parents telling their children, the study concluded that 'there was a discrepancy between the intentions of the legislation and how parents act

9 Claes Gottlieb et al., 'Disclosure of Donor Insemination to the Child: The Impact of Swedish Legislation on Couple's Attitudes' (2000) 15 *Human Reproduction* 2052.

10 Ibid.

11 A. Lalos, C. Gottlieb and O. Lalos, 'Legislated Right for Donor-Insemination Children to Know Their Genetic Origin: A Study of Parental Thinking' (2007) 22(6) *Human Reproduction* 1759–1768.

12 Ibid., p 1759.

13 Ibid.

in relation to them'.[14] A major influencing factor was that healthcare staff had impacted on the parents' way of thinking – a majority of those who had been encouraged to tell their children had done so. Lalos et al., therefore, suggested that to improve compliance, 'it is crucial to organize education, support and ethical discussion among professionals, and to offer parents, and parents-to-be, counselling, support and group sessions with other DI families.'[15]

In 2011, a study by Isaksson et al.[16] found that 90 per cent of participants supported disclosure and honesty to offspring concerning their genetic origin and had told other people about their donation treatment. Between 26 per cent and 40 per cent of participants wanted additional information and support about parenthood following donation treatment. The study concluded that two decades after the Swedish legislation of identifiable gamete donors, recipient couples of donated sperm and oocytes[17] were relatively open about their treatment and support disclosure to offspring.

Support surrounding disclosure

In the 2011 study, Isaksson et al. noted that recipient couples might benefit from more information and support regarding parenthood after gamete donation, and that further studies are required to follow up on the future parents' *actual* disclosure behaviour directed to offspring.

The suggestion for support might also be relevant for those who obtain information, because once a donor-conceived person has information, it is easy for him or her to find the address of the donor (through tax authorities). Although the donor is aware that contact can be made, there are no mechanisms for support or regulation.

In fact, it is unknown how many donor-conceived people have actually made requests for this information.[18] Such data would be held (presumably) by the hospitals, however, despite the author making contact with all ten hospitals, as well the representative of the National Board of Health and Welfare also contacting people with more practical experience, as part of a research study in 2012, there was no response to the inquiry. Follow-up surveys were also sent to all possible contacts; however, there was again a lack of response. Further research since then has not been able to reveal anything more. Therefore, the author cannot

14 Ibid.

15 Ibid.

16 S. Isaksson, A. Skoog Svanberg, Gunilla Sydsjö, A. Thurin Kjellberg, P.O. Karlstrom, N.G. Solensten and C. Lampic, 'Two Decades After Legislation on Identifiable Donors in Sweden: Are Recipient Couples Ready to Be Open about Using Gamete Donation?' (2011) 26(4) *Human Reproduction* 853–860.

17 Perhaps definition here for 'occytes' i.e. 'an immature egg cell which may form an ovum.'

18 S. Allan, 'A Cross-Jurisdictional Study of Regulatory Requirements and Practice Regarding the Recording of Donor Information and Its Release to Donor Conceived People 2012.' Report prepared for the Winston Churchill Memorial Trust.

definitively state whether or not donor-conceived people receive support when making requests.[19]

Nevertheless, a study conducted in Sweden and published in 2014 looking at donor attitudes to disclosure found that a majority of oocyte and sperm donors supported disclosure to donor offspring (71–91 per cent) and had positive or neutral attitudes toward future contact with offspring (80–87 per cent)[20]. Few donors reported a need for more counselling regarding the consequences of their donation.[21]

Australia

Victoria, Australia, was the second jurisdiction in the world to legislate regarding the recording and release of information. However, it is important to recognize that Australia is a federation, having a national government along with state and territory governments. Regulation of assisted reproduction, the status of children and matters pertaining to health fall to the separate states and territories of Australia. Although all Australian states and territories in one way or another provide for information release, four of the eight states have information release systems enshrined in the law,[22] while the remaining states are governed by National Health and Medical Guidelines which have stated since 2004 that anonymous donation is not acceptable.

Of the states that have legislative provisions, three – Victoria, Western Australia and New South Wales – maintain central registers administered by the Department of Births, Deaths and Marriages; the Health Department; and an independent government-funded reproductive authority, respectively. In South Australia, access to information occurs via the clinic where donor conception took place, with a proviso in the legislation that the Minister may set up a donor register, which is imminent. The remaining states and territories require people seeking information to make inquiries with the relevant clinic, hospital or GP, and there are no laws regulating or enforcing information release. The respective systems are discussed next with particular details of the development of the law in Victoria, as that state has shown the most progressive and evolving approach to access to information not only in Australia but also in the world.

Before moving to that discussion, however, it should be noted that over the past few years, and at the time of writing, laws continue to develop, both within and across states and territories. This development followed a national inquiry

19 Ibid.

20 C. Lampic, A. Skoog Svanberg and G. Sydsjö, 'Attitudes Towards Disclosure and Relationship to Donor Offspring Among a National Cohort of Identity-Release® Oocyte and Sperm Donors' (2014) 29(9) *Human Reproduction* 1978–1986 first published online 15 July 2014, doi:10.1093/humrep/deu152.

21 Ibid.

22 Victoria, Western Australia, New South Wales, and South Australia.

conducted in 2010 by the Australian Senate Legal and Constitutional Affairs Committee into issues relating to donor conception. In the report handed down in February 2011, the Senate Committee made seventeen recommendations that related to the preservation, recording and release of records concerning identifying and non-identifying information[23] about donors to donor-conceived people.[24] The recommendations called for the establishment 'as a matter of priority' of a national register of donors[25] that should operate according to principles which provide for donor-conceived people to be able to access identifying information about their donor.[26] The Senate Committee's report left a number of issues open for further debate at state level noting the structure and powers of government in Australia, including whether the recommended legislation should provide for the *retrospective* release of information about donors to donor-conceived people.[27] The Federal Government responded to the Senate Committee's recommendations that although it agreed in principle with its recommendations, it ultimately fell to the states to regulate assisted reproduction, and thus each state was called on to further consider and/or act on them. Developments and debates at a state and territory level have since ensued, continue in the present day and will continue into the future.

Victoria

EARLY INQUIRIES: THE WALLER COMMITTEE

In May 1982, the Victorian Government established the Committee to Consider the Social and Legal Issues Arising from In Vitro Fertilization, chaired by Professor Louis Waller (the Waller Committee). The Waller Committee was 'to consider whether the process of in vitro fertilization (IVF) should be conducted

23 Identifying information would include the donor/donor-conceived person's name, date of birth and address; non-identifying information might include education (level and qualifications); eye colour; hair colour; height; weight; marital status; number of children (if any); sex; year of birth; place of birth; nationality/culture with which the donor identifies; religion (if any); reason for becoming a donor; number of offspring born through other donations; identity of other offspring born through other donations; interests/hobbies/sporting activities; anything else the donor considers central to their personality. (It is difficult to delineate some of the information as identifying or non-identifying as some information in combination might lead to the identification of a person, but alone would be considered non-identifying.).

24 Senate Legal and Constitutional Affairs References Committee, Donor conception Practices in Australia (2011), pp 103–109, (see Recommendations 3, 5–14, 19–21, 25, 31–32).

25 Ibid., p 104, Recommendation 5.

26 Ibid., pp 104–105, Recommendation 9. Such a register may also enable donors to receive information about their offspring, and donor-conceived siblings to receive information about each other.

27 Ibid., p 114 at [7.26]:

in Victoria and, if so, the procedures and guidelines that should be implemented in respect of such processes in legislative form or otherwise'.[28]

The committee published two reports in 1982 and 1983. The second report focused on the use of donor gametes in IVF and in donor insemination.[29] In that report, the committee stated that donor insemination had become 'established in the Victorian community'[30] as part of the management of fertility, and recommended that the use of donor gametes should be permitted in Victoria.[31] However, it also emphasized honesty and integrity as being crucial to family formation,[32] and considered that donor-conceived offspring had a right to non-identifying information about their donor. The committee recommended that the gamete donor's 'genealogical background, medical history and personal characteristics may be transmitted to the recipients of the gametes, any child or children born as a result of the donation and, if necessary, any medical practitioner treating such child or children'.[33] It also recommended that detailed information about gamete donors should be maintained by the Health Commission and hospitals conducting IVF programs.[34]

THE LAW

Alongside Sweden, Victoria was one of the first jurisdictions in the world to subsequently pass laws recognizing a right of access to information by donor-conceived people. It was the first jurisdiction in the world to establish a central register to record information about donors, recipients and donor-conceived people. In 1984, the Infertility (Medical Procedures) Act 1984 established a donor conception register to contain information about donors, recipients and donor-conceived people for all donations that resulted in a child and occurred post-1988. Unlike Sweden, however, such laws did not prohibit anonymity completely. Information that identifies the donor (or donor-conceived person) could only be released with the consent of the person about whom it relates.

28 Committee to Consider the Social, Ethical and Legal Issues Arising from In Vitro Fertilization, Parliament of Victoria, *Interim report* (1982) 2.

29 Committee to Consider the Social, Ethical and Legal Issues Arising from In Vitro Fertilization, Parliament of Victoria, *Report on donor gametes in IVF* (1983) 26–28. (*Waller Committee Report*), 38–41.

30 Ibid., 9.

31 *Waller Committee Report*, 10, 12.

32 Ibid., 26.

33 Ibid., 20.

34 Committee to Consider the Social, Ethical and Legal Issues Arising from In Vitro Fertilization, Parliament of Victoria, *Report on donor gametes in IVF* (1983) 26–28. (*Waller Committee Report*). 'his or her genealogical background, medical history, and personal characteristics may be transmitted to the recipients of the gametes, any child or children born as a result of the donation and, if necessary, any medical practitioner treating such child or children'. *Waller Committee Report*, 20.

34 *Waller Committee Report*, 26.

The laws in Victoria have, however, developed and changed over time.

In 1995, the Infertility Treatment Act 1995 changed the law to *require* consent to release of information prior to donation of gametes. The changes to the law removed anonymity completely for donations made after the law came into force on 1 January 1998. These laws meant that children born because of donations made post-1998 were able to access identifying information about their donor. Donors continued to be able to access information about their donor-conceived offspring, subject to consent. Such information also continued to be recorded on the central register.

The changes to the law over time in Victoria, however, meant that different people had different rights to access information in the same state jurisdictions dependent on when the sperm (and later eggs) with which they were conceived was donated. People conceived with sperm donated before 1988 were not granted access to information because there were no laws governing ART at that time; those conceived with sperm donated between 1988 and 1998 were granted access to non-identifying information, and only to identifying information if the donor consented;[35] and those conceived with sperm donated after 1 January 1998 were granted both identifying and non-identifying information when they turned 18 as the law required the donor to consent to such release prior to donation.[36]

FURTHER CHANGES TO THE LAW: A MODEL FOR LAW REFORM

The impetus to change continued to grow in Victoria as more donor-conceived people came forward seeking information. Hundreds of donors had also placed themselves on the voluntary register which had been established alongside the central register (described further next). At the time of the Federal Senate Committee inquiry, a state inquiry on the issue of access to information by donor-conceived people had been also under way in Victoria. The Victorian Law Reform Committee inquiry had commenced in the 56th Parliament, in 2010, and an interim report recommended it proceed into the 57th Parliament, which it did in 2011 to 2012. Many people came forward during this time and continued the call for information release.

On the issue of retrospectivity, this author put forward to both sessions of the Victorian inquiry that under Australian law, there was no impediment to passing such laws.[37] What needed to occur in deciding whether to pass such

35 *Infertility (Medical Procedures) Act 1984* (Vic), ss 20 and 23.

36 *Infertility Treatment Act 1995* (Vic), s 17 (repealed); *Assisted Reproductive Treatment Act 2008* (Vic), s 57 (application for information on Central Register), s 58 (with respect to parents of a person born as result of donor or donor treatment procedure), s 59 (person born as result of donor treatment procedure) and s 60 (person descended from person born as result of donor treatment procedure).

37 See for example, S. Allan, 'Submission to the Victorian Parliament Law Reform Committee Inquiry into Access to Information by Donor Conceived Individuals about Their Donors'

laws, however, was consideration of the possible injustices to one party (some donors may have not wanted to disclose information) and whether these were outweighed by the need to rectify injustice to others (donor-conceived people searching for information, donors wishing to release their information and parents wanting to tell their children).[38] It was to this end that it was put to the inquiry that 'contact vetoes/preferences' would provide a way to balance the rights of donor-conceived people to access information with the right to privacy of any donor.[39]

Given the ethical, social and legal issues that were raised, experts in relevant areas of law and practice, as well donor-conceived people, recipients and donors, were also called on[40] to consider further the issues regarding the rights and interests of donor-conceived people to information,[41] how to balance these rights with the right to privacy of donors,[42] whether there existed a contract for anonymity,[43] the comparison between the approach taken for the release of information to adoptees and that which might be taken for donor-conceived people,[44] and of course whether and if so how information could be released.[45] The outcome of this research further supported the release of information to donor-conceived people, with a number of articles supporting the contact veto/preference approach.[46]

(2010); S. Allan, 'Psychosocial, Ethical and Legal Arguments for and against the Retrospective Release of Information about Donors to Donor-Conceived Individuals in Australia' (2011) 19(1) *Journal of Law and Medicine* 354.

38 Ibid.

39 Ibid. The contact veto/preference approach to information release, which was eventually adopted in Victoria is further discussed in Chapters 8 and 9 in part III of this book.

40 The author guest edited a special edition of the *Journal of Law and Medicine*, in which numerous experts in the field were commissioned to research and write articles in these areas.

41 D. Adams and C. Lorbach, 'Accessing Donor Conception Information in Australia: A Call for Retrospective Access' (2012) 19(4) *Journal of Law and Medicine* 704; Eric Blyth, Marilyn Crawshaw, Lucy Frith and Caroline Jones, 'Donor Conceived People's Views and Experiences of Their Genetic Origins: A Critical Analysis of the Research Evidence' (2012) 19(4) *Journal of Law and Medicine* 769.

42 J. Tobin, 'Donor Conceived People and Access to Information About Their Genetic Origins: The Relevance and Role of Rights' (2012) 19(4) *Journal of Law and Medicine* 742; See also S. Allan, 'Access to Information about Donors by Donor Conceived Individuals: A Human Rights Analysis' (2013) 20 *Journal of Law and Medicine* 655.

43 Anne Rees, 'Keeping Mum about Dad: "Contracts" to Protect Gamete Donor Anonymity' (2012) 19(4) *Journal of Law and Medicine* 758.

44 R. Chisholm, 'Information Rights and Donor Conception: Lessons from Adoption?' (2012) 19(4) *Journal of Law and Medicine* 722; Naomi Cahn, 'Legal Parent Versus Biological Parent: The Impact of Disclosure' (2012) 19(4) *Journal of Law and Medicine* 790.

45 See S. Allan, 'Donor Conception, Secrecy, and the Search for Information' (2012) 19(4) *Journal of Law and Medicine* 631; Louise Johnson, Kate Bourne and Karin Hammarberg, 'Donor Conception Legislation in Victoria, Australia: The "Time to Tell" Campaign, Donor-Linking and Implications for Clinical Practice' (2012) 19(4) *Journal of Law and Medicine* 803.

46 Adams and Lorbach, above n 41; Allan (2012), above n 45; Chisholm, above n 44; Cahn, above n 44.

A further seventy-seven submissions were made to the inquiry.[47] Fifty-two supported releasing information to *all* donor-conceived people in Victoria;[48] two suggested that donors be given an option to decline information release, subject to review by the regulatory authority about the best interests of the child;[49] eleven submissions supported a 'consent first' approach, in which a donor could decide whether identifying information would be released;[50] four submissions were against information release and wished to maintain the status quo.[51] Three were confidential and, therefore, their contents were not publicly available.[52]

The submissions to the inquiry demonstrated qualitatively where preferences lay. Notably, public hearings conducted by the Victorian Law Reform Committee also reflected preferential support for the full release of information to all donor-conceived people. However, the Victorian Law Reform Committee reported it was most significantly influenced in its decision making by the evidence given by donor-conceived people, recipient parents and donors. Some told stories of devastation and grief, others told tales of successful relationships being forged between donors and their offspring. Mostly, there were consistent and heartfelt

47 Note seventy-five submissions contained differing material as the Fertility Society and VARTA made the same submissions twice: Submissions 32/59 and 19/76, 9 August 2010 and 12 August 2011 (16 August 2012) http://www.parliament.vic.gov.au/lawreform/article/1469.

48 These included submissions from recipient parent(s)/families (x12); donor-conceived people (x5); academic experts (x6); Monash IVF; the Public Interest Law Clearing House; representative groups (including adoption groups (x2)), Rainbow Families, Tangled Webs, the Donor Conception Support Group; members of the public (x2); a record specialist; a lesbian-parent family (self-identified); infertility counsellor groups (x2); Murdoch Children's Research Institute; an adoptee; the Australian Christian Lobby; the Australian Family Council; the Institute for Judaism and Civilisation; and the Victorian Equal Opportunity and Human Rights Commission ('VEOHRC'). Submissions 2, 3, 4, 5, 6, 7, 8, 9, 10, 11, 12, 14, 17, 18, 20, 21, 23, 24, 25, 26, 27, 28, 29, 31, 33, 34, 37(sup), 38, 39, 41, 42, 43, 44, 45, 49 (sup), 50, 51, 52, 53(sup), 55, 56, 57, 60, 61, 62 (sup), 63 (sup), 64, 67 (sup), 68, 72, 74*, 75 to Victorian Parliamentary Law Reform Committee, *Inquiry into Access by Donor Conceived People about Their Donor* (16 August 2012), available at http://www.parliament.vic.gov.au/lawreform/article/1469.

49 This option was supported by the Adhoc Interfaith Committee and the VEOHRC as an alternative to information release to all.

50 These included submissions from one donor, two ITA/VARTA employees (one former, one current) in their independent capacity, VARTA in its official capacity, the Victorian Infertility Support Counsellors, Melbourne IVF, one doctor, the Office of Victorian Privacy Commissioner regarding donor privacy, the Western Australia Reproductive Technology Council, the Fertility Society of Australia (doctors representative group), and the Australian Medical Association. Submissions 1, 16, 19, 22, 32, 35, 46 (sup), 54, 58, 65, 66, 71 to Victorian Parliamentary Law Reform Committee, *Inquiry into Access by Donor Conceived People about their Donor* (16 August 2012), available at http://www.parliament.vic.gov.au/lawreform/article/1469.

51 These included one donor, one lesbian couple (self-identified), one doctor and one donor-conceived person. Ibid., submissions 13, 30, 40, 77.

52 Ibid., submissions 15, 36, 69.

appeals for equality, truthfulness and openness in the law. Their life experiences demonstrated the need for change.

Considerations concerning donor anonymity, while balancing of interests of donors who had been promised anonymity (some of whom might be opposed to information release), also weighed heavily on the committee. While such donors did not appear to be in the majority,[53] their interests in privacy needed to be respected. The key point in the proposed model for releasing information became the option of the person about whom information was to be released to be able to use a contact veto/preference. The Committee Chairman, Clem Newton Brown, said:

> When the Committee commenced this Inquiry, it was inclined toward the view that the wishes of some donors to remain anonymous should take precedence – as they made their donation on that basis – and that identifying information should only be released with a donor's consent. Upon closer consideration, however, and after receiving evidence from a diverse range of stakeholders – donor-conceived people, donors, parents, medical and counselling professionals, department representatives, and academics – the Committee unanimously reached the conclusion that the state has a responsibility to provide all donor-conceived people with an opportunity to access information, including identifying information, about their donors. [However], the Committee also recognized the importance of ensuring that there will be no unreasonable interference in donors' lives should donor-conceived people have access to identifying information. Consequently, one of the Committee's recommendations is that donors, and donor-conceived people, have the ability to place a veto on contact from each other. It is also important that donors, and all of the people affected by donor conception, have comprehensive counselling and other support services available to them.[54]

As such, the Victorian Law Reform Committee's inquiry resulted in recommendations that all records in Victoria be opened on request by a donor-conceived individual for information about his or her donor, regardless of when they were conceived, pursuant to adopting the suggested contact veto system.[55]

Narelle Grech lived to see the handing down of the committee's report, but not the final changes to the law.

53 Notably there are more than 120 donors on the voluntary register in Victoria, and many donors supported information release.

54 Victorian Law Reform Committee, Inquiry into Access by Donor Conceived People to Information about the Donors (March 2012), xvii–xviii.

55 Victorian Law Reform Committee Report, *Access by Donor Conceived People to Information about Their Donors* (2012), available at http://www.parliament.vic.gov.au/57th-parliament/lawreform/article/1468.

Interim changes

Following the Law Reform Committee's recommendations, the then liberal government did not move to support full retrospective release, but did enact changes to legislation, once more giving some further rights to donor-conceived people in Victoria. Laws changed on 29 June 2015 to allow all people conceived with gametes donated in the state before 31 December 1997 to have access to non-identifying information and to access identifying information *if the donor gave his or her consent.*[56] That is, the law as it applied to those born between 1988 and 1998 was extended retrospectively to apply to all people conceived with donated gametes prior to that date. The extension of the law also applied to donors who wish to access information about donor-conceived people.

Access for all donor-conceived people to information about their donors

Donor-conceived people, recipients and donors continued to share their stories and their plight, calling for access to information pursuant to the contact veto system. In 2015, a national conference was held in Victoria, along with a subsequent campaign about being donor conceived, both of which drew further attention to the issues faced by these groups.[57] A discussion paper released by the newly appointed Labor Government undertook to introduce further legislation. 'The Right to Know' outlined how the proposed changes would work in practice and was released for public consideration and comment.[58]

The Assisted Reproductive Treatment (Amendment) Bill 2015 was introduced into the Legislative Assembly in late November 2015, where it was passed with a free vote of 56 to 27. It moved to the Legislative Council in February 2016, and again received bipartisan support, via another free vote resulting in the bill being read into law. Donor-conceived people, their parents, donors, children and their supporters watched from the galleries. Members of Narelle Greche's family were also there to see the passing of the law.

The law to support access to information for all, subject to expression of a 'contact preference', was passed on 23 February 2016. The model adopted is a world first concerning donor conception.

56 *Assisted Reproductive Treatment Act 2008* (Vic), s 59.

57 See further Are You Donor Conceived (RUDC) Campaign, available at http://www.areyoudonorconceived.org/, accessed 16 March 2016.

58 Victorian Government, The Right to Know Your Identity: Giving Donor-Conceived People the Right to Access Information Identifying their Donor (Discussion Paper, Victorian Government, 29 June 2015).

The Victorian Minister for Health, Jill Hennessy, made the following statement afterward:

> We believe all donor-conceived people should have the right to know about their genetic heritage, no matter when their donors donated. . . . If this information is available, it shouldn't be kept from them.[59]

The new law is scheduled for enactment on or before 1 March 2017.

Voluntary register

Because access to information in Victoria had not been available to all donor-conceived people, voluntary registers were set up years ago to enable information exchange by people not governed by the legislation (i.e. those conceived with sperm donated and used prior to laws enabling access) as well as for siblings and people whose records may not exist or have been destroyed. There have been various iterations of such voluntary registers by the former Infertility Treatment Authority (the government authority whose name was subsequently changed to the Victorian Assisted Reproductive Authority [VARTA] in 1995), which were then transferred in 2010 to the Victorian Registry of Births, Deaths and Marriages.

In 2015, the following people could lodge information and apply for access to information held on the voluntary register: a donor-conceived person (e.g. born prior to 1988 or searching for siblings); a parent of a donor-conceived person; a relative of a donor-conceived person; a descendant of a donor-conceived person; a donor; or a relative of a donor. If there is a 'match', information that the person has agreed to release will be given to the other person. For example, if both the donor-conceived person and the donor place their name on the voluntary register, they may be matched and the information they have agreed to release will be shared. People who want to register on the voluntary register must fill in a voluntary register application form. There is no fee for this service.

From 2017, further changes to the law will transfer all register functions to VARTA, including the voluntary register. In addition to maintaining the voluntary register, there is further provision for people to place a photograph, toy, jewelry or other item approved by the Authority that the person has asked to enter in the register.

59 Premier of Victoria, the Hon Daniel Andrews MP, Media Release: New Law Gives All Donor Conceived Victorians the Right to Know Their Heritage, available at http://www.premier.vic.gov.au/new-law-gives-all-donor-conceived-victorians-the-right-to-know-their-heritage/, accessed 16 March 2016.

Notification of donor-conceived status

Victoria was the first in the world to implement a system that notifies people of their donor-conceived status.[60] Since 2010, Victorian law has required an addendum to the birth certificate of a donor-conceived person.[61] On applying for a birth certificate at age 18, a donor-conceived person will be told there is more information about them held on the register. Parents are therefore encouraged to discuss their child's donor-conceived status early.

Support surrounding disclosure

In Victoria, the independent government authority, VARTA, runs a 'Time to Tell' campaign aimed at encouraging and supporting parents to share information about the method of conception and the donor with their children.[62] Over the years, the government authority has had varying responsibility for linking biologically related parties.

The Victorian 'Time to Tell' campaign was based on research that found parents often find it difficult to tell their children about their donor origins or to know when to tell them. Therefore, the work of VARTA is aimed at raising awareness of the implications of legislation in Victoria that provide for information release, to inform parents of donor-conceived children about the benefits of telling children about their donor, and to assist them in telling their children about their donor origins. VARTA has used media advertising, public relations campaigns, and a website to disseminate information about donor conception and resources such as brochures and podcasts to advise parents about how to communicate with children of various ages about their donor origins. Community education activities are also conducted, including public seminars for parents, donor-conceived people and donors, along with ART clinics and consumer groups. Johnson et al. emphasize how attendance at such seminars has steadily grown and have had significant reach.[63]

60 Other countries now include Ireland, and Argentina. In Croatia, the law obligates parents to tell their children they are donor conceived prior to their 18th birthday, but has no system that will alert them to their status. In Estonia donor-conceived adults may apply to the authorities to establish their donor-conceived status, however this does not equate to notification rather, it allows donor-conceived people who suspect their status to confirm (or deny) it. In the United Kingdom, two people wishing to marry may apply to the HFEA to establish they are not donor-conceived siblings.

61 *Assisted Reproductive Treatment Act 2008* (Vic), s 153; *Births, Deaths and Marriages Registration Act 1996* (Vic), s 17B(2).

62 Louise Johnson, Kate Bourne and Karin Hammarberg, 'Donor Conception Legislation in Victoria, Australia: The "Time to Tell" Campaign, Donor-Linking and Implications for Clinical Practice' (2012) 19(4) *Journal of Law and Medicine* 803–819. The Time to Tell Campaign has been said to have been modelled on, or to mirror, the very successful workshops run by the United Kingdom Donor conception Network: 'Telling Children About Being Donor Conceived'.

63 Ibid., p 811.

Johnson et al. also detail the donor-linking services model that was employed by the earlier Infertility Treatment Authority, which have become a function of the current VARTA.[64] The model used in Victoria is similar to those operated in a number of other jurisdictions (including Western Australia, the Netherlands and the United Kingdom) and was established at around the same time as those jurisdictions. It involved steps for applications to the Central Register upon which mandatory identifying and/or non-identifying information may have been held and counselling at all levels regardless of whether information was available and whether it was identifying or non-identifying.[65] In cases where identifying information was available, the applicant was assisted to establish contact via a letter drop service with the person about whom information was available, and the authority acted as an intermediary between the parties in relation to how much information they wished to exchange.[66] Again, counselling and/or support services are available for guidance throughout the process.

In relation to the voluntary register(s), people are supported in placing their information on the register, searching for a match and counselled in relation to whether such a match existed, and if so, how to proceed.

Such services will be maintained and enhanced under the new legislation in March 2017.

Western Australia

The law

In Western Australia, people conceived using gametes donated after 2004 can access identifying information about their donor when they turn 16.[67] People conceived prior to 2004 may access non-identifying information that is held on the register, noting that information has only been held on the central register since 1993. Many people still must approach the clinic involved in their conception. Acess to information will depend on a clinic's record keeping and policies.

Voluntary register

A voluntary register also exists in Western Australia to facilitate the exchange of identifying information for those not able to access identifying information about donors or siblings. Such information is entered on the voluntary register if a person completes a properly signed and witnessed written registration form. Access is based on mutual consent between donors and donor-conceived individuals. Related donor-conceived offspring may also have access to identifying

64 Ibid., p 812.
65 Ibid.
66 Ibid.
67 *Human Reproductive Technology Act 1991* (WA), ss 49(1a), 49(2d) and 49(2e).

information about each other if all parties have consented. This access may be done without identifying the donor.

Although the Western Australia voluntary register may include details of people involved in donation since ART started in Western Australia in the early 1970s, its operations are influenced by whether the donation was made before or after the Human Reproductive Technology Act 1991 came into operation on 8 April 1993, since central records have only been stored since that date. The only records available before that time are those held by the fertility clinics and medical practitioners that provided such services. Because detailed records were not always kept in the early days of ART, the registry notes that it is difficult to match records for donors and donor offspring where donations were made before the early 1980s.

Notification of donor-conceived status

In 2002, the Western Australia Reproductive Technology Council produced a pamphlet on 'Talking to Children about Donor Conception', which was circulated to relevant organizations and groups to provide practical assistance to parents of donor offspring in telling their child about the method of his or her conception. The Western Australia Reproductive Technology Council also continues to conduct workshops during which people involved in the donor conception process may explore issues such as: 'With whom should they share their experiences?'; 'Should the children be told?'; 'At what age is it best to tell?'; and 'Where is help and support available?'

Support surrounding donation and disclosure

When disclosure or sharing of identifying information about donation is being considered, counselling is required by a person approved by the Commissioner of Health.

New South Wales

The law

Laws were introduced in New South Wales to establish a central donor register on 1 January 2010. The Central Register contains mandatory information that providers must submit to the NSW Ministry of Health for inclusion on the register. Mandatory information includes information regarding every child born because of ART treatment using donated sperm, eggs or embryos, or born through surrogacy, and whose conception occurred after 1 January 2010. It contains the full name, sex and birth date of the child born because of ART treatment by the ART provider, the name of the woman who gave birth to the child, and the full name and date and place of birth of the gamete donor. The ART provider must also supply identifying information about the donors who donate sperm, eggs or embryos. Donors must provide the following Mandatory Information to ART providers for inclusion on the Central Register:

- full name, residential address, date and place of birth
- ethnicity and physical characteristics
- medical history or genetic test results of the donor or the donor's family that are relevant to the future health of:
    - a person undergoing ART treatment involving the use of the donated sperm, eggs or embryo, or
    - any offspring born as a result of that treatment, or
    - any descendent of any such offspring
- sex and year of birth of other offspring arising from the donation
- name of each ART provider who has previously obtained donated sperm, eggs or embryo from the donor and the date on which the sperm, eggs or embryos were obtained

ART providers must also collect non-identifying information about the year of birth and sex of any offspring a donor has who have not been born as a result of ART treatment. This information is also entered on the register; however, it is only with that offspring's consent that identifying information about him or her can be shared.

All children conceived using gametes or embryos donated after this date might access identifying information when they turn 18.[68] Those conceived using gametes or embryos donated prior to 1 January 2010 need to contact the clinic in which they were conceived for non-identifying information if such records still exist.

Parents of children conceived after 1 January 2010 because of ART treatment using donated gametes can apply to the Central Register for non-identifying information about their child's sperm, egg or embryo donor. Identifying information can only be provided to the parent in the event of a medical emergency or life-threatening situation and must be reasonably necessary to prevent serious damage to the child's physical or psychological health.

When sperm, egg or embryo donation resulted in offspring conceived after 1 January 2010, mandatory non-identifying information held by the New South Wales Ministry of Health on the Central Register can be provided to the donor. The law currently provides that the information that will be shared includes the sex and year of birth of each offspring.

People who want to apply for information need to fill in a specific form found on the NSW Department of Health's website.

68 *Assisted Reproductive Technology Act 2007* (NSW), s 37; Assisted Reproductive Technology Regulation 2009 (NSW), regs 15 and 16.

Voluntary register

In New South Wales, people who were donor conceived before 1 January 2010 and those who fall within the time of the ART Act coming into effect can register any of the above information about themselves on the Central Register. Donors who donated sperm, eggs or embryos before 1 January 2010 can also register their details. When both the donor and donor-conceived person have given their express consent to do so, information about each other can be exchanged.

Support surrounding disclosure

There is no legislative requirement in New South Wales for people who want to apply for information to undergo counselling; however, the New South Wales Department of Health 'strongly recommends' people seek counselling before applying for information held on the register.

Further amendments afoot

In 2013, the New South Wales Parliamentary Committee on Law and Safety completed an inquiry into managing donor conception information and made several recommendations relating to ART treatment. The NSW committee did not mirror the Victorian position, instead following the 'interim position' taken by the then Victorian Liberal Government in 2013 by recommending that pre-2010 donor-conceived individuals should have a right to access de-identified information about their donor but that identified information should *only be disclosed with consent*. They also recommended an addendum to donor-conceived people's birth certificates notifying them of their status as per the Victorian approach.[69]

In 2016, the NSW government introduced a bill to enable access to non-identifying information by donor-conceived people born because of gametes donated prior to 2010, the preservation of records for a period of seventy-five years, penalties for destroying or tampering with records and a *voluntary* addendum to the birth certificates of donor-conceived people.[70] In response, there was great concern by the donor conception community that there was no provision that records be passed to the Central Register to be preserved. This was seen as particularly important because it had been revealed that in one NSW hospital, eighty-four records were stripped of their donor codes because the doctors claimed it was the 'ethics of the time'.[71] Furthermore, such changes would

69 See New South Wales Law and Safety Committee Inquiry into Management of Information Relating to Donor conception 2013; and New South Wales Law and Safety Committee Inquiry into Donor Information on the Birth Registry 2012.

70 Assisted Reproductive Technology Amendment Bill 2016 (NSW).

71 Belinda Hawkins, Breaking the Code: Donor Conceived Children Search for Identity of Fathers and Biological Heritage, *ABC News*, 18 August 2014, available at http://www.abc.net.au/news/2014–08–18/code-breaking3a-abc-journalist-sarah-dingle/5676544,

provide little more information to donor-conceived people than they currently had, not even going so far as to put forward in bill form the recommendations of the NSW Law and Safety Committee. Nevertheless, the bill proceeded to a debate in Parliament and was passed subject only to one amendment that provided for review of the legislation in twelve months. A review of the NSW position is therefore required to occur in 2017.

South Australia

The law

South Australia, like Victoria, introduced legislation regulating assisted reproduction early on. South Australia's Reproductive Technology Act 1988 created a statutory body, known as the South Australian Council for Reproductive Technology (SACRT), with responsibility for licensing and developing a code of ethical practice governing assisted reproduction. The SACRT was devolved in 2010 following changes to the act and there is currently no statutory body providing oversight of ART in South Australia.

In relation to donor conception, the early South Australian law provided statutory protection for the anonymity of donors, making it a criminal offence, subject to a penalty of $5,000 or six months' imprisonment, for revealing the identity of a donor without consent.[72] However, the identity of the donor could be revealed if the donor consented. Children born as a result of the use of donated gametes were also permitted to access to non-identifying information about donors once they reached the age of 16, with prospective parents receiving non-identifying information at the time of the donation.

In April 2000, the SACRT issued a discussion paper that made a number of recommendations concerning donor conception, the main being that children born from donor gametes should have access to identifying information about their biological origins.[73] The SACRT recommendation was to be prospective only, recommending that past donors should be contacted and invited to provide information to their donor offspring. It also recommended that a voluntary register be established to collate information relating to donors, children and recipients. That same paper also recommended that recipients tell their donor offspring of their method of conception.

However, by 2005, no further legislation had been enacted. The South Australian Social Development Committee (SDC) and the SACRT again raised

---

accessed 16 March 2016; Harriet Alexander, 'Fast and Loose Days of Sperm Donation, When Records Were Deleted', *The Sydney Morning Herald*, 5 December 2015, available at http://www.smh.com.au/national/health/fast-and-loose-days-of-sperm-donation-when-records-were-deleted-20151203-glepqz.html, accessed 16 March 2016.

72 *Reproductive Technology Act 1988* (SA), s 18(1).

73 Discussion Paper of the South Australian Council on Reproductive Technology, Conception by Donation (SACRT, 2000).

concerns about the lack of access to identifying information about gamete or embryo donors in South Australia and recommended that donor registration be addressed. In 2007, the SDC again recommended that legislation be amended to ensure that people conceived through donor conception have access to information about their genetic parentage should they request it.

Changes to the Assisted Reproductive Treatment Act 1988 (SA) were introduced to Parliament in 2008 and came into force in 2010. In relation to donor conception, changes included a provision that the Minister *may* keep a register of donors of human reproductive material used in assisted reproductive treatment and resulting in the birth of a child. The law currently provides the register must contain, in relation to each donor on the register, the following:

- donor's full name and nominated contact address
- full name and nominated contact address of the person to whom assisted reproductive treatment using the donor's human reproductive material was provided
- full name of any child born as a consequence of such assisted reproductive treatment (if known)
- any other information required by the regulations and other information that the Minister thinks fit[74]

However, the use of the word 'may' means that such a register is not compulsory. To date, there is no central register that holds this information and thus no further regulations regarding its operation nor a mechanism for the release of information without the donor's consent. Without such consent, a person releasing information could be subject to a fine of up to $10,000 or six months' imprisonment.[75] Note, the current situation is that the act requires adherence to the NHMRC guidelines, which have required all donations since 2004 to have occurred only with consent to release of identifying information. People born as a result would likely be able to access identifying information from clinics when they reach 18. (However, note the NHMRC guidelines don't address what should happen if the donor retracts such consent, and without clear legislative provisions on the matter, access to information release may not be guaranteed.)

In 2013, a call for submissions regarding draft regulations pertaining to the register was seen as indicative of the intention of government to establish the register; however, subsequently nothing occurred.

In 2016, under a mandated five-year legislative review of the 2010 changes to the act, the issue was considered again. The author of this book was appointed by the Minister of Health to lead the review with particular focus on the operation and effectiveness of the act in relation to it being required that the welfare of the child being born as a result of assisted reproduction is considered paramount

74 *Assisted Reproductive Treatment Act 1988* (SA), s 15(2).
75 Ibid., s 18.

and the provision for the Minister to establish a donor register (among other things). That review again revealed a significant demand for access to information by all donor-conceived people and a call for laws similar to those enacted in Victoria. Support was shown by health professionals, donor-conceived people, recipients, donors and numerous other submissions to the review for the establishment of the donor register, including centralizing all past records to ensure their preservation and access for all donor-conceived people. The South Australian government will need to enact further legislation and regulations to make this possible. It was expected that this would occur.

National Health and Medical Research Council (NHMRC) guidelines

In addition to state regulations in Australia, there are national guidelines promulgated by the National Health and Medical Research Council (NHMRC), which is an independent statutory agency established by the NHMRC Act (Cth). The NHMRC Act provides for the NHMRC to pursue activities designed to:

- raise the standard of individual and public health throughout Australia;
- foster the development of consistent health standards among the various states and territories;
- foster medical research and training and public health research and training throughout Australia; and
- foster consideration of ethical issues relating to health.

In 2004, the NHMRC published *Ethical Guidelines on the Use of Assisted Reproductive Technology in clinical practice and research.*[76] All states and territories must adhere to the NHMRC guidelines pursuant to a self-regulatory accreditation system operated by the Reproductive Technology Accreditation Committee of the Fertility Society of Australia and in order to receive Medicare funding (public funding for services). Nevertheless, such guidelines do not have the same force as law. Since 2004, the NHMRC guidelines have required:

6.1 Persons conceived using ART procedures are entitled to know their genetic parents. Clinics must not use donated gametes in reproductive procedures unless the donor has consented to the release of identifying information about himself or herself to the persons conceived using his or her gametes. Clinics must not mix gametes in a way that confuses the genetic parentage of the persons who are born.

76 NHMRC published ethical guidelines on the use of assisted reproductive technology in clinical practice and research (2004) (Updated 2007).

6.1.1 Clinics should help potential gamete donors to understand and accept the significance of the biological connection that they have with the persons conceived using their gametes. Donors should be advised that the persons conceived are entitled to knowledge of their genetic parents and siblings.

6.1.2 Clinics should help prospective recipients to understand the significant biological connection that their children have with the gamete donor. Recipients should be advised that their children are entitled to knowledge of their genetic parents and siblings; they should therefore be encouraged to tell their children about their origins.

6.1.3 Working with relevant professional organizations, clinics should use forums for public information to encourage people who were donors before the introduction of these guidelines, and those previously conceived using donated gametes, to contact the clinic and register their consent to being contacted by their genetic children or genetic siblings and half-siblings, respectively.[77]

However, there have been mixed anecdotal reports from donors, recipients and donor-conceived people concerning the extent to which the guidelines are (or are not) implemented in relation to encouraging information release – some clinicians show strong opposition to information disclosure, while other clinics engage in donor-linking and support donors, recipients and donor-conceived people to exchange information. Given that when a register does not exist, donor-conceived people must contact the clinic to see if it holds any information and whether it will release that information, consistency in approach across clinics is essential. The lack of consistency has been one reason for the call for legislative provisions mandating information release.

It is also important to note that the NHMRC ethical guidelines were under review at the time of writing this book. A draft copy of suggested amendments to the guidelines released in 2015, while continuing to place value on children born because of donor conception having access to information about their genetic heritage, also placed greater emphasis on privacy and autonomy of donors and recipients. Although these suggestions appear contrary to the legislative movement in Australia to increase access to information, and increasing calls for information release for all, they also illustrate different philosophical views and emphasis by some academics and industry members who have strong influence over such guidelines. In some instances, such parties are not supportive of information release and the issue has not been clearly resolved.

77 NHMRC Ethical Guidelines on the Use of Assisted Reproductive in Clinical Practice and Research (2007).

Austria

The law

Austria was the third jurisdiction to enact laws concerning assisted reproduction. In Austria, sperm donation is permitted only in circumstances of a married couple who are experiencing infertility. The law prohibits egg donation; said to have been formulated to avoid the creation of 'unusual' personal relations (e.g. a child with two biological mothers). Austria has also stated that the aim of its law has been to avoid 'exploitation and humiliation of women, especially those from economically disadvantaged backgrounds' who may be pressured to donate egg cells to infertile women so they can receive IVF treatment they could not afford otherwise.[78]

The laws requiring the release of information about donors to donor-conceived children – which therefore relate to sperm donation – were enacted in 1992.[79] Access to information requires contact with the clinic or hospital in which conception took place. The law provides that the clinic or hospital record the following information about a sperm donor: first and last name, place of birth, nationality and place of residence; first and last names of his parents; date of donation; the results of medical investigations carried out at the time as per current medical knowledge to ensure mother and child are not at risk; and whether there are other families who have used the donor's sperm.

In addition, the law stipulates that a donor-conceived person, upon request, after having reached the age of 14, may inspect the records of the clinic that holds this information. Earlier inspection may occur in medically justified cases subject to court authorization.

The practice

In one major clinic that the author visited,[80] the following practice regarding counselling couples prior to the use of donor sperm was outlined.

> The couple comes to the clinic for treatment – they are counselled about what they think the outcome of using donor sperm will be, any fears they have, and who they would tell. The couple is asked about whether they intend for the donor conception to be kept secret and if so for how long. The doctor

78 Francesco Paolo Busardò, Matteo Gulino, Simona Napoletano, Simona Zaami and Paola Frati, 'The Evolution of Legislation in the Field of Medically Assisted Reproduction and Embryo Stem Cell Research in European Union Members' 14 *BioMed Research International* (2014), Article ID 307160, available at http://dx.doi.org/10.1155/2014/307160, accessed 16 March 2016.

79 Fortpflanzungsmedizingesetz. 275 Bundesgesetz, 1 July 1992.

80 S. Allan, A Cross-Jurisdictional Study of Regulatory Requirements and Practice Regarding the Recording of Donor Information and Its Release to Donor Conceived People 2012. Report prepared for the Winston Churchill Memorial Trust.

> providing counselling will make comparisons with adoption, emphasizing it has been shown to be advantageous that a child knows from the beginning its donor status. The parents are informed that the best approach is to wait until the child asks how they were conceived and then explain the nature of their conception. This should proceed step-wise, so that the child grows up knowing their donor status and that it is a normal thing. However, it is important to note that the ultimate decision and disclosure method is left to the parents.[81]

The doctor reporting on the clinic's practice noted that parents are told 'of course you may keep the secret but you may have problems, psychological, guilt and so on, because it is the clinic's experience that keeping the secret is not advantageous'.[82] The doctor also reported that parents are warned that if a child finds out later in life – which may often be the case – the devastation of being lied to all of his or her life may be very damaging. Therefore, counselling aims at taking the fear out of telling – if the child is told the truth about his or her biological father, the love he or she holds for the social father should not be reduced.

However, it was the clinic's experience, and anecdotally by way of its communication with the other seven clinics in Austria that practice donor conception, that few inquiries are made. It is believed that the lack of inquiries is because most couples in Austria do not, and will never, tell the children of the method of conception. Those who want to tell them, or do tell them, only ask information about the donor if there are special reasons. For example, the clinic in central Austria reported that one child was not growing properly and pediatricians asked about the height of the donor father.[83] Otherwise, they do not seek information.

Non-disclosure may be reinforced by the practice in Austria of matching the donor as closely as possible to the father. The doctor makes note of all characteristics of the donor, including looks and blood group, and a photo is taken. This information is used to find as close a match to the rearing father as possible. Parents are also told that to narrow too much is not good because Austria does not have a large pool of donors. (In Austria, a donor can only donate for three couples until they have completed their families.)

In that same research, it was revealed that clinics might take different approaches depending on the circumstances in which information is sought. For example, one clinic informed the author that occasionally an inquiry would be made by a mother at the time of divorce. In such instances, the clinic said it would counsel the mother about whether it is the right time to tell. It was reported that this is perceived as a moment when the woman needs some support – 'it is important that she has someone who knows, and to whom she can speak'.[84] In the clinic

81 Personal communication by clinician to author, during Churchill Trust funded research; Allan, Churchill Report, above n 80.

82 Ibid.

83 Ibid.

84 Ibid.

that the author visited in 2012, such support was provided by the doctor along with a psychologist.

Regarding inquiries from children, in all the time that the clinic had been operating, the doctor interviewed remembered only one direct inquiry by a donor-conceived person for information – a seventeen-year-old girl. He described the situation in which her mother had called first; however, information in this jurisdiction is not disclosed to the mother. Following the mother's inquiry, the doctor contacted the donor and told him that maybe in the future the daughter might contact him. The donor said that he was worried about timing, his job was changing and he was not in a secure position. The daughter then came to the clinic and asked to inspect the file. She arrived with a friend, and was told about how her parents had wanted a child, what they did and she looked at the file that contained the name, date of birth and address of the donor at the time of donation. The doctor did not explain the donor's position because the daughter said that 'she did not want contact, she just wanted information'. In the doctor's view, 'it is important that they know the name, but that was it for this girl.'[85]

Record keeping

In Austria, clinical records are kept closed in a safe for at least thirty years, and then they have to be given to the Health Ministry of the state. Beyond the clinic-based information, there is a central registration system of donor conception through the notaries. That is, all of the contracts signed by the recipient parents are kept forever at the state office, so if the children want to know where the treatment took place, they can go to that office and find out.

There is also government oversight from the Health Ministry stipulating that clinics have to report every year how many cases and the results. However, the clinics only report global statistics. These numbers are used because social insurance pays for IVF – half by insurance, half by the Health Ministry. However, the statistics refer to IVF generally and not donor statistics. The government has the potential to control and enforce the law more thoroughly, yet so far, it appears that the focus has been on patient safety and not as much on donor insemination. The clinician the author spoke to emphasized that as donor conception is not the norm and 'numbers are so small – perhaps 40 to 50 cases per year – that the focus has not been on this issue'.[86]

85 Ibid.

86 Note, the author contacted all other clinics in Austria that may be carrying out donor conception and requested an interview. No replies were received. A follow-up survey was sent to each clinic asking the questions covered in the above material – again no replies were received. To gain a fuller understanding of practice and implementation of the law in Austria, follow-up with these clinics is necessary.

Switzerland

The law

In 1992, Switzerland incorporated into its constitution a guarantee of access to data concerning lineage for children born because of donor conception. The Swiss Federal Act on Medically Assisted Procreation 1998, which came into effect in 2001, further provides for access to information by all donor-conceived people at age 18 (or earlier where there is a legitimate purpose for obtaining it). The access is provided for those conceived with sperm donated both before[87] and after[88] the act – with the source of information based at clinics in the former case, and on a government-established register in the latter.

Specifically, Article 18 of the Swiss law provides that before donating sperm, the donor must be informed in writing of the child's right to obtain information. Article 24 stipulates that information recorded should include family name and first name, date and place of birth, place of residence, place of origin in Switzerland or nationality, occupation and education; date of the sperm donation; results of the medical examination; and information about physical appearance. Article 27 then provides that once the child has reached 18 years of age, he or she may request information from the Federal Office about the donor's physical appearance and personal data. In addition, the child may, at any time, request information on all data relating to the donor if he or she has a 'legitimate interest' in obtaining it. Before the Federal Office discloses personal data, it shall inform the donor if possible. If the donor does not wish to have personal contact, then the child must be informed and made aware of the donor's rights of privacy and his family's entitlement to protection. If the child insists on his or her right to obtain information, the information shall be provided.

In addition, Article 41 provides for retrospective application of the act. It states 'Articles 18 and 24–27 also apply if sperm cells have been donated before, but are only used after, the commencement of this Act'.[89] It further creates a requirement that 'in all other cases, physicians who have used assisted reproductive techniques using donated reproductive cells must provide information, with the provisions of Article 27 applying *mutatis mutandis*'.[90]

The system implemented in Switzerland supports retrospective release for those conceived prior to the date of the law's enactment and was the first in the world

87 *Federal Act on Medically Assisted Procreation 1998* (Switzerland), Art. 41 provides that if sperm cells were donated before, but used after, the commencement of the Act, the information release provisions still apply. In addition, in all other cases, if a donor-conceived person makes a direct inquiry to the clinic physicians who used assisted reproductive techniques using donated reproductive cells must provide information, with the provisions of the act applying *mutatis mutandis* regardless of when such cells were donated.

88 *Federal Act on Medically Assisted Procreation 1998* (Switzerland), Art. 27.

89 Ibid., Art. 41.

90 I.e. changing only the things that need to be changed.

to do so. However, the law requires that those conceived with sperm donated before the legislation must contact clinics that are required to give information, while those conceived with sperm donated after the enactment of the legislation may request information from the Federal Office register.

The practice

In practice the Swiss authority reports that treatments before 1 January 2001 cannot be traced because documents were destroyed after ten years. Attempts from individuals conceived before the new law came into force (FMedG 2001) to get information have ended negatively. Many are told it is impossible to find the donors before that time. Regarding post-2001 donations, the authority said 'Today, the 'child' must be of legal age (18) to get data from the donor. The first insemination was theoretically on 1 January 2001 with delivery at the end of 2001. As such, the first request for donor information will reach the Federal Department only in 2018 or 2019 at the earliest. We thus have no experience.'[91]

The Netherlands

The move to end donor anonymity in the Netherlands was originally a move from religious politicians in the early 1980s to limit semen donation and reduce access by lesbians and single parents to donor insemination. This move did not find much support. Over time, however, the debate shifted to focusing on the needs of donor-conceived offspring and increased recognition of their right to information.

Between 1990 and 2004, a dual system was introduced giving parents a choice between anonymous donors (A donors) and donors who could be traced if the child requested identifying information about them (B donors). Both A and B donors provided a type of 'passport' of autobiographical information. However, the information contained in the passports varied. Sometimes 'it was not very accurate, not complete, some got lost, some forms were not filled in properly, [and] some things got mixed up'.[92]

Public awareness on the issue reportedly grew because of recurring discussions in the media (newspapers, radio and television) including real-life stories involving some donor-conceived people. Public opinion increasingly supported and called for information release. It is noted that reported fears during the fifteen years of debate about a decrease in donor numbers or access to donor insemination by certain groups of people were not realized. A final draft of the law was sent to the Dutch parliament in 2001, and following parliamentary debate and a number of amendments, it was accepted almost unanimously by parliament in

91 Personal communication to Sonia Allan, 2013.
92 Allan, Churchill Report, above n 80.

2002.[93] The law came into force in June 2004, giving offspring conceived by semen or oocyte donation the right of access to information identifying their donor once they turn 16 years of age.

The law

In the Netherlands, there is now a combination of mandatory register for people born or conceived post-2004 (operated by the Foundation for Donor Information) and voluntary register for those born pre-2004. In addition, the Netherlands utilizes DNA testing in searching for genetic relatedness. Thus, there exists the central government register and a separate DNA databank/support system currently run by an independent (but government funded) agency known as FIOM. These two linked systems work in unison to achieve information release and support for all people who make an inquiry. The government and regulatory authority reported spending considerable energy implementing the law, making practical rules, safeguarding the recruitment of new donors and educating parents, donors and the public of the consequences of the law.[94]

The Foundation for Donor Information (the register)

The Foundation for Donor Information is part of the Ministry of Health, Welfare and Sport. It records all information regarding donor conception in the Netherlands and manages the data in terms of information release. Since 1 June 2004, donors may only donate if they have no objection to the registration of their data or to the possibility that this information will be released to any resulting offspring. When doctors perform a treatment with donated sperm, egg or embryo, they are required to report all details concerning the donor to the register. Women who have undergone treatment are required to report to the clinic when there has been a live birth. If they do not, it is assumed that there has been a live birth.

The register's board consists of seven members: a lawyer; ethicist; child psychologist; chairman (currently a gynecologist); three members who work in the field of ART (embryologist, gynecologist and psychologist). The board meets four times a year to discuss applications. The register is staffed and administered by a person who is legally trained (i.e. a jurist or lawyer) who maintains the register; has contact with the Ministry of Health; liaises with FIOM (the provider of counselling and support services); liaises with the Ministry of Justice; is responsible for record keeping, addressing policy questions and maintaining the website. This person is also responsible to write the reasons for any 'weighing of interests' (it was decided that a lawyer was best placed to make decisions about the weighing of the interests of the child and formulating documentation that

93 Wet donorgegevens kunstmatige bevruchting, 2002.

94 Allan, Churchill Report, above n 80.

will be acceptable before a judge). The role also deals with other issues on medical law and beyond ART including euthanasia, late-term abortion and withdrawal of treatment of neonates.

The register is digital, so information can be entered directly on the Internet from any computer. Anyone who wants to enter information needs a 'token', which is a form of safety identification to enter the site. Although clinics can input information themselves, they can only see information that they have filled in. The register can see all of the information.

Information held on the register includes identifying information, which contains the donor's first name, last name, address and date of birth. This information is kept secret until the child reaches age 16. It also includes the following non-identifying information:

- medical history
- blood type
- genetic information
- physical
- height
- weight
- hair colour
- eye colour
- social information
- age at time of donation
- highest education
- occupation
- marital status
- with whom donor lives
- number of children
- gender of children
- age of children
- reason for donating
- details about donor (34 characteristics donor scores regarding personality/ interests etc.)

A variety of people may access the register including a doctor who can obtain medical information, parents who can ask for physical and social information until their child is 12 years old and a donor-conceived person who at age 12 can access physical and social information, and from age 16 can access identifying information.

Contact and consent approach for past donations

In the two years before the law became operational in the Netherlands, between 2002 and 2004, clinics were obliged to contact all donors that they had used in the past and ask them to sign a statement about whether they would agree to the release of identifying information. If the donor said no, he was required to sign a 'confidentiality statement', which the clinics must send to the register.

Whether or not clinics state there is a confidentiality agreement, all clinics are obliged to give all information they have about donors to the register. At the inception of the legislation, not all clinics agreed to this policy; however, legal advice was sought and the decision was that the law is clear: all information regardless of donation date *must* be given. If the clinic stated there was a confidentiality agreement, this simply means that the donor cannot be contacted when there is an inquiry for information to ask whether such information may be released. This policy ensures that donor records are kept, regardless of whether in the present day they may be released.[95]

The contact and consent approach for donations made prior to the introduction of the law was and continues to be seen by some as equivalent to an 'information veto',[96] which in itself is seen as unacceptable by some because it fails to balance the rights of donors and donor-conceived people by giving an absolute right of veto to the donor. It has been further suggested that leaving such capacity thwarted the underpinning values of the act to release information to, and support, donor-conceived people.[97] People searching for information who were conceived from these dates have turned to the DNA register provided by FIOM.

The practice for release of identifying information

At age 16, when a child asks for information, the register does a search for the donor's current address (establishing the address is relatively straightforward in the Netherlands). There are then two paths taken depending on the time of the donation.

First, if the donor donated *before* 2004 and there is no confidentiality agreement, the donor is contacted in writing stating there has been a request and asked for permission to release information. If the donor says no to the request, no further steps are taken and information is not released. If the donor says yes, the register moves to the information release process.

Second, if the donor donated *after* 2004, the register will write to the donor letting him or her know that the register has received an application from the child who was informed by the register that he or she is the donor. The register asks permission whether they can release information. If the donor says no, the law states that the interests of the donor and the donor-conceived person must be weighed. The law also states that the best interests of the child come first and that generally the weight of decision making will reside with the child unless the donor has some extreme reason to say no. Of course, this scenario will only be relevant after 2020 when eligible donor-conceived people have turned 16. It is unknown (including to the register) what might constitute an acceptable reason to prevent the release of information.[98] However, the register has made clear that age, marital status and not having disclosed to wife or family members about donating are not satisfactory reasons. The register imagines an example might be when they contact a donor who had just lost his or her own child and it was permissible to wait. Some people want the possibility that the register may refuse information if the donor is in prison or has psychiatric problems.

95 Allan, Churchill Report, above n 80.

96 An information veto refers to the ability to 'veto' information release.

97 Communications to author during Churchill Fellowship; Allan, Churchill Report, above n 80.

98 Allan, Churchill Report, above n 80.

Once information is able to be released, the support services of FIOM are engaged.

All processed inquiries are reported in the annual reports (available in Dutch at http://www.donorgegevens.nl/stichting/documentatie/). Each year, the reported number of inquiries is growing. That is, while people who have a child conceived prior to 2004 in the Netherlands are aware that there was no law and therefore are less likely to inquire, for people who had a child post-2004, the numbers of inquiries are climbing each year. Because parents are told that they can ask information, they are coming forward and asking. The register has also coupled with FIOM to help support people in disclosing and talking about donor conception.

Sibling matching – practice

Formally, the law is silent on sibling matches. However, it has been the practice of the register to recognize when donor children share donors in the Netherlands. The children will be asked if they would be interested in having contact with half-siblings. In the register's experience, the children have all said yes and are very interested. The register will therefore link them. The register has done that for both identified and non-identified donors (but could not if there was one donor-conceived child who has information and one donor-conceived child who does not know).[99]

Support services: DNA register and intermediary services

The law in the Netherlands states that people should be supported by counselling and intermediary services; however, the register does not have counselors themselves. When they have a match, the register contacts FIOM which provides social work support services and acts as an intermediary.

FIOM is a national social work agency whose primary role is to assist with decision making regarding abortion, adoption and donor conception. It provides counselling and support services for questions that have a deep impact on human life. It merged with the International Social Services, which is an international non-government organization that focuses on providing social work support and intermediary services for those seeking information (and reunions) about intercountry adoptions and family reunifications. Together, FIOM and ISS continue to provide these services as well as being responsible for the DNA register for donor-conceived people and providing intermediary services for all people in relation to information release about donors to donor-conceived people. The provision of support and intermediary services occurs throughout a process that includes DNA testing and donor linking.

99 Ibid.

DNA TESTING

The DNA laboratory used by FIOM collaborates with nineteen hospitals throughout the country, so there are nineteen different places that people can have their blood taken, with actual testing performed at the central hospital. People are obliged to show their identity card and a form with a special code. On the blood vial, only their code is recorded to protect privacy. Because the laboratory does not know whose blood it is, they can only say that they have a match between numbers. Under the current system, donors or donor-conceived people have to pay for the DNA test themselves; however, because of the numbers of people, the laboratory keeps the price down as low as possible. To help donors to come forward, the price for them is lowest: at around 100 Euros. Donor-conceived people pay 225 Euros. To find a match between a half brother or half sister if there are no donor details, the laboratory may use the mother – which costs 100 Euro. This is important because it increases the likelihood of establishing a link. Two brothers or two sisters are easiest to test. There are more than 600 people currently on the database.

People may voluntarily place themselves on the database and hope that there is a match with a donor or sibling who has done the same.

DONOR LINKING

Government funding in the Netherlands to date has recognized the need for counselling and intermediary services. FIOM has acted as the central agency, but may use other practitioners on an as needed basis (e.g. due to location). This way there is a national agency that keeps high-level expertise and then local-level support that sometimes needs to work with adopted or donor-conceived people and that can call into the national agency.

Where there has been a DNA test, the following steps are taken:

1. the codes go to FIOM which then informs the local social worker (who is chosen based on proximity to donor);
2. the social worker first talks with the donor (with the view that donors should be assisted in feeling as much at ease as possible);
3. the same social worker talks to the donor-conceived person/people (separately);
4. the social worker establishes how to exchange information and also whether a meeting is desired and/or possible between all parties;
5. if the social worker establishes that a meeting is possible, then a meeting is proposed to all parties in a local office or elsewhere;
6. once the first meeting occurs, the parties may proceed with having direct contact, but there is always the possibility that they may go back to the social worker.

When people have been referred by the government register, they may or may not undergo DNA testing; however, the process from steps 2 to 6 is the same.

It is noted that FIOM has extensive experience with adoption and the need for counselling and intermediary services at different stages of the process. Its follows a similar vein with people who are engaging in donor conception or who are donor conceived. It was FIOM's view that 'it is becoming more and more known that knowing one's origins (or rather not knowing them) does affect someone's life very much. This is particularly so if a person keeps asking where they come from and is not provided answers. The view in the Netherlands is that this is a fundamental question which later on can cause all kinds of problems in a person's life.'[100]

Aftercare and expectation management

FIOM stresses that 'just like with adoption' the aftercare a person receives is important. Expectation management is also critical since people may have different aspirations regarding the donation and there can be great disappointment when these are not met. For example, it is FIOM's experience in the Netherlands that often donor children already have a 'dad' but that the donor might also wish to become a parent. They report that sometimes the donor-conceived person just seeks one meeting with his or her donor and that is enough. FIOM reports that after initial meetings take place, generally contact with their donors goes down (often resulting in only one or two further meetings, then a letter or a phone call, then gradually less and less). However, it was reported to the author that with donor siblings they often keep in contact more frequently and extensively.[101]

Norway

The law

In Norway, artificial insemination remains restricted to use by a woman who is married or lives with her male partner. Egg donation is not permitted. In relation to the release of information about donors, Norway enshrined donor anonymity in its laws from 1994 to 2003.[102] Following much discussion and debate about needing to focus on children's rights to have information, the law changed and after 2003 has provided for 'the child's right to information about the sperm donor'.[103] It dictates that 'any person who is born as a result of medically assisted reproduction using donated sperm has a right to information on the sperm donor's identity at the age of 18'.[104]

100 Ibid.
101 Ibid.
102 Bioteknologiloven av 1994 (Act on Biotechnology 1994).
103 Ibid.
104 Bioteknologiloven av 2003 (Act on Biotechnology 2003) (Norway), § 2–7.

The law also requires the Ministry to 'establish a register for registration of the identity of sperm donors, so that children can exercise their rights pursuant to [the act]'.[105] However, in 2016, a register still did not exist.

The practice

A media report published in 2013 noted that approximately 26,000 children had been conceived with the help of assisted reproduction in Norway since treatment began in 1984, with an estimated 1,000 pregnancies having resulted from the use of sperm obtained via an anonymous donor. The article reported that 'Lars Ødegård, chairman of Norwegian Biotechnology Advisory Board, [said] that Norway should consider offering assistance to any children who want to find out more about their biological father, or indeed find any half-siblings'.[106] It also reported that 'a recent survey showed that only 25 per cent of parents who used artificial insemination with the help of a donor had told their child about how they were conceived'.[107]

Further information detailing the practices in Norway was not found.

The United Kingdom

The United Kingdom again demonstrates changes in social views and laws over time. It initially supported secrecy and anonymity as illustrated by statements made by the 1982 Committee of Inquiry into Human Fertilisation and Embryology (the Warnock Committee) in its report published in July 1984.[108] The Warnock Committee unanimously agreed that there was a 'need to maintain the absolute anonymity of the donor' to 'give legal protection to the donor' and to 'minimiz[e] the invasion of the third party into the family'.[109] The committee maintained donor anonymity despite its view that 'it is wrong to deceive children about their origins' and that '[while] couples who achieve pregnancy may come to look on their [artificial insemination by donor] child as a true child of the marriage . . . the sense that a secret exists may undermine the whole network of family relationships'.[110]

It recommended limiting the amount of information available to recipients to basic facts about the donor, such as ethnic group and genetic health, to avoid 'the possibility of prospective parents seeking donors with specific characteristics [in

105 Ibid., § 2–8.

106 Ann Tomkvist, Norway Ponders Sperm-Donor Register, *The Local Norway News in English*, 17 July 2013, available at http://www.thelocal.no/20130717/norway-ponders-sperm-donor-registry, accessed 16 March 2016.

107 Ibid.

108 Ibid.

109 Ibid., 25.

110 Ibid., 21.

the] hope to give birth to a particular type of child'.[111] It also recommended that on reaching the age of 18 'the child should have access to the basic information about the donor's ethnic origin and genetic health and that legislation be enacted to provide the right of access to this'.[112] It further recognized that couples might conceal that a child had been conceived using donor sperm to 'hide the fact that the husband was infertile and to avoid unfavourable reactions amongst relatives and friends' and may also lie when registering the birth by stating the husband was the father (thus committing an offence). Therefore, it recommended changes to the law to permit the husband to be registered as the father, stating that such a legal fiction would be 'consistent with the husband's assuming all parental rights and duties with regard to the child'.[113]

Despite their actions, the Warnock Committee stated that 'people should be encouraged to be open about this form of treatment' to make easier the legal changes they had recommended, and to increase the provision of treatment, which might lead to donor insemination being viewed as a 'more acceptable . . . means of relieving male infertility'.[114] In addition, they said that consideration should be given as a matter of urgency to making it possible for the parents in registering the birth to add 'by donation' after the man's name.[115] This latter suggestion was never enshrined in the law, thus not only was anonymity established, but secrecy also prevailed.

The law

Laws were enacted in 1990 in the United Kingdom to regulate assisted reproduction,[116] and records began to be kept for offspring born starting on 1 August 1991. However, while a right to the small amount of non-identifying information would be made available (for those who reached the age of 16 to rule out a possible genetic tie to a potential marriage partner, and for those who reached 18 and sought confirmation of their donor-conceived status), a shift to recognizing the right of donor-conceived people to have identifying information about their donors would not occur until some fifteen years later (and then, only prospectively) in 2005.

Access to information in the United Kingdom by donor-conceived people now depends on when they were conceived, whether before or after 1991 (which marked the enactment of the Human Fertilisation and Embryology Act 1990 [UK]) and the establishment of a central register of information or whether before

111 Ibid., 24.
112 Ibid., 25.
113 Ibid.
114 Ibid., 28.
115 Ibid., 26.
116 *Human Fertilization and Embryology Act 1990* (UK).

or after 2005 (after which anonymous donation was prohibited).[117] Depending on these dates, donor-conceived people seeking information about their donor (or siblings) may be able to obtain information about donor(s) and/or sibling(s) via the Human Fertilisation and Embryology Authority (HFEA) register; the UK Donor Conceived Register (which is a voluntary register, which also uses DNA testing); or clinics. Each option is discussed in turn next.[118]

The HFEA register – for post-1991 conceptions

The Human Fertilisation and Embryology Authority has kept records of all births that have resulted following assisted reproductive treatments in all licensed UK fertility clinics since its inception on 1 August 1991. The type of information that is available to people from this register depends on when they were born and to whom the information pertains.

INFORMATION AVAILABLE ABOUT DONORS

For people conceived between 1 August 1991 and 1 April 2005 The HFEA collected both identifying information and non-identifying information about the donor. Non-identifying information included the physical description (height, weight, eye and hair colour); the year and country of birth; ethnicity; whether the donor had any children at the time of donation; and any additional information the donor chose to supply such as occupation, religion, interests and a brief self-description (noting, however, that not every donor provided all of this information). People conceived using a donor between 1991 and 2005 can access non-identifying information when they turn 16. The HFEA advises 'relevant counselling' prior to making an inquiry so that information seekers are able to cope with finding less information than they desire.

Some people conceived between these dates may also be able to access 'identifying information' (i.e. a name and address) of the donor at age 18. This is incumbent on the donor to 're-register' with the HFEA as identifiable. To date, approximately 153 donors have done so, noting that there does not appear to have been a large public campaign (or any campaign at all) to make it known that donors could do so and a decision was taken not to directly contact donors to ask them to re-register.

117 The *Human Fertilisation and Embryology Act 1990* (UK) was subsequently repealed and re-enacted as the *Human Fertilisation and Embryology Act 2008* (UK).

118 Note – beyond that discussed in the text, in the United Kingdom, there may also be the possibility that identifying information about a donor may be released in special circumstances if a Court orders it to be released 'in the interests of justice' pursuant to s 34 of the 1990 Act, or for example, if a clinic is the subject of civil proceedings concerning the congenital abnormality of a child conceived using donor-gametes.

For people conceived post–1 April 2005 The information collected by the HFEA regarding donors post–1 April 2005 is more extensive. When donor-conceived people who were conceived after 1 April 2005 reach the age of 16, they will be able to access the following information about their donor: physical description (height, weight, eye and hair colour) if provided by the donor; year and country of birth; ethnicity; whether the donor has any children, how many and their gender; marital status; and medical history. A 'pen-portrait' and/or a 'goodwill message' may also have been left voluntarily and will be accessible. When the donor-conceived people reach the age of 18, they will also be able to obtain identifying information (the donor's name, date of birth and last-known address).

There was a window between 1 April 2005 and 1 April 2006 where anonymous donor gametes that were stored could still be used. In addition, people may store anonymous donor gametes for up to ten years to conceive a genetically related sibling for a child already born. People conceived using these anonymous gametes, even if post-2005, do not have similar access to identifying information.

INFORMATION AVAILABLE ABOUT GENETICALLY RELATED SIBLINGS

Donor-conceived people are also entitled to anonymous information about any donor-conceived genetically related siblings which they may have from age 16. This excludes information about the donor's own legal/natural children. This information consists of year of birth, details on the number of donor-conceived siblings and the sex of the siblings.

In the United Kingdom, the HFEA has also established a donor sibling register. From 2010, when donor-conceived people reach the age of 18, they have been able to place their contact details on a voluntary sibling contact register called Donor Sibling Link, administered by the HFEA. The HFEA states that it will facilitate the exchange of contact details between siblings who consent to be on this register. Consequently, it will be possible for donor-conceived adults to trace their siblings, based on mutual consent, through the voluntary sibling contact register. It is not possible for parents to trace their child's siblings through the voluntary contact sibling register.

Note that two people who intend to get married or have intimate relations may contact the HFEA register and inquire whether they are genetically related.[119]

INFORMATION AVAILABLE TO RECIPIENT PARENTS

In the United Kingdom, parents are granted a discretionary right of access to information by the authority. The HFEA states that they will be given everything held about the child's donor except for that which could identify them. Only information which could not on its own or in conjunction with any other

119 *Human Fertilisationand Embryology Act 2008*, s 31ZB.

information be used to trace or identify the donor will be given. Therefore, different donors will have provided different amounts and types of information. As such, parents may get some or all of the following: a physical description of the donor (height, weight, eye and hair colour); year and country of the donor's birth; donor's ethnicity; whether the donor had any children at the time of donation, how many and their gender; the donor's marital status; the donor's medical history; and/or a goodwill message from the donor to any potential children. However, over time, there have been reports of some lack of clarity about what information combined might be identifying and that parents desired greater openness regarding the information available.

How is information collected?

Information about donors is collected at the time of donation in the United Kingdom. Under the act, there is a duty to contact the donor when an inquiry is made by a donor-conceived person about the donor's identifying information. However, such contact can only be made when there is a recent address on record. Donors are advised to update their address in eighteen years and that it is not necessary to update each time they move.

When a recipient uses donor eggs, sperm or embryos to conceive, it is incumbent on them to report back to clinics regarding outcomes of any pregnancy that results. This reporting is voluntary. It is, however, in the clinic's interest to follow up with parents so that the clinic may report their success rate, and in this way, clinics actively seek information about live births that result from donor conception.

Support services

Although the people working on the Central Register in the United Kingdom have some training regarding difficult or personal conversations, for some time, it was not seen to be a part of the HFEA's remit to provide counselling to donor-conceived people, donors or the recipient parents. Although there was reference to 'implications counselling' in the guidelines, such counselling was often provided by the clinics. The view was expressed by the HFEA during interviews conducted by the author in 2012 that 'one cannot force someone to engage in counselling where there is not a personal need.'[120] As such, the past practice of the HFEA has been to provide people with advice that counselling might be required and desirable and to make available information about where such counselling might be found.

However, in June 2015, the HFEA launched a new professional support service for people affected by donation. The service is provided by the nationwide post-adoption agency PAC-UK on the HFEA's behalf, and offers advice and

120 Allan, Churchill Report, above n 85.

support by phone, online and face-to-face meetings. It is available to everyone affected by donations that took place in licensed clinics after August 1991.

Under the new scheme, two free sessions of information, support and/or intermediary services are offered to:

- donor-conceived people over age 16 considering applying for non-identifying information and, after 18 years of age, identifying information about their donor or donor-conceived siblings
- pre-2005 donors who are considering re-registering as identifiable, and those who are aware that a donor-conceived person has applied for their identifying information

Family and friends of donors and donor-conceived people who have also been affected by the donation experience will be able to access the service for a fee.[121]

Voluntary DNA register – for pre-1991 conceptions

There were approximately 8,700 babies born following fertility treatment between 1978 and 1991 (noting that the first baby born after her mother underwent IVF treatment at a clinic in the United Kingdom was in 1978). For people conceived prior to 1991, there was no central repository of donor information. As such, UK DonorLink, the world's first DNA-based voluntary register service for donor-conceived adults, was opened in 2004. UK DonorLink was established as a government pilot program to test the need for such services and explore how best to provide services to donor-conceived people seeking information. It specifically serviced donor-conceived people who did not have a legal right to access information (i.e. those conceived prior to 1991) and was run by post-adoption services based in Leeds (After Adoption Yorkshire).

The UK DonorLink program was declared a success by the Public Health Minister in 2010; however, its future (particularly with regard to funding) was uncertain. On 1 April 2013, the operations of UK DonorLink were taken over by what is now known as the UK Donor Conceived Register. The UK Donor Conceived Register is not described as a separate or new service to that offered by UK DonorLink. Rather, it is a more permanent voluntary register, which has had a name change, but continues the work of UK DonorLink – and, in fact, states that it was established in 2004 as DonorLink was.[122] The UK Donor Conceived Register notes that 'because of storage and distribution practices it is possible that donor conceived born until December 1992 could find donor-conceived

121 Human Fertilisation and Embryology Authority, *Support and Intermediary Service*, available at http://www.hfea.gov.uk/9757.html, accessed 16 March 2016.

122 UK Donor Conceived Register, available at http://www.donorconceivedregister.org.uk/, accessed 16 March 2016.

half-siblings or their donor on the register'.[123] DNA analysis is now conducted by DNA Analysis, King's College London, and is further discussed here.

Support services for the voluntary register

The UK Donor Conceived Register continues the approach established by UK DonorLink in that support services are provided on an individual, as-needed basis. It describes the provision of support as follows:

> Registrants will receive adequate support during the whole process which can include full discussion with DNA specialists on the implications of taking a DNA test and free specialist (intermediary) support. Support requirements will be discussed and agreed on a case-by-case basis. There is free mandatory specialist support for all parties involved in the case of a possible or confirmed match.[124]

If there is a match, both sides are informed by a specialist intermediary support worker. The respective parties will be independently invited to state how they would like any contact to proceed. This contact may include exchange of information/communication through a specialist intermediary support worker, exchange of non-identifying biographical information, exchange of email addresses, exchange of identifying information (e.g. name, address, telephone number, email address) or face-to-face meeting(s).

The UK Donor Conceived Register then provides a specialist intermediary support worker to engage with both sides to help manage the contact, based on the preferences expressed by both parties. The UK Donor Conceived Register states that:

> The key principle followed will be that neither party will be expected to go beyond the level of contact they are comfortable with. Typically, there will be sequential progression through the contact process, over a period of many months, with either party free at any time to withdraw from the process or further contact.[125]

What is the process for registrants to have DNA testing?

As there is insufficient or little information available from clinics or other records pertaining to most donor conception arrangements prior to 1991, DNA testing

123 Ibid.
124 Ibid.
125 Ibid.

is seen as a vital part of the services offered in the United Kingdom for those conceived prior to this date.

DNA testing for UK registrants is carried out at DNA Analysis, King's College London. Among other administrative, data control, privacy and practice procedures, the agreement between the UK Donor Conceived Register and King's College provides that the UK Donor Conceived Register will supply DNA analysis at King's with the full names, dates of birth and contact information of all clients from whom a sample is sent. The DNA tests used are known as short tandem repeat (STR) tests in which about thirty-six markers are used (ESS and HDPlex). Testing involves statistical analysis that takes account of linkage between markers and the results provided are given as a likelihood ratio. A statement is provided to those being tested as to the strength of the evidence. One original copy of the genetic results is provided to each client, but not to the UK Donor Conceived Register. A report is also provided to each client with a copy to the UK Donor Conceived Register. The report indicates whether any significant relationships have been revealed (LR >10) after testing and comments on any equivocal relationships and what attempts are being undertaken to resolve these. Linked individuals are only identified by a unique number, although information about the identity of the linked donor is provided to the UK Donor Conceived Register. Reporting time is approximately five to six weeks. DNA analysis at King's will provide written or verbal explanations to the client, or the UK Donor Conceived Register, of any results as requested at no additional cost.

It is important to note here that DNA testing is used to identify *potential* genetic links between donors, donor-conceived offspring and their genetically related siblings, but DNA testing can never be 100 per cent conclusive. The former operators of UK DonorLink noted that identifying genetic relationships between donors and their donor-conceived offspring is more straightforward; and half-siblings are more complicated (and less certain).[126] Development of new tests may provide for better accuracy.

It appears that all voluntary registrants were retested when UK DonorLink was transitioned to the UK Donor Conceived Register, as there is reference to 'initial bulk' testing in the agreement between UK Donor Conceived Register and DNA Analysis, King's College London.

Finland

The law

The regulatory system in Finland comprises a regulatory authority – the National Supervisory Authority for Welfare and Health (VALVIRA) – that maintains the donation register Louteri for donated gametes and embryos. A child born

126 Allan, Churchill Report, above n 80.

because of gamete or embryo donation may consult the register at age 18 to learn the donor's identity.

The Act on Assisted Fertility Treatments (1237/2006) in Finland came into force on 1 September 2007. Drafting had commenced in 1980; however, issues relating to a complete prohibition on surrogacy, the right of donor-conceived people to access information about the identity of their donor and allowing access to donor services by single women or lesbian couples delayed legislation.

Following extensive debate regarding such issues and the passing of legislation, reasons for giving access to information included a variety of factors. First, it was considered that since information on a person's origin would be held somewhere in a government office or fertility office, the person to whom that information related had a right to such information (i.e. an interpretation of the donor-conceived person's right to privacy, it would be a breach of that privacy to allow third-party access to information that directly pertains to the donor-conceived person while continuing to deny the donor-conceived person access).

Second, the view was that the legal rights of people born because of donations should come first, above donors and recipient parents. This view stemmed from cases where couples had infertility treatment and then separated. The social father could claim the child was not his and paternity laws in Finland would support his claim, leaving the child vulnerable. Subsequent changes to the law recognized the social father as a legal parent, but called for the law to provide that the child should have access to information about the donor.

Third, the Finnish Constitutional Law Committee of Parliament argued that the right to personal identity came within the scope of the right to privacy guaranteed under the Finnish Constitution. This includes the right to obtain information about one's origins.

Fourth, the doctrine regarding the interests of the child is seen to overpower every other interest and consideration. To be consistent with this doctrine – and with Finland being a state party to international agreements, including the UN Convention on the Rights of the Child – it was necessary to allow for information access.

What information is recorded?

In Finland, section 17 of the act provides that prior to a donor donating gametes, a consent document must be completed. This document shall contain the following information:

- donor's identification code
- confirmation of performance of physical examination
- confirmation of receipt of counselling
- conditions imposed on use of gametes (if any)
- consent to the gametes being used in assisted reproduction treatment

- consent to confirmation of paternity (noting that in Finland the donor may consent to be recognized as the legal father – a provision usually used in known donor situations where parties wish to co-parent the child)
- period of consent
- date and signature of donor providing service with consent

Section 18 requires that the service provider collecting the donation shall 'without delay' notify the donation register of the donor code, identification data and whether the donation consisted of sperm, eggs or embryos, as well as whether consent to paternity has been given. No data other than this is recorded on the Louteri register. For example, there is no information about nationality, ethnic origin or place of residence of the donor. Nor does the register contain information on the children born because of the donation.

If the clinic does not provide the register with this information, it is committing an 'offence of violation of child identity' which may be subject to a fine or one year's imprisonment.

What information is (will be) released?

DONOR-CONCEIVED PEOPLE

Section 23 of the act provides that a person who may have been born from a donated gamete or embryo shall, upon attaining the age of 18, be entitled to obtain from the service provider a copy of the consent to treatment and the donor code. The donor-conceived person may then provide the donation register with the code to learn the identity of the donor.

As no donor-conceived people have yet reached the age of 18 in Finland, there have not been any applications for information. (Although technically there is nothing preventing donors who donated prior to the act, placing information on the register and a child now 18 accessing such information.)

It is expected that when a donor-conceived person makes an application to the register, he or she will be given the donor's name and social security code. This will assist the donor-conceived person in tracing the donor if he or she wants to.

RECIPIENT PARENTS

In Finland, recipient parents do not receive information about donor characteristics. It is an offence to release information collected concerning the physical examination. The act further prohibits influencing the characteristics of the child to be born via gamete or embryo selection and this is interpreted as a prohibition on providing information about external features or other characteristics of the donor to the clients seeking treatment.

Recipient parents are not given identifying information about the donor *unless* the donor has consented to be recognized as the legal 'father' of the child.

THE DONOR

A donor may be informed of whether any children have been born because of using his or her gametes. Some donors have expressed concern that they will die before the time that the child reaches 18 years and have offered to prepare a personal profile that the child may access. However, the act does not permit access to information in this manner.

Has the change in law resulted in fewer donations?

The great worry with the changes of the law was that people would not donate; however, while the numbers initially dropped, they later picked up. In Finland, the number of donor-conceived treatments increased by 20 per cent within two years over the number of treatments performed before the law was passed.

Implementation of the register

Of the twenty-five clinics in Finland, not all use donated gametes. Those that do used to mail the information on a form to the register and it was entered into the computer. In 2011, VALVIRA started using an electronic system, so immediately after donation a clinic is required to send information about the donor to the register. It seemed, at first, that this system took some time to get used to as the information to some degree lagged behind. However, over time, this information entry has improved.

The other problem faced in Finland related to using sperm from Denmark included a problem with recording the Danish men's names on their register – some have first and last names that are the same and clinics do not know how to enter this information. In addition, giving information out in the future may be a problem because the report is based on a social security number, making it difficult to track how many times a donor donates if a social security number is the only number used. The register has, however, subsequently added a donor identification number to help resolve these issues.

Support services

At present, because no donor-conceived people are of the age necessary to request information, support services do not exist in relation to accessing the information. In research conducted by the author in 2012 in Finland, a representative of VALVIRA said that generally the method would be that people are given information on a form and would most likely deal with that information on their own.[127] The general view of VALVIRA has been that the provision of

127 Ibid.

psychological support is best arranged by the fertility clinic referring the person to necessary support systems and counselling providers when the person arrives at the clinic to collect the donor code. The register and clinics have nevertheless tried to encourage the Ministry of Health and Social Affairs to move toward establishing support services.

That said, at the time the law was passed, it responded to three major issues that had been debated for twenty-five years: access to information by donor-conceived people; access to ART for lesbians and single women; and a ban on surrogacy to prevent both financial and emotional exploitation of women. These steps were so important that perhaps it will take some time to correct the infrastructure.

The challenge for the donation register Louteri resides in the sensitivity of its data, the requirement for absolute reliability and the long duration envisioned for the maintenance of the register. The first access to the register is not envisaged to be for more than a decade, at which point it is anticipated that procedures will be in place for governing the process for release of information – including whether support services will be offered.

Notification of donor-conceived access?

In Finland, debate continues as to whether there should be notification to donor-conceived people about their donor-conceived status.

New Zealand

The law

In New Zealand, donor information record keeping by clinics commenced in 1983 in Wellington, in 1985 at the Fertility Center in Christchurch, and generally during the 1990s at other clinics.[128] This record keeping coincided with clinics generally not accepting donations unless a donor agreed to information later being released.

However, there is currently no legal right to information collected prior to the laws enacted in 2005.[129] People born before 2005 may therefore contact the clinic they were conceived in, but there is no guarantee they will be given access to information. People conceived prior to the 1990s are generally entirely reliant on DNA testing or serendipity.

128 *Law Commission* (New Zealand), *Report 88: New Issues in Legal Parentage* (NZLCR88) (2005), p 124.

129 See *Human Assisted Reproductive Technology (HART) Act 2004* (NZ), Part 3.

On 22 August 2005, laws came into operation that gave the right to donor offspring to access identifying information at age 18 about their donor.[130] They can also access information about donor-siblings if the sibling consents.[131]

DONOR-CONCEIVED PEOPLE

Donor-conceived people under the age of 18 are currently entitled to non-identifying information pursuant to the Human Assisted Reproductive Technology Act 2004 (NZ) (HART Act).

In addition, a donor offspring who is 16 or 17 years of age can apply to the Family Court to be treated as though he or she is 18 years of age for the purposes of providing information for inclusion on the register, or for applying to access identifying information about a donor or related donor offspring. A Family Court Judge will only give approval if he or she is satisfied that it is in the best interests of the donor offspring to have access to the information or to provide information for inclusion on the register.

RECIPIENT PARENTS (GUARDIANS)

Guardians (for example rearing parents) of donor-conceived people can apply for information about a donor when the child is under the age of 18.[132]

DONORS

Donors can access information if a donor-conceived person over the age of 18 consents to the release of his or her information.[133]

Information recorded

Information that must be kept by providers of assisted reproduction concerning a donated embryo or a donated cell includes the following:

- donor's name
- donor's gender
- donor's address
- date, place and country of the donor's birth
- donor's height
- colour of the donor's eyes and hair
- donor's ethnicity and any relevant cultural affiliation
- in the case of a Māori donor, the donor's whanau, hapu and iwi, to the extent that the donor is aware of those affiliations

130 Ibid.
131 Ibid., s 58.
132 Ibid., s 50(2).
133 Ibid., s 59.

- any aspects considered significant by the provider, of the medical history of:
  - donor
  - donor's parents and grandparents
  - donor's children (if any)
  - donor's siblings (if any)
- donor's reasons for donating[134]

The HART register

The Human Assisted Reproductive Technology (HART) Act 2004 establishes the HART register, which has been operational since 22 August 2005. The HART register is maintained by the office of Births, Deaths and Marriages within the Department of Internal Affairs.

Only donations made on or after 22 August 2005 that result in a birth are automatically included on the register. Information to be held on the register includes the donor's name, address and date and place of birth; the offspring's name, gender and date and place of birth; and the guardian's name and address. After fifty years (or if the clinic goes out of business), fertility clinics will give Births, Deaths and Marriages more detailed information about the donor and offspring including family history and cultural affiliations.

In New Zealand, access to information held on the register is restricted. Only the people named on the register, or the guardians of offspring under the age of 18, can access the information.

Voluntary register

People who donated sperm, eggs or embryos prior to 22 August 2005 and people who were born because of those donations (and their guardians), can choose to provide information about themselves for inclusion on the HART register. Donor linking occurs when there is a match of information on the register for people who voluntarily register.

Support services

Counselling in New Zealand is not compulsory but is recommended for people considering accessing information about their donor, offspring or siblings who share the same donor. A counsellor may also be able to advise on the usefulness of DNA testing to confirm a genetic link. The HART register advises that people seeking information may choose to approach the fertility clinic where the

134 Ibid., s 47(1).

treatment took place, or speak to an independent counsellor. The person seeking the counselling is responsible for any cost incurred.

Washington State, United States of America

The law

The state of Washington, since July 2011, has recognized the rights of donor-conceived people to having access to information about their donors.[135] Gamete donors must provide identifying information about themselves and their medical history when donating gametes. Donor-conceived children may contact the clinic that provided the gametes when they reach 18 years of age to request identifying information about their donor and their donor's medical history.

The law, however, does not provide for complete access to information, because it permits the donor to veto disclosure and prevent the clinic from revealing his or her identifying information. If this occurs, the donor offspring will still be entitled to the anonymized medical history. The legislative system in Washington State therefore appears to be much more like the systems described next where people are able to choose between open identity and anonymous gametes. Nevertheless, while the law in reality means that identifying information may not be available to all, Washington is the first U.S. state to legislate on the matter. It also shifts the starting point of donation to being identity release, rather than anonymous.

Croatia

The law

Croatia updated its laws in 2012 concerning assisted reproduction. In its law on medically assisted reproduction, promulgated on 13 July 2012, it regulates the conditions for exercising the right to medically assisted conception and the rights, obligations and responsibilities of all participants in the procedures of medically assisted conception.[136] This includes the recording of information about donors of gametes and embryos and its release to donor-conceived people. That is, a person conceived and born with the help of medically assisted conception using donated sperm, ova or embryos has the right to have access to 'all information about their biological origins, including identifying information about the donor(s)'.[137]

135 Wash Rev Code Ann §26.26.750.

136 Zakon O Medicinski Pomognutoj Oplodnji (Law on Medically Assisted Reproduction, 12 July 2012) (Croatia), No: 71–05–03 / 1–12–2, Article 1.

137 Ibid., Article 15(1).

A central register

Information about donors of gametes and embryos in Croatia is held on the National Register of Medically Assisted Reproduction of the ministry responsible for health.[138]

Notification of donor-conceived status

Parents are obliged under law in Croatia to inform the person conceived and born with the help of medically assisted conception using donated sperm, ova or embryos, the nature of their conception no later than the age of 18.[139] How such a law is (or will) be enforced is unclear.

Other access

In Croatia, the legal guardian of a donor-conceived person or a medical doctor with consent, may access information about a donor's gametes should such access be medically justified or for the well-being of the donor-conceived person.[140] Such access needs approval by a court or government body.[141] Information released for this purpose must be kept secret in accordance with special regulations.[142]

Uruguay

The law

Laws enacted in November 2013 in Uruguay provide that it is in the best interests of the child born through assisted human reproduction to know the method of their conception and that they are 'entitled' to such information.[143]

The law also provides that donation of gametes is anonymous and altruistic;[144] however, the law also asserts that the donor's identity may be revealed on application to the court by the child or his or her descendants if approved by a competent judge.[145]

138 Ibid.
139 Ibid., Article 15(2).
140 Ibid., Article 15(3).
141 Ibid., Article 15(4).
142 Ibid., Article 15(5).
143 Law Regulating Human Assisted Reproductive Techniques (22/11/2013 No 19.167), Article 10. Available at http://archivo.presidencia.gub.uy/sci/leyes/2013/11/msp_512.pdf or http://www.ninrial.com.uy/de-interes/legislacion/leyes/ley-no-19167/, accessed 16 March 2016.
144 Ibid., Article 12.
145 Ibid., Article 21.

Such approval is to be granted in accordance with Articles 22, 23 and 24 of the law which provide respectively that:

1 information regarding donors of gametes must be protected by those professionals performing tasks related to donor conception, and that when information is released to a child or his descendants, that they too must maintain confidentiality;
2 the action requesting information release may be brought by the donor-conceived child or their legal representatives and, if he has died, by their lineal descendants to the second degree, by themselves or through their representatives; and
3 that unless the request is manifestly inadmissible, the Court should order release and information must be provided by the institution where the assisted reproduction was performed. To ensure confidentiality, the identity of the donor shall be notified personally to the applicant.

The law further stipulates that the information provided does not imply any advertising of the identity of the donor nor produce any legal effect in relation to filiation.[146]

Notification of donor-conceived status

Although the law states that the child is entitled to know his or her method of conception, it is unclear whether the law will further provide a mechanism (such as registration on birth certificate or otherwise) to ensure this.

Argentina

The law

Argentina introduced new laws under its Código civil y comercial de la nación (Civil and Commercial Code of the Nation) that were approved by Law 26, 994 on 1 October 2014. Such laws provide for the 'right to information of those born by assisted reproduction'.[147]

Notification of donor-conceived status

Information regarding the person born by the use of assisted human reproduction with gametes of a third party must be included in the corresponding base file for birth registration. Thus, it appears that donor-conceived people will be made

146 Ibid.
147 Código civil y comercial de la nación, Article 563.

aware of their status when they obtain this document, if their parent(s) have not told them previously.[148]

Access to information

Article 564 of the law provides that at the request of people born through assisted human reproduction,

a health information regarding the medical records of the donor may be obtained from the center that holds the medical records of the donor; and
b the identity of the donor may be revealed based upon duly founded reasons as evaluated by a local judicial authority.

The Argentinian system, therefore, does not provide for a central register or direct application to a clinic, but rather requires judicial evaluation of the application prior to information release.

Ireland

In the twenty-first century, Ireland has seen a number of significant reports and changes that have collectively led to legislative reform enabling access to information by donor-conceived people, recipient parents, donors and donor-siblings in varying circumstances.

First, in 2000, the Minister for Health and Children established a Commission on Assisted Human Reproduction to prepare a report on the possible approaches to the regulation of all aspects of assisted human reproduction and the social, ethical and legal factors to be taken into account in determining public policy in the area. There was no regulation on the specific issue at the time.

The commission delivered its report in 2005[149] following extensive consultation and public debate, as well as consideration of laws in other jurisdictions. The report included many recommendations concerning the regulation of assisted reproductive treatment, including recommendations that children born through donated gametes should be entitled to know the identity of their genetic parents[150] (and that children born as a result of surrogacy should be entitled to know the identity of the surrogate mother and of any donors of gametes).[151] The commission's view, as expressed in the report, was that 'the welfare of children born as a result of AHR in terms of their personal identity and their experience of family relationships should not be compromised by the circumstances of their

148 Ibid.
149 Commission on Assisted Human Reproduction, *Report of the Commission on Assisted Human Reproduction* (April 2005), available at http://hdl.handle.net/10147/46684, accessed 16 March 2016.
150 Ibid., pp xiii, 50, Appendix VIII.
151 Ibid., p xvii, 55.

conception'.[152] In addition, in considering arguments for and against information release presented to them, the commission said:

> The main argument in favour of withholding information centres on the fear that there would be no supply of sperm donors were identification to be adopted. However, countries where donor identification is permitted have found that reduced supply does not continue beyond a relatively brief period. The arguments in favour of disclosing information include the value of openness and honesty and the avoidance of identity confusion. In addition, the need of children to discover their genetic heritage is met. Having access to genetic origins is potentially of profound importance for people's understanding of their identity in a psychological, genetic and historical context. The Commission considered and discussed the arguments for and against anonymity and concluded that the safeguarding of the best interests of the child born through AHR necessitates access for all children to information that would enable them to identify their genetic origins.[153]

The recommendation thus followed that 'any child born through use of donated gametes or embryos should, on maturity, be able to identify the donor(s) involved in his/her conception'.[154]

Second, in 2010, a report by the Law Reform Commission[155] considered how the law in Ireland dealt with the relationship between children and their parents and how the law dealt with the relationship between children and other adults who have – or have taken on – parental responsibility for children. In that report, the Law Reform Commission recognized the right of children to have accurate information available to them on their birth certificates. It referred to Article 7.1 of the 1989 United Nations Convention on the Rights of the Child which requires that the child shall be registered immediately after birth and shall have the right from birth to a name, the right to acquire a nationality and, as far as possible, the right to know and be cared for by his or her parents. The Law Reform Commission noted that:

> the recognition of this right is important in ensuring that the child develops a sense of identity, which is in the best interests of the child. From a wider perspective the Commission considers that accurate registration of birth information is important for society.[156]

152 Ibid., p 31.
153 Ibid., p 50.
154 Ibid.
155 Law Reform Commission Reports, *Legal Aspects of Family Relationships* (December, 2010) (LRC 101–2010). (The report followed an earlier consultation paper: Law Reform Commission, *Consultation Paper on Legal Aspects of Family Relationships* (LRC CP 55–2009).
156 Ibid., p 17.

Third, The Civil Partnership and Certain Rights and Obligations of Cohabitants Act, which was enacted in 2010, provided for same-sex civil partnerships and shared rights within non-marital relationships, but did not address the issue of children within those relationships. Further impetus to addressing the issue therefore arose.

Fourth, the Thirty-first Amendment of the Constitution was approved at referendum in 2012 (but not signed into law until 28 April 2015), and as such, article 42a of the Constitution now provides that the State 'recognizes and affirms the natural and imprescriptible rights of all children and shall, as far as practicable, by its laws protect and vindicate those rights'.[157]

In 2014, proposed legislation to regulate assisted human reproduction was circulated, including provisions concerning the welfare and best interests of children born as a result of donor conception and information release. The details of the legislation, as passed in 2015 and relevant to donor conception and the release of information, are discussed next noting first that when the bill was discussed in Parliament by Deputy Frances Fitzgerald, she said:

> The Bill is incredibly child centred. Under it, we must have clear rules on consent in [donor assisted human reproduction] and information, that is, children knowing their biological origins. We are creating a situation where clear information must be available. The position is unregulated and a child has no right to information on his or her biological inheritance. We are changing this and moving in a child-centred way from anonymous to identifiable donation. This is in the interests of the child having access to that information. The golden thread running through the legislation is child centred. It is not about parental rights but a child's parentage.[158]

The law

The current Irish law provides that only a medical practitioner or nurse may perform a donor assisted human reproductive treatment.[159] Clinics, or places in which donation takes place,[160] must acquire at the time of donation of gametes[161]

157 Bunreacht Na heireann Consitution of Irenland D'achtaigh an Pobal an 1 Iúil, 1937 Enacted by the People 1st July, 1937 I ngníomh ón 29 Nollaig, 1937. In operation as from 29 December, 1937.

158 House of the Oireachtas, Seanad Éireann Debate Vol. 239 No. 2, 30 March 2015.

159 Children and Family Relationships Act 2015 Act No. 9 of 2015, s 25(1).

160 Referred to in the act as a 'donation facility', which is defined as 'a place where a person donates his or her gametes and a place in which donor human reproductive treatment occurs'. Ibid., s 4.

161 Children and Family Relationships Act 2015 Act No. 9 of 2015, s 24(1).

or embryos,[162] the donor's consent to the donation of gametes or embryos[163] and the following information about the donor:

- name
- date and place of birth
- nationality
- date on which, and the place at which, he or she provided the gamete
- contact details[164]

Information about the recipient(s) of donor treatment must also be collected, including name, date and place of birth and contact details.[165]

The operator of a donor assisted human reproduction facility must report that the donor procedure has been performed (no later than six months after its performance), and the information recorded about both the donor and the intending parent(s). They must also report (if known) whether the procedure has led to the pregnancy of the intending mother, and if so, the date on which the intending mother is expected to give birth. When the pregnancy has come to an end, the provider must also report whether the pregnancy resulted in the birth of a live child, and if so, the name, date and place of birth, sex and address of the child.[166]

The information provisions apply to all donor conception, including where donor gametes are obtained from other states outside of Ireland.[167]

National donor-conceived person register

The law in Ireland also provides that a register, known as the National Donor Conceived Person Register, be established and maintained.[168] All information collected about the child, recipient parent(s) and donor are to be entered into the register, in addition to the date on which the donor procedure took place and the name and address of the facility in which the donor procedure was performed.[169]

Access to certain information from register

NON-IDENTIFYING INFORMATION

Donor-conceived person and/or recipient parent A donor-conceived child who has attained the age of 18 years, or the parent of a donor-conceived child who has

162 Ibid., s 24(2) (in the case of embryos each donor's consent and information about them must be obtained).
163 Ibid., s 23.
164 Ibid., s 24(3).
165 Ibid., s 25(3).
166 Ibid., s 25.
167 Ibid., s 26.
168 Ibid., s 33.
169 Ibid.

not yet attained the age of 18 years, may request that the Minister provide him or her with the following information from the register:

- information other than the relevant donor's name, date of birth and contact details, that is recorded on the register in respect of the relevant donor
- the number of persons who have been born as a result of the use in a donor-assisted human reproduction (DAHR) procedure of a gamete donated by the relevant donor and the sex and year of birth of each of them[170]

Donor A donor may request the Minister provide him or her with information from the register on the number of persons who have been born as a result of the use in a donor procedure of a gamete donated by the donor and the sex and year of birth of each of them.[171]

IDENTIFYING INFORMATION

Donor-conceived person A donor-conceived person who has attained the age of 18 years may request from the Minister the name, date of birth and contacts details of his or her donor, as recorded in the register.[172] However, information release is not guaranteed.

Section 35 of the Irish legislation provides that when the Minister receives such a request, the donor is to be sent a notice informing him or her of the request, and twelve weeks after sending the notice, the information is to be released to the donor-conceived person unless the relevant donor makes representations as to why the safety of the donor, or the donor-conceived child, or both, require that the information not be released.[173] If such representations are made, the Minister is to consider them and have regard to the right of the donor-conceived child to his or her identity. Nevertheless, if satisfied that sufficient reasons exist to withhold information, the request for information may be refused. In such cases, the reasons for the refusal may be explained, including the contents of the refusal. If not satisfied that sufficient reasons have been given to withhold the identifying information, the information will be released to the donor-conceived person concerned.

In circumstances in which a refusal has been made by the Minister, the donor-conceived person may appeal to the Circuit Court.[174]

Information to be provided to donor In Ireland, identifying information can be released to a donor, with the consent of a donor-conceived person. The consent may be given before or after a request by the donor is made.

170 Ibid., s 34(1).
171 Ibid., s 34(2).
172 Ibid., s 35(1).
173 Ibid., s 35(2).
174 Ibid., s 35(5).

First, at the age of 18 years a donor-conceived person may request the Minister record on the register a statement of his or her name, date of birth and contact details and confirm that he or she consents, on the making by the relevant donor of a request, to the release of that information to the donor.[175] Second, a donor may request from the Minister the name, date of birth and contact details of a donor-conceived child who has attained the age of 18 years and in relation to whom he or she is a relevant donor.[176]

When a request is made by a donor for identifying information, the donor-conceived person will be sent a notice informing him or her of the request, and unless the donor conceived refuses such release within twelve weeks, the information shall be released to the donor.[177]

Siblings Provision for identifying information release about siblings that share the same donor is also made. A donor-conceived child who has attained the age of 18 years may request the Minister to record on the register a statement of his or her name, date of birth and contact details and confirmation that he or she consents to the release of information to that person. As per the process for donors described previously, the release of information then relies on a request being made. When such a request is made, the donor-conceived person about whom it relates will be notified and information will be released within twelve weeks unless the donor-conceived person refuses.[178]

Requirement for counselling

All donors, recipient parents and donor-conceived children must receive counselling on the implications of his or her recording information on the register or, as the case may be, receiving such information. This must happen prior to any information being recorded or released.[179]

Notification of donor-conceived status (interaction of the register with register of births)

Ireland, like Victoria and Argentina, now includes notification on the register of births that a person is donor conceived. When an entry is made on the National Donor Conceived Register, the Minister must also notify the tArd-Chláraitheoir (The Registrar General) that they hold a record in the register in respect of the child concerned.[180] An tArd-Chláraitheoir must then note the entry in the regis-

175 Ibid., s 36(1).
176 Ibid., s 36(1)–(4).
177 Ibid., s 36(1)–(4).
178 Ibid., s 37.
179 Ibid., s 38.
180 Ibid., s 39.

ter of births that the child is donor conceived and that additional information is available from the register in relation to that child.[181]

Like Victoria, when a person reaches 18 years of age and applies for a copy of his or her birth certificate – and the register of births contains a note that he or she is donor conceived – an tArd-Chláraitheoir shall, when issuing a copy of the birth certificate requested, inform the person that further information relating to him or her is available from the register. The note shall be released only to the child concerned.[182]

Jurisdictions that have judicially supported a right to information

Germany

The law

A number of judgments in German courts have supported a donor-conceived person's right to know his or her genetic heritage.

In 1989, Germany's Constitutional Court decided that individuals should have the right to know their genetic identity. A further ruling on tissue donation in 2007 declared that files on specific donations must be held for thirty years. On 6 February 2013, the Higher Regional Court in Hamm, Germany, granted a 21-year-old donor-conceived woman the right to access the identity of her donor.[183] The court ruled that the interest of the plaintiff in ascertaining her parentage was higher than the interests of the defense and the right to a nondisclosure of donor information. Furthermore, it was held that an agreement between a clinic and rearing parents to maintain the anonymity of a sperm donor was an illegal contract as it was to the detriment of the offspring. The Federal Association of Reproductive Medical Centers described the decision as improving the legal position not only for children of sperm donors but also of doctors. Because physicians would be obliged the share the information, the court decided, they could not be held culpable for breaking doctor-patient confidentiality by doing so. Flowing from this decision, it was considered that children over the age of 16 could access identifying information.

Then, on 28 January 2015, the German Supreme Court (Bundesgerichtshof) further held that all children have a right of access to information, regardless of age, and that right trumps any right the donor has to privacy.[184]

181 Ibid.
182 Ibid.
183 Oberlandesgericht Hamm, I-14 U 7/12, available at http://www.justiz.nrw.de/nrwe/olgs/hamm/j2013/I_14_U_7_12_Urteil_20130206.html, accessed 16 March 2016.
184 BGH, Urteil vom 28 January 2015 – XII ZR 201/13.

This Supreme Court's decision concerned two sisters, age 12 and 17, who were both fathered from donor sperm. The sisters had appealed to the Supreme Court after a reproductive clinic refused to provide the biological father's identity because the girls' legal parents had initially waived the sisters' right to know who the donor was.

The court derived the right of the child to know his or her heritage from Articles 2(1), 1(1) of the German Constitution, which held the right to a claim for information between two private individuals if a civil claim exists between the parties.[185] The German Civil Code §242 was also seen as important because it established such a civil claim. The contract entered into by the parents and the doctor constituted a third-party beneficiary contract for the benefit of the child and this contract could be the basis of the right of the child to know the donor's identity.[186]

The German Supreme Court dismissed the lower court's argument that a minimum age of 16 should apply to children seeking information about their donor as the judges saw no foundation in existing laws to support this age requirement. The judges argued that it had to be assumed that a child would have a desire to know his or her parents independent of age and that naturally such a desire does not emerge only when a child turns 16.[187]

It further determined that 'the right of the sperm donor to informational self-determination, i.e. deciding himself which details about his private life to disclose to the wider public, based on Articles 2(1), 1(1) of the German Constitution, was trumped by the right of the child to know his or her heritage'.[188] The court, among other things, argued that in the balancing test between the fundamental rights of the child and the donor, it had to be taken into account that the donor had willingly participated in the procreation of the child and that he had to accept a certain social and ethical responsibility toward the child. In addition, the court reasoned that the donor's economical interests were insignificant as part of the balancing test. [189]

The right of the child to know his or her heritage was seen by the court as also surpassing the right of the doctor not to disclose information about his patients as part of his or her professional freedom derived from Article 12(1) of the German Constitution. [190]

185 Child rights international network, Supreme Court of Germany decision XII ZR 201/13, summary, available at https://www.crin.org/en/library/legal-database/supreme-court-germany-decision-xii-zr-201/13, accessed 16 March 2016.
186 Ibid.
187 Ibid.
188 Ibid.
189 Ibid.
190 Ibid.

Practice

Approximately 100,000 people fathered by sperm donations are currently living in Germany, and somewhere between 1,500 to 5,000 children are conceived annually using donor sperm. Most of them are not told they were donor conceived. Those who do know, and wish to find information, generally have a difficult time. In addition, while egg donation and surrogacy are not allowed in Germany, some people may travel abroad for treatment and, in those cases, there is no information available for the child. There is also no central registry or entry of donor conception on the birth registry.

Dr Petra Thorn, a German counsellor and academic who specializes in this area, notes also that the rights of people conceived between 1997 and 2007 are unclear.[191]

In addition, barriers exist to encouraging people to disclose their children's status or to share information. For example, in Germany citizens have a right to contest paternity. This right is granted to donor-conceived people living with heterosexual parents during the two years following disclosure. Calls for such laws to be abolished have been made, emphasizing that while offspring are interested in and curious about the sperm donor, they do not wish the donor to be granted legal parenthood. (NB: The German legal system does not provide the possibility to contest maternity after egg donation.)

Sperm donors currently may also be held to legal paternity if their sperm is used for same-sex couples not in a civil relationship and where, therefore, the social mother cannot adopt the child. They may also be considered the legal father when donating to single women.

Thus, while fundamentally, the Supreme Court judgment of 2015 upholds the right of children to information, regardless of their age, there is ongoing public debate in Germany and calls for legislative reform. In particular, there are calls to clarify the paternity of donors and legal fathers of donor-conceived children, which may in turn support people in telling their children about their donor-conceived status and in the release of information. Calls have also been made for a central register collecting all data about donor insemination.[192] Support groups such as Spenderkinder, which represents donor-conceived people, also continue to advocate for an end to anonymous donation, the right to information for donor-conceived persons and for more openness about donor conception practices.[193] The view is that ultimately there is a need for a comprehensive legal framework to ensure the rights of donor-conceived people.

191 Petra Thorn, Court Decision in Germany Supports Rights of the Donor Conceived to Access Their Donor's Identity, *BioNews*, 18 February 2013, available at http://www.bionews.org.uk/page_257189.asp.

192 Ibid.

193 See Spenderkinder, available at http://www.spenderkinder.de/english/, accessed 16 March 2016.

Discussion

Since 1984, there have been a growing number of jurisdictions that recognize donor-conceived people have a legal interest and/or right to access information about their donors. This chapter has shown that prohibitions on donor anonymity and openness about identity started as early as 1984 and continue to be adopted across the globe into the modern day.

However, there are some interesting distinctions to be drawn among such jurisdictions in terms of their approach. That is, while all such jurisdictions have banned anonymous donations, at least from the date of enactment of legislation onwards, the approaches vary within such jurisdictions in terms of whether the laws apply only to people born after the enactment (i.e. prospectively) – in most jurisdictions – or give further or total rights to donor-conceived people who are donor conceived, regardless of when the donation took place or when they were conceived or born (retrospectively). The model adopted for information release also differs, as does whether donor-conceived people are notified of their status, and if so, how; and the age at which people may access information.

Retrospective access to identifying information

Retrospective access was made possible by law in Switzerland in 2001, which set up a register of donor information for all future children but also included provision for children born before that date, which states that clinics must release information about donors to donor-conceived people on request. It was the first country in the world to provide for access to information by donor-conceived people regardless of when they were born. However, retrospective access may prove difficult because many files held by clinics there are said to have been destroyed.

In 2014–2016 in Australia, the states of Victoria and New South Wales considered laws that would give access to information by donor-conceived people born prior to the current laws in those jurisdictions. Both conducted inquiries that recommended expanding laws to allow access to information in Victoria with full retrospectivity, while in NSW this was subject to the consent of the donor. These states have moved to enact legislation to varying degrees. This includes Victoria adopting world-first legislation in the application of a contact veto/preference system for the release of identifying information about donors, regardless of when the donation took place. NSW has taken the more cautious 'consent first' approach. South Australia is currently considering what it will do in relation to access to information about past donors.

The consent first approach has also been followed in the Netherlands and the United Kingdom. In the Netherlands, legislation introduced in 2004 allowed access to information for all donor-conceived people conceived after that date; however, all donors that donated prior to that date were also asked to consent to release of information. If the donor consented, people conceived prior to the law were also able to have information about their donor. Such a consent model, while not giving retrospective access to all donor-conceived people, nevertheless recognized that those people clearly also have an interest in accessing information. A voluntary DNA register exists for those not able to access information otherwise.

Similarly, laws and practices introduced in the United Kingdom in 2005 to ban anonymity and provide for the release of information, also allow people who donated between 1991 and 2005 to 're-register' so as to give their consent to the release of information. This practice again may have provided access for some, but not all those searching for information.

Models of information release

The models for information release also vary among jurisdictions. Some provide for the release of identifying information under the law, but provide for no central register that holds information. These jurisdictions include Sweden, Austria, Norway, Switzerland (pre-2001) and some states of Australia, where information may be accessed via the clinic or hospital at which the donation or conception took place.

Others jurisdictions provide for registers, but not support services. These jurisdictions include Switzerland, New South Wales, Finland and Croatia. The view in these nations is that while information should be made available, it is up to the person accessing such information to decide whether he or she needs support services. In addition, there is some view in these jurisdictions that the clinic should provide such support services if or when needed.

Yet, others provide for registers *and* support services, including the Netherlands, the Australian states of Victoria and Western Australia, the United Kingdom (at present). Such support services include counselling about the information release system, and in most cases, also an intermediary service to support people if they wish to make contact. The systems in these jurisdictions appear to be effective in helping people manage their expectations and to form the kind of relationships they wish to pursue.

In Argentina and Uruguay, approval by a judicial authority is required before information will be released. How such a process will work is yet to be seen due to the respective pieces of legislation having only just been introduced.

Voluntary registers

While many jurisdictions have established central compulsory registers, administered by government entities, there may also exist voluntary registers operating for those who do not fall under the remits of the law due simply to when they were born. These registers exist in Victoria, Western Australia, New South Wales, the Netherlands and the United Kingdom.

However, it is important to note that voluntary registers are often less effective because they rely on all parties placing their names on the register, whereas compulsory registers are a mandatory recording of information regarding donor conception. Some jurisdictions, such as the United Kingdom and the Netherlands, have therefore also established DNA registers or databases for those born prior to the laws enabling access to information, to aid in matching genetic relatives where records may not be available whether they not accessible due to lack of legal right or because they have been destroyed. New legislation in Victoria will also enable DNA testing to confirm genetic relatedness when there is doubt.

Notification of donor-conceived status

Three states – Victoria, Croatia and Argentina – now carry information about the method of conception on the birth register.

Victoria and Ireland explicitly state that such information will be provided to the donor-conceived person on application for their birth certificate at age 18.

One jurisdiction – Croatia – mandates disclosure by parents to the child regarding his or her donor-conceived status no later than age 18, although how such a provision will be enforced is unclear.

Age to access information

Depending on the jurisdiction, different ages are specified for release of information; in the Netherlands, a donor-conceived child must be 16 to access information about his or her donor. In other countries, they must be 18 years of age, or in Sweden, the law vaguely specifies that a donor-conceived person be in their 'upper teens' to access information. A number of jurisdictions have also moved to allow for access to identifying information by recipient parents, donors and donor-conceived siblings – subject to the consent of the party about whom such information is sought. In such circumstances, again the systems vary in whether such consent is *actively* sought or whether some kind of 'voluntary register' operates in which a 'wait and see' approach is taken.

Access for all?

In concluding this chapter, it is important to note that even in the juridictions discussed in this chapter, there remain thousands of donor-conceived people in existence who will continue to find it difficult – if not impossible – to gain information about their donors. Although some do not seek such information, others engage in extensive searches, to no avail. Many issues thus remain. Whether anonymous donation should be prohibited, whether the choice to access information should be given to all donor-conceived people (i.e. whether laws should have retrospective effect), and best practice approaches to the release of information are discussed further in Part III of this book. The focus of this part of the book, however, remains in detailing approaches to information release and anonymity and any processes that have surrounded the development of and/

or changes to the law. As such, the discussion now turns to jurisdictions that while increasingly recognizing the interests and rights of donor-conceived people to information, have moved to dual-track approaches to access – dependent on choices made by donors to be 'open identity' or 'anonymous' and subsequently potential recipients in the donor they choose.

5 Jurisdictions that enable both open-identity and anonymous donation

Introduction

Within some jurisdictions such as Canada, Denmark, Iceland, Hungary and the United States the practice of allowing for both open-identity and anonymous gamete donation – sometimes referred to as the 'choice' or 'double-track'[1] approach – may be found. These jurisdictions are similar to the jurisdictions discussed in Chapter 4 in that they also illustrate a growing recognition of the need for access to information by donor-conceived people, with efforts and approaches taken to allow such access. Again, these jurisdictions create a situation where access to information will not be possible for all who seek it.[2] Some have set up voluntary registers (albeit non-government based) in the hope of helping and supporting these people.

In the 'choice' jurisdictions, there are also significant differences from the systems discussed in Chapter 4 that are worth noting. These include, but are not limited to, the way that open-identity systems operate, where the choice lies (i.e. with donors and recipient parents – and not the child) and whether they place the interests of the child above others. In addition, in jurisdictions like Hungary, open-identity donation applies only to egg donation, while sperm donation remains anonymous.

Overview of open-identity systems

Generally, the open-identity approach may be seen as one that is given effect either by providing for choice within the law (such as in Hungary in relation to egg donation, or Denmark for sperm and egg donation) or via a system that is

1 Guido Pennings, 'The "Double Track" Policy for Donor Anonymity' (1997) 12 *Human Reproduction* 2839.

2 Noting that to date most jurisdictions that require non-anonymous donations and allow for access to information by law also leave many donor-conceived people without information due to the laws operating prospectively and not retrospectively and/or some jurisdictions still requiring the donor's consent in certain circumstances.

implemented by a clinic or sperm bank on a voluntary (albeit usually contractual) basis (such as in the Canada and the United States).

The first step to a donation being classified open-identity is that the donor must consent when making his or her donation to provide identifying information and being open to contact by any offspring that result. Contact protocols and practices vary between jurisdictions and providers of gametes, but generally when a donor-conceived person reaches the age of 18, he or she can contact the clinic (or sperm bank) that provided the gametes to obtain the identity of the donor(s) as well as contact information. In the alternate, when gametes are provided anonymously, both the provider and the recipients agree that the donor wishes to remain anonymous to the recipients and offspring (and vice versa).

The second step is the choice by recipients as to whether to use open-identity or anonymous donations when accessing donor conception services.

Of course, for information release to occur, more steps will also be involved. A donor-conceived person needs to be told of their status, and then he or she can make a choice about whether to ask for further information.

To illustrate approaches that allow for choice at the point of donation by the donor, and use by the recipients, regarding identity release or anonymity of donated gametes, detailed examples are given here from a number of jurisdictions that allow for both open-identity and anonymous donations – noting that discussion of a U.S. example in depth is used to facilitate understanding of how the process operates via clinics, and description of similar clinical practice in other jurisdictions is limited so as not to provide repetitive information. However, respective laws and/or systems in each jurisdiction are detailed, particularly when differences are apparent. Hungary is also noted as a point of difference because, while allowing for choice, it does not provide the same type of program found in the other countries discussed. The discussion of the different jurisdictions also includes reflection on the varying approaches presented and how the choice or double-track approach may affect donor-conceived people searching for information.

The United States

In the United States, the open-identity option is not generally governed by legislation.[3] It is provided by some clinics and sperm banks; however, it is not practiced uniformly across the country. While the American Society for Reproductive Medicine recommends the indefinite retention of records regarding gamete donation and encourages every U.S. clinic to have an information-sharing

3 See above for discussion of the only state that requires non-anonymous donation in the United States – Washington State.

policy,[4] many clinics do not. In fact, there is wide variation across clinics in relation to record keeping and donor anonymity.

Nevertheless, the United States does provide the first example in the world to allow for open-identity donation as an option alongside anonymous gamete donation, with the Sperm Bank of California (TSBC) having had such a program in place since 1983. In addition, most U.S. sperm banks today have an option for exchange of information and/or contact between donor-conceived people and their donor and/or siblings, with the rate of 'open' donation increasing. The next subsection discusses TSBC as a case study to illustrate how voluntary open-identity donation systems might work, before discussing other U.S. practices more broadly that either support or hinder information release.

Case study: The Sperm Bank of California (TSBC)

The Sperm Bank of California (TSBC) developed its Identity-Release® Program in 1983 with the view of providing donor-conceived adults with access to information about their donors. As noted, it was the first program in the world that actually offered such release. It is worth examining as a case study illustrative of how such programs might operate. The following section provides an overview of reasons for the program being set up and its approach to information release.

Why was the program implemented?

TSBC reports that initial requests for the program came from prospective parents who 'wanted to leave the door open for their children to get more information in the future'.[5] They state that the program is offspring focused in that it does not involve the release of the names of rearing parents and their children to donors.

Who chooses whether a donor is in the Identity-Release® Program?

The Identity-Release® Program operates via contractual arrangements in which donors agree to their identity being released. The donor signs a contract authorizing TSBC to reveal his identity (noting TSBC is a sperm bank and so they only deal with male donors) when specific requirements are met.

4 American Society for Reproductive Medicine, 'Informing Offspring of Their Conception by Gamete or Embryo Donation: A Committee Opinion Ethics Committee of the American Society for Reproductive Medicine' (2013) 100 *Fertility Sterility* 45–49.

5 The Sperm Bank of California, Identity-Release® Program, available at https://www.thespermbankofca.org/content/identity-release-program, accessed 16 March 2016.

What are the requirements for information release?

TSBC is permitted to reveal the donor's identity under the following circumstances:

- A donor's identity can be released only to the donor-conceived individual.
- The donor-conceived individual must be at least 18 years old.
- The donor-conceived individual must request the donor's identifying information in writing and go through a release process before the identity is released.
- The information is not automatically released.

When a request is received, before releasing any information to donor-conceived adults, TSBC contacts the donor and asks him to fill out an updated profile. He is also asked to specify his preferred form of contact (such as phone, email or letter). Following this contact, the donor's full name, birth date, place of birth, updated profile and contact information (if available) are released. TSBC notes:

> There is no guarantee that donor-conceived adults will request their donor's information, nor that those who do request information will initiate contact with their donor. Our experience so far is that about 30 per cent of eligible adults have made requests and that at least half of those who received their donor's information have contacted him.[6]

Furthermore, choosing to participate in the Identity-Release® Program does not obligate donors to meet their offspring; although TSBC states that its 'research shows that the majority of donors in the program expect to have contact with donor-conceived adults'.[7]

Anonymous donors

An anonymous donor similarly signs a contract, but in that case the contract prohibits TSBC from revealing the donor's identity under any circumstance. The contract does, however, permit TSBC to contact the anonymous donor in the future should a donor-conceived adult petition for the release of identifying information. It then remains the donor's decision whether to remain anonymous or to release his identity.

Can donors change their minds?

An Identity-Release® Program donor signs a contract that allows TSBC to release his identity to donor-conceived adults on request (and to no other party). 'Yes' donors do not have the option of changing their minds and becoming 'no' donors.

However, donors who initially opted to remain anonymous have the option of becoming 'yes' donors at a later date and agree to be contacted by the clinic should an adult make a request to be given the option of changing his mind.

6 Ibid.
7 Ibid.

Who makes the choice to use an open-identity or anonymous donor?

Whether a donor is Identity-Release® or anonymous is advertised by TSBC in their catalogue. Recipients ultimately make the choice of which sperm donor they use. However, TSBC encourages recipients to consider whether an Identity-Release® Program donor or anonymous donor is best for their family. While they know some prospective parents simply feel more comfortable using an anonymous donor, they find that the Identity-Release® Program provides parents and donor-conceived individuals with more options and control – making it important for all families to consider. They emphasize that parents choosing Identity-Release® Program donors:

- have *flexibility* should their life or perspective change
- have the *choice* of what to tell children about their donor origins and when to tell them
- give their future children *options* that are not available with an anonymous donor

TSBC further notes the decision is one that has long-term implications and that they find 'parents sometimes feel different about these options after their child is born, so we want to take a moment to present some important information that may be overlooked'. They also provide the information contained in the following box quotes which appears intended to allay fears about using an Identity-Release® donor.

I do not want the donor involved in my child's life.

The donor will not be involved in the upbringing of your child. He can only be identified at the request of your then-adult child. Identifying information about your family is never released to the donor. This protects the family (and the donor) legally and psychologically.

I am not planning to tell my child that she or he was conceived using donor sperm.

The decisions of whether, when and what to tell your child about his or her conception origins remain parental choices regardless of what type of donor you choose. It is not uncommon for parents to be more inclined toward openness and disclosure after their child is born and parents often report that disclosure is easier if they have an Identity-Release® donor.

I do not want information about my family released to the donor.

No identifying information about our families is ever released to donors. Ever.

My partner feels more comfortable with choosing an anonymous donor.

We encourage all recipients and their partners to learn the facts about the Identity-Release® Program. Some partners express concern that the Identity-Release® Program will place their parenting rights in jeopardy. Donors in the Identity-Release® Program do not have any of the rights or responsibilities of parenthood based on California law. (Note: Regardless of where the insemination takes place, the donor's parental rights are terminated based on California law because the donation was provided in California.) However, we understand this concern and this is part of the reason that donor-conceived individuals must be 18 years old to receive their donor's identity.

Another concern expressed by partners is that choosing an Identity-Release® Program donor will make the donor more important to their child and thus diminish the non-biological parent's role in their child's life. Our published research indicates that youth feel that being donor-conceived has a neutral to positive impact on their relationship with their parents. While it is true that many donor-conceived adults are curious to learn more about their donor, this is expressed as an interest in *learning more about themselves and their genetic origins*, and not as a desire for their donor to be their parent. There is no way to know in advance how curious any specific donor-conceived individual will be about their origins. Choosing an Identity-Release® Program donor leaves the door open in case your child, as an adult, wishes to learn more.

If I choose a donor in the Identity-Release® Program, will you release my information to the donor when I get pregnant? Can the donor access MY information once I am pregnant?

No to both questions. TSBC does not release identifying information about parents or their children to donors. In fact, we do not release any identifying information about our families to other parties except when requested to do so by families who choose to participate in our Family Contact List.

It doesn't really matter so we are choosing an anonymous donor.

Research from TSBC and elsewhere indicates that many donor-conceived youth and adults have a healthy curiosity about their donor. Therefore, whether or not the donor is open-identity may be more important to your future child than it is to you. Regardless of which type of donor you ultimately choose, we encourage you to consider this an important decision that will have future implications for your child.

Does the Identity-Release® Program give parental rights to the donor? If I choose a donor in the Identity-Release® Program, the donor could seek custody, right?

No, a TSBC program donor, regardless of their Identity-Release® Program or anonymous status, does not have the right to seek custody of your child. Donors in our program do not have any of the rights or responsibilities of parenthood based on the Uniform Parentage Act that is part of California law. Furthermore, the donor will not know who you are or who your child is. Remember, if you choose an Identity-Release® Program donor, your child will not have access to the donor's identity until the child is 18 years old or older and is legally an adult. (Note: If you are considering working with a donor who is personally known to you through our Directed Donor or Known Donor programs, we strongly encourage you to seek legal advice regarding the issue of parental rights.)

While TSBC also does not obligate donors to be Identity-Release®, they state that they believe the program 'leads to the best outcomes – not just for the donor-conceived individuals and their parents but for donors as well'.[8] They note that donors participate in this program for a variety of reasons, with the most

8 Ibid.

commonly stated reasons including the donor felt that donor-conceived adults should have the right or chance to know their donor's identity; the donor would want to have this option, if he were donor conceived; the donor said he was curious about future offspring; and the donor has a personal connection, such as having a friend who is donor conceived. One TSBC donor is quoted on his website as having said: 'I tried to put myself in the shoes of someone who was the result of such a donation. I might not actually look up the donor, but it would be reassuring to have the option to do so'.[9]

Costs and fees

Of note regarding TSBC, the costs to recipients, and payments to donors, are the same whether anonymous or Identity-Release® sperm donation is chosen.

They state that in the past, Identity-Release® sperm provided by TSBC was more expensive to cover the costs of running the program, but that an unintended consequence of this was that more women selected anonymous donors as a financial decision rather than based on what they felt was ideal for their family. To eliminate the influence of price on such decisions, TSBC brought them back to the same cost level.

Similarly, TSBC ensures that all donors are compensated the same on a per sample basis regardless of which program they choose, it being noted that they 'want men to choose the Identity-Release® Program because they believe in the program, not because they get paid more for being in it'.

Other U.S. donor programs

Although laws across a number of U.S. jurisdictions protect the legal rights and responsibilities of recipient parents and free the donors of such rights and responsibilities, open-identity options and variants thereof, are still not the preferred donor program in the United States. Nevertheless, although the majority of gamete and embryo donation in the United States remains anonymous, there has been increasing numbers of open-identity donors.

For example, in 2012 it was reported that nearly 80 per cent of sperm donors were anonymous.[10] Such a figure was based on research by Bryn and Ireland that considered numbers of anonymous donors listed by three U.S. sperm banks in mid-2011.[11] The author conducted the same search in December 2015, with the figures showing a decrease in anonymous sperm donors to 70 per cent across these three banks. These figures are shown in Table 5.1.

9 Ibid.

10 Mary P. Byrn and Rebecca Ireland, 'Anonymously Provided Sperm and the Constitution' (2012) *Faculty Scholarship Paper* 232, available at http://open.mitchellhamline.edu/facsch/232.

11 Ibid.

Table 5.1 Numbers and percentages of anonymous sperm donors at three U.S. sperm banks

Sperm bank	*2011 – Anonymous donors*	*2015 – Anonymous donors*
California Cryobank Inc.	220 out of 274 (80 per cent)	312 of 538 (58 per cent)
Cryogenic Labs	85 out of 101 (84 per cent)	50 out of 60 (83 per cent)
Fairfax CryoBank	137 out of 179 (77 per cent)	275 out of 406 (68 per cent)

DIFFERENTIAL PRICING

Interestingly, unlike TSBC, prices at these sperm banks are differential in relation to anonymous and open-identity donors – the latter being more expensive. The following tables 5.2 and 5.3 illustrate the differential pricing at each of these sperm banks.

Table 5.2 California CryoBank – fees for anonymous v. open-identity donors

Anonymous donors	*2015*	*2016*
Premium ICI (Intracervical Insemination)	$640	$690
Premium IUI (Intrauterine Insemination)	$740	$790
Open-Identity donors		
Premium ICI (Intracervical Insemination)	$740	$790
Premium IUI (Intrauterine Insemination)	$840	$890

Table 5.3 CryroGenic Labs advertised fees in 2016[12]

Donor category	*Intracervical (ICI)*	*ICI ART*	*Intrauterine (IUI)*	*IUI ART*	*IVF*
Anonymous	$505/dose	$460/dose	$585/dose	$530/dose	$350/dose
ID option	$640/dose	$535/dose	$760/dose	$645/dose	$480/dose

Table 5.4 Fairfax CryoBank advertised fees in 2016[13]

Donor category	*Intracervical (ICI)*	*ICI ART*	*Intrauterine (IUI)*	*IUI ART*	*IVF*
Fairfax anonymous/ Fairfax anonymous graduate	$650/dose	$590/ dose	$775/dose	$705/ dose	$470/ dose
Fairfax ID option/ Fairfax ID option graduate	$770/dose	$695/ dose	$880/dose	$805/ dose	$630/ dose

12 As advertised at Fairfax Cryobank website, available at https://fairfaxcryobank.com/us/fees, accessed 16 March 2016.

13 Ibid.

More about U.S. information at a cost

Interestingly, not only do open-identity sperm donors usually cost more in the United States than anonymous donor sperm, even at the initial stages of choosing a donor, although some information is free, cost increases the more information that is sought. The following table 5.5. provides an example of fees from one such provider for various types of information (referred to as 'product') about the donor:

Table 5.5 Fairfax CryoBank fees for information about donor ('product')

Product	*Website download*	*Mailed copy**
Summary profile (1–3 pages)	Free	On-line only
Essay	Free	On-line only
Audio clip	Free	On-line only
Staff impression	Free	On-line only
Medical profile (12–15)	Free	$23
Personal profile (9–14)	$26	$29
Childhood photo	$13	$23
Silhouette	$27	$29
Audio interview	$37	$40
Lifetime series photo set	$95	$95
Adult/Childhood photo (2 photos total)	$65	$65
Childhood photo/Silhouette set	$30	$33
Profile set: personal, medical, audio, childhood and silhouette	$83	$98
Partial profile set: personal, medical and audio	$55	$56
Donor unlimited access packages: Access to all donor information	$54.95–$194.95	N/A
Tier ll childhood photos	$54.95	N/A
Tier ll except Keirsey and Lifetime	$124.95	N/A
Tier ll including Keirsey and Lifetime	$194.95	N/A
Club Fairfax	$294.95 / year	N/A
Personality Testing Keirsey Donor Report	$24	N/A
Personality Testing Take the Keirsey	$24	N/A
Shipping/handling of donor information		
USPS	$10	N/A
FedEx overnight letter	$30	N/A
FedEx letter saturday delivery	$45	N/A
FedEx outside USA	N/A	N/A
Profile by fax	$10 profile	N/A

Research on the double-track approach in the United States

In the United States, some research has been done regarding recipient choices between anonymous donations and open-identity. For example, a study by Scheib et al. published in 2000, which investigated recipient preferences for open-identity to anonymous donors at TSBC, found that 79 per cent of recipients wanted an open-identity donor.[14]

In comparison, a study published in 2009 by Ottey et al. regarding clients who purchased donor sperm at the Fairfax CryoBank and Cryogenic Laboratories, Inc. (CLI),[15] reported that 66–69 per cent of recipients purchased anonymous sperm and 31–34 per cent purchased Identity-Release®.[16] Of those that purchased anonymous sperm, 35–40 per cent rated anonymity as important in their decision, 85–90 per cent rated the available medical and genetic information as important, and 79–81 per cent rated physical characteristics as important. Interestingly, the Fairfax study reported that 'approximately 80 per cent of this population planned to reveal the use of donor sperm to the resulting offspring'– despite not being able to tell the offspring the identity of the donor.

Fairfax clients who purchased Identity-Release® sperm were found to rate the importance of the sperm being Identity-Release® as much higher than those from CLI (being 78 per cent and 35 per cent, respectively). Some 68–82 per cent of these purchasers rated medical and genetic information as important; 55–68 per cent rated donor physical characteristics as important; 82–90 per cent of that population planned to reveal the use of donor sperm to the resulting offspring.

Notably, the study by Ottey et al., and final recommendations made by the authors, focused on demand and sales to recipient populations, and not on access to information by the children who may result. Their conclusion states:

> This data and sales data support the need for both AD [anonymous] and ID [Identity-Release®] sperm donors. The choice of AD and/or ID sperm donor varies by client and is dependent on several factors including the clients' priority for ethnicity, phenotype, education level, and availability of these factors in the ID category. Informing offspring varies dependent on: sexual orientation, marital status, and parenting philosophy. Sperm banks should provide choices of both anonymous and ID release donors with accurate comprehensive non-identifying donor information *in order to meet the needs of the recipient population.* [emphasis added][17]

The study did not investigate the influence or impact of differential pricing on open-identity to anonymous donors on choice of potential recipients.

14 J.E. Scheib, M. Riordan and P.R. Shaver, 'Choosing Between Anonymous and Identity-Release Sperm Donors: Recipient and Donor Characteristics' (2000) 10 *Reproductive Technology* (formerly Assist. Reprod. Rev.) 50–58.

15 Note CLI was purchased by Fairfax Cryobank in 2010.

16 M. Ottey, A. Erickson-Hagen, S. Seitz and S. Pool, 'Anonymity vs Identity Release: Choices in Donor Sperm' (2009) 92(3) *Fertility and Sterility*, Supplement, S251.

17 Ibid.

Online forums and voluntary registers in the United States

Other methods of seeking and providing information in the United States are not limited to open-identity donation programs or buying information about the donor. Some clinics and/or sperm banks have moved to provide online forums in which recipients and offspring can connect with other recipients and/or offspring on a variety of issues, including identifying those who share the same donor. For example, Fairfax CryoBank has a number of forums for people seeking to use or who have used donor conception, including (but not limited to) private forums for recipients who want to connect over offspring and donor-conceived adults who want to connect with siblings.[18] Another sperm bank, Xytex International, announced in 2014 that it was 'beta testing' (i.e. letting users trial) a forum called xyConnect, which would allow exchanges between patients, donors and offspring.[19] The success and use of such forums is unknown.

In addition (and perhaps in contrast in terms of use) are voluntary registers that have been set up independently by those affected by donor conception. One of the best-known registers of this kind is the Donor Sibling Registry (DSR),[20] established in 2000 by Wendy Kramer, a recipient mother, and her then 10-year-old donor-conceived son, Ryan. It was the first of its kind that specifically focused on linking siblings. There are currently 47,081 members registered from around the world.[21] It is reported that most of those members have either used, donated or been conceived at large U.S. sperm banks, as well as smaller clinics and facilities in cities and towns worldwide. The advocacy work undertaken by Wendy and Ryan Kramer in relation to highlighting the need for information exchange has been highly significant in bringing the issue to the fore in numerous settings – and particularly in the United States.

Denmark

Assisted insemination has been practiced in Denmark for many years, with more technical forms of assisted reproduction becoming increasingly prominent since the 1980s. Early practices were seen as best left to the medical profession to decide on, and in relation to the practice of sperm donation, anonymity had been implemented by the medical community since its inception; said to have been expected by both recipient parents and donors. The earliest guidelines therefore presupposed anonymity as natural, focusing on safety as well as

18 See http://blogandforum.fairfaxcryobank.com/forum/index.php, accessed 16 March 2016.
19 See https://www.xytex.com/xyconnects/views/login_view.cfm, accessed 16 March 2016.
20 The Donor Sibling Register, www.donorsiblingregistry.com, accessed 16 March 2016.
21 Wendy Kramer and Naomi Cahn, *Finding Our Families: A First-of-Its-Kind Book for Donor Conceived People and Their Families* (2013).

quality of care (particularly in light of HIV) and legislation specifically regarding insemination.[22]

Arguments in relation to anonymity were put forward comparing donor conception with general population statistics concerning unknown biological fatherhood running at approximately 5–10 per cent (i.e. for 'naturally conceived' offspring where the husband was not in fact the father).[23] Consideration of legislation in neighboring Sweden that was enacted in 1985 – giving rights to donor-conceived people to access information about their donor – was dismissed. A working group argued:

- artificial insemination was primarily a fertility treatment to replace a natural function and that the child's upbringing and place in the family therefore ought to take place as close to the normal and natural way as possible;
- the interests of the donor, who acted for altruistic reasons, did not reflect any desire whatsoever to be recorded as the origin of any offspring; and
- the Swedish law did not have a significant legal importance, since it did not place an obligation on parents to tell the child that it had been conceived with donor sperm, noting, that without such information it would be hard to fulfil the right of the child which was at the centre of the Swedish law.[24]

In addition, the view that the Swedish law had resulted in fewer sperm donations in Sweden and an increased number of Swedish women being treated in Denmark was relevant to decision making.[25]

When in 1997 the first piece of legislation in Denmark on artificial fertilization was adopted, it stated that the existing practice of anonymity in sperm donation was to be continued, creating a legal obligation for sperm banks to ensure anonymity. No specific reasons were given for this provision, but Herrmann suggests they were simply upholding the original reasons for anonymity.[26]

Egg donation at that stage was prohibited between known parties, especially between family members as this would create 'unfortunate and confusing familiar relations'.

22 Janne Rothmar Herrmann, 'Anonymity and Openness in Donor conception: The New Danish Model' (2013) 20(5) *European Journal of Health Law* 505, 505–511. Note, in this paper Associate Professor Janne Rothman Herrmann from the Faculty of Law, University of Copenhagen comprehensively explains the regulation of assisted reproduction in Denmark, and Denmark's stance in relation to anonymous donation. The information contained in this section is primarily drawn from her paper, summarizing the main points about views regarding information release, legislative provisions, and changes in legislation and practice over time in Denmark. The points discussed are illustrative not only of what the law is, but of the reasoning that lays behind it. For more comprehensive discussion of the law, see Herrmann's paper.

23 Ibid., p 507.

24 Ibid.

25 Ibid.

26 Ibid., p 508.

In the 2006, the legislation was reviewed and amended, and again, anonymity was explicitly upheld. This time, the following listed reasons were given:

- there was not a demand from donors or families to change the law;
- the interests of the child could not be viewed in isolation from the family in which it lived;
- the total welfare of the family might be affected if a third party was to be involved in the child's life;
- there were the interests of society to consider. This included that:
    - if anonymity was abolished, the number of donors would decline and Denmark would face the same problems with providing treatment as seen elsewhere in the world (i.e. the alleged drop in sperm donor numbers);
    - the need for more complex treatment such as IVF would increase; and
    - business interests were at stake. (Herrmann notes that 'for the legislator the sperm industry had become an export success' and that 'the fact that big industry interests were at stake was used as one of the winning arguments by the previous government to maintain donor anonymity').[27]

It is important, however, to note that since 1997 the act had only applied to treatment performed by doctors. Simple insemination that did not require medical intervention was not governed by the act. It was performed by midwives or others (partners/self-insemination), and had long seen the use of 'open donors', primarily by gay families. Further amendments in 2012 were therefore not surprising when the legislature adopted a model in which a choice between anonymous and known donors could be made. The amendments made it possible to choose an open or an anonymous donor in medical and fertility clinics as well as 'continuing to accommodate those lesbian couples who wish to make up the nuclear family without the presence of a third party'.[28] Anonymity was upheld for the same reasons as given earlier, but the option to use open or known donors was added to 'secure individual freedom and choice for donors, women and couples'.[29]

The most recent iteration of the legislation, therefore, did not give the right to access information to donor-conceived people. Rather, whether access to information is possible, depends on the choice of the recipient parent(s) of whether they wish to use an anonymous donor and their agreement with the sperm bank when selecting a donor.[30] At a clinic level, Denmark now offers the choice between anonymous and open-identity donors. The system is the same as that in

27 Ibid.
28 Ibid., p 509.
29 Ibid.
30 Christina G. Jeppesen de Boer and Annette Kronborg, 'The Rights of the Child: Danish National Report' in Olga Cvejic Jancic (ed.), *The Rights of the Child in a Changing World:*

the United States with choices being made by the donor in regard to whether he or she wishes to be anonymous and the recipient person(s) in regard to whether they wish to use anonymous or open-identity gametes. Interestingly, a rudimentary survey of two of the primary sperm banks in Denmark in December 2015 revealed that the numbers of anonymous donors remained high at one leading sperm bank, being 387 out of 475 donors (82 per cent) on the Cryos website[31] (Cryos bills itself as 'the world's largest sperm bank'); while at another, the figures were much lower – being 99 out of 236 (42 per cent) anonymous donors on the Nordic/Europe Sperm Bank (clinic country that Denmark selected).

In relation to egg donors, the removal of laws that made it illegal to use a willing sister or friend as donor have 'given the clinics more tools to attract more female donors'. They may also result in donor-conceived people having access to information about their egg donors.

Embryo donation remains prohibited, as it has always been a requirement in the act that there must be a genetic link between the couple and the embryo. That is, a couple must be able to provide either egg or sperm themselves and cannot rely on both gametes being donated.

Broader issues for donor-conceived people – cross-border donation

Herrmann comments on what she titles 'Anonymity and the Free Movement of Goods', which is particularly relevant in terms of donor-conceived people seeking information, when they may have been conceived as a result of Danish sperm sent to other countries. She states:

> The Danish legal framework on anonymity in donation has been a key element in making the Danish sperm bank industry a major business globally. The EU tissue directive paves the way for the free movement of cells and tissues. If a sperm bank is a licensed tissue centre according to the EU tissue directive it can deliver tested and screened donor sperm to anybody, even to private patients for home insemination. Consequently, a Danish sperm bank can ship anonymous donor sperm to countries where anonymity is illegal, such as Sweden, the United Kingdom, Switzerland, Austria and the Netherlands, because the license of the sperm bank does not regulate what can be delivered to whom. In the EU goods can move freely from country to country, and the sperm bank is generally not responsible for the legality of imports in the recipient country. Furthermore, in most countries a

25 Years after the UN Convention on the Rights of the Child (Springer, New York, 2016), p 101.

31 See Cryos Denmark website, available at http://dk.cryosinternational.com/donor-search/, accessed 16 March 2016.

prohibition to use anonymous donor sperm will only apply to physicians and/or licensed tissue centres in the country in question.[32]

In this case, donor-conceived people who become aware of their donor-conceived status must consider whether the sperm they were conceived with came from the country in which they live. Perhaps for these people, if they seek information, the only hope is DNA testing and sleuthing as set out in Chapter 3, as a clear path to information does not appear to exist, and at least in Denmark, does not seem to be something that will be forthcoming in the near future.

Canada

In Canada, both federal and provincial laws govern matters relevant to assisted reproductive technologies. The Assisted Human Reproduction Act, S.C. 2004, c. 2 (AHRA)[33] is the most significant piece of federal legislation governing the use of third-party reproductive technologies, while provincial law governs issues of legal parentage (to varying degrees across provinces).[34]

Notably, in December 2010, the Supreme Court of Canada released a decision (an advisory opinion in response to a question from the Quebec government) which struck out several provinces of the AHRA as being outside the law's permissible reach – specifically finding that much of the legislation did not fall within the federal jurisdiction's constitutional powers, but rather under provincial jurisdiction as a matter related to health.[35] However, most provinces have not enacted legislation in the areas that were struck out, leaving certain issues unregulated. Thus, while the federal law provides for prohibitions on commercialization, certain health and safety considerations, and consent provisions (within regulations), much else in terms of the practice of assisted reproduction occurs in a regulatory void.

In addition, information release for donor-conceived people is currently not covered in the legislation. The current practice of some clinics in Canada is to offer both open-identity and anonymous donors, noting that the system is similar to that described earlier in relation to the U.S. ReproMed. The Toronto Institute for Reproductive Medicine had forty-five out of sixty-one (74 per cent) listed

32 Herrmann, above n 22.

33 Assisted Human Reproduction Act, 2004, s.c. 2004, c.2, available at http://laws-lois.justice.gc.ca/eng/acts/a-13.4/, accessed 16 March 2016.

34 See for example, *Children's Law Act*, RNSL 1990, Chapter C–13 s 12 (Newfoundland); *Revised Statutes of Yukon*, Chapter 31, *Children's Act* s 13; *Civil Code of Quebec* SQ 1991, Title 2, Filiation, Chapter I.1.

35 See Supreme Court of Canada, Reference re Assisted Human Reproduction Act 2010 SCC 61, available at http://scc.lexum.org/en/2010/2010scc61/2010scc61.html, accessed 16 March 2016.

donors who were anonymous in December 2015. The institute also notes the following:

1 Using an Identity-Release® Donor does not automatically enroll the recipient in the Identity-Release® Donor Program.
2 If recipients would like to participate, they have to register for the Identity-Release® Program. They can choose to register immediately after the birth of their child or at any time later.
3 Registration can be done by completing a Live Birth Report and indicating on the form that the person would like to register in the Identity-Release® Program.
4 Once the report is received, the recipient will be contacted by a member of ReproMed's Patient Services Team and asked to provide supporting documentation such as medical records, sample order confirmation or an invoice. In addition, the recipient will need to sign consent for participation in the program.
5 The completed registration information will be securely kept at ReproMed. After the child turns 18, he or she may contact ReproMed requesting the donor's identity information release.
6 ReproMed *does not* provide semen donors with any offspring information unless an identity release request has been made by an offspring who is older than 18 years or the recipient mother of an offspring who is older than 18 years.[36]

Such requirements illustrate that at least in this example, recipients choosing open-identity sperm need to actively participate in ensuring their child will be able to access information when he or she turn 18 – the choice itself is not enough to guarantee such access.

Notably, only 5–10 per cent of sperm used in Canada is from Canadian donors. Most is sourced from the United States and ReproMed lists XyTec, Fairfax and CryoGenic Labs Inc. as other suppliers of sperm. Although payment to donors for donating is prohibited in Canada, there are fees by the clinics for accessing services and donor sperm. The pricing is again differential based on whether the sperm is open-identity or not, and where the sperm comes from.[37] It is possible that such differential pricing would affect decision making by potential recipients in choosing which sperm donor they will use, and thus access by donor-conceived people to information about their donor(s) in the future.

Concerning donor-conceived siblings, ReproMed operates the ReproMed's Sibling Registry that allows recipient parents and children to interact with families

36 ReproMed, Identity Release (Open ID) Canadian Donors, available at http://www.repromed.ca/open_id, accessed 16 March 2016.

37 See ReproMed Fee Schedule, available at http://www.repromed.ca/fertility_fees.html, accessed 16 March 2016.

that have used the same donor. Access to the registry can occur immediately after the birth of the child or at any time later. The author could not ascertain the level of use of the registry.

Iceland

Although not as much information was available in English on Iceland, it was noted that the dual-track approach also exists there.

In Iceland, assisted reproduction, including donor conception, is governed by the Act on Artificial Fertilisation and use of Human Gametes and Embryos for Stem-Cell Research.[38] The act allows the donation of sperm and eggs, but not embryos. The decision lies with the donor in the first instance, Article 4 of that act allowing the donor to choose whether he or she will be anonymous. Should a donor request anonymity, health workers must ensure that this wish be respected. In such cases, information may not be provided to the donor about the couple receiving donor gametes or about the child, while the couple or the child may not receive information on the donor.

Should the donor not request anonymity, the institution shall keep information on the donor in a special file. Should the donation of gametes result in the birth of a child, data on the child and on the couple who received the donated gametes shall be kept in the same file.

A child conceived because of a donation of gametes, where the donor did not request anonymity, may at the age of 18 request access to the records to acquire information on the name of the donor. Should a child receive information on the gamete donor from the institution, the institution shall, as soon as possible, inform the donor that the information has been provided.

Hungary

Even less information can be found about Hungary; however, the law there continues to provide for anonymous sperm donation, while allowing egg donors to elect the amount of information to be disclosed. It is unclear if the recipient would have a say in choosing an egg donor on this basis.[39] Any access to information about egg donors would be via the clinic in which the conception took place, and may or may not occur at the time of the agreement.

38 [Act on Artificial Fertilisation and use of Human Gametes and Embryos for Stem-Cell Research] 1) No. 55/1996 1) Act No. 27/2008, Article 9 as amended by Act No. 65/2006, Act No. 27/2008, Act No. 54/2008, Act No. 55/2010 and Act No. 65/2010.

39 See Act on Health, Chapter IX, 20/2007; Ministerial Decree 30/1998 – Annex 7 of 30/1885 (VI.24) NM Regulation, available at http://net.jogtar.hu/jr/gen/hjegy_doc.cgi?docid=99800030.NM, accessed 16 March 2016.

Discussion

The choice or double-track approach allows for both open-identity and anonymous gamete donation in certain jurisdictions. While some argue that the *option* for open-identity donation emphasizes the best interests of the child in having access to identifying information, such access ultimately depends on the choices of others: the donor(s) and recipient parents. When anonymous donation is chosen, most often the donor-conceived person will not have access to information (unless a system operates in which the donor will be approached and asked if he or she has changed his or her mind). Again, such an approach both illustrates a growing awareness of the need for access to information while simultaneously creating a situation where such information will not be possible for all who seek it.

Interestingly, choices of recipients at the stage of selecting a donor are based on personal preference for anonymous donation or may be influenced by cost. That is, they may not ultimately be driven by what may be in the 'best interests of the child' that will be born as a result, but rather by their own personal preference or beliefs and/or their current financial situation. In the United States, Canada and Denmark, price differentials for open-identity sperm in some cases might constrain or influence such choice thus further limiting the possibility of access to information by donor-conceived people.

In cases of either anonymous or open-identity donation, access to other information about donors at the time of selection may also be driven by recipient choice and the fact that some types of information are provided only for a fee by certain clinics.

The level of information available in different jurisdictions and at different clinics can also vary. Some jurisdictions provide (for a fee) extensive profiles including audio, personality tests, silhouettes and more, while others provide only rudimentary information.

Differences can also be found in whether the clinic provides the opportunity for connection between people who have shared the same donor(s). Some clinics now provide forums or registers that allow such interaction, albeit reliant on other parties also engaging in such places.

Thus, while there is clearly a move toward providing more choice in some jurisdictions (or in particular clinics or sperm banks), providing such choice often appears to be driven by sales or the commercial nature of the enterprise, rather than being focused on the interests of donor-conceived people who will be born as a result and who may seek identifying information. This appears to be the case, for example, in Denmark, where donor anonymity is seen as having assisted in making the Danish sperm bank industry a major business globally. The EU tissue directive ensures free movement of cells and tissues by licensed practitioners, thereby enabling the industry to ship anonymous donor sperm globally. Donor-conceived people, therefore, must consider when seeking information, whether their donor even comes from the same country in which they live. If they are the result of anonymous sperm shipped around the world, donor-conceived people in any country will find it next to impossible to discover information about their donor if that donor came from a country that upholds donor anonymity.

Clearly in such jurisdictions, as well as those jurisdictions to which they export gametes, tens of thousands of children born as a result of donor conception who may seek information will be denied access because of the decisions other people made prior to, and at the time of, their conception. This is true not only of recipient parent choice – of whether to use open-identity donated gametes (or embryos in some cases) – but also in whether the child is subsequently informed of his or her method of conception. That is, none of the jurisdictions discussed in this chapter have a mechanism to notify children of their status. Therefore, inequity continues to exist regarding whether the donor-conceived person in such jurisdictions may choose to access information.

For those who are aware of their status, voluntary registers – such as the Donor Sibling Registry in the United States – play an important role in assisting people in their search. In fact, because they are the only form of register in such jurisdictions, they are an important point of hope. DNA testing may also provide an important role. Nevertheless, they can provide no guarantee that the information sought will be found.

Although there has been increased recognition that donors, recipients and donor-conceived people may have an interest in exchanging information – and a definite increase in the availability and preference for open-identity donation – it does not guarantee access to information for all. Nevertheless, this marked shift is likely to continue to be explored and modified over time.

Chapter 6 moves to those jurisdictions that do not provide any option regarding access to information – jurisdictions that maintain secrecy and anonymity.

6 Jurisdictions that have laws enshrining anonymity

Introduction

In this chapter, examples of jurisdictions that continue to enshrine anonymous donation in law are highlighted. A consideration of the details of such laws illustrates that not all of the jurisdictions are the same. One cannot simply list jurisdictions that have laws enshrining anonymous donation because while all jurisdictions noted in this chapter have anonymity (or confidentiality) in common, some provide for the release in varying degrees of other information. Access to information by donor-conceived people thus ranges from no information to scant information about blood type and age to more detailed non-identifying information.

Reasons for maintaining anonymity are discussed in jurisdictions where the author was able to discern them; however, explicit reasons for maintaining anonymity were difficult to find in some instances. Consideration and/or critiques of such reasons, and the law, within jurisdictions are noted. Any groups or organizations that exist to assist people searching for information are also identified.

Belgium

Gamete donation in Belgium is regulated by the law 'regarding medically assisted reproduction and the destination of supernumerary embryos and gametes' as of 17 July 2007. The law stipulates that donation to others is anonymous and must be altruistic (compensation is prohibited). There is no central register for information. Clinics, including all employees, must guarantee the confidentiality of all data that might lead to the identification of the donor. For example, clinics are not permitted to tell recipients even the physical characteristics of the donor, since such information is viewed as having no medical value. Professor Guido Pennings from Ghent University in Belgium reported that when the law was being discussed, all amendments in which even non-identifying information about the donor would be provided to children were rejected. He explained the position as illustrating 'the classic view in which the donor is reduced to a sperm or egg and in which the donation is a medical treatment completely separated from the person of the donor'.[1]

The exception is Article 57 of the Belgian law which provides that 'non-anonymous donation based on the consent of the donor and the recipient(s) is allowed'. This article is currently interpreted as allowing donations in which the donor and recipient know each other prior to donation; for example, in situations of a close family member or friend. It does not provide for the open-identity situation described in Chapter 5 in which the donor is not previously known to the recipient.

All medical records of the mother may be destroyed after thirty years – that is, during the lifetime of a donor-conceived person.

In Belgium, the organization DonorKinder represents people who are calling for information.[2] Amongst other things, they seek an end to anonymous donation, the establishment of a global registration system and the breaking of the taboo on infertility and treatments with donor material. They would also like to see a cross-border DNA bank, recognizing that gametes have been exchanged across countries and that there is also a need to identify genetic siblings, and they ask for international cooperation on these matters.

Recently, the DonorKinder group has indicated that they are moving to establish a DNA database with a connection to the FIOM DNA database in the Netherlands (see Chapter 4), or to expand the FIOM DNA database in the Netherlands further, given Belgian donor children may already sign up there. There are also moves to expand existing Belgian organizations to enable Belgian donor-conceived people to be helped in their own country. One such step was to gain confirmation from the Minister of Health that a public organization known as Caw de Term and Caw de Mare, which provides counselling for 'life and family questions', would be able to support parents and donor-conceived people with personal and relational issues.[3]

Bulgaria

In Bulgaria, assisted reproduction is governed by the Bulgaria Health Act of August 2004[4] and by Order 28 on Assisted Reproduction Activities 2007 (amended 29 July 2011) of the Bulgarian Ministry of Health. According to Article 129 of the Bulgaria Heath Act, 'assisted reproduction shall be applied, where the condition of the man or the woman prevents the natural performance of their

1 Guido Pennings, 'Belgian Laws on Medically Assisted Reproduction and the Disposition of Supernumerary Embryos and Gametes' (2007) 14 *European Journal of Health Law* 251–260.

2 See DonorKinder, available at http://www.donorkinderen.com/#!news/cg4g, accessed 16 March 2016.

3 Ibid.

4 Bulgarian Health Act 2004, Part 2, Chapter 4. A translation of this Act was obtained from http://solicitorbulgaria.com/index.php/bulgarian-health-act-part-2, accessed 16 March 2016.

reproductive functions'.[5] Assisted reproduction is legally available to unmarried couples, single women and women-only couples. Sperm and egg donation are permitted, although egg donors should have at least one live birth and a maximum of five live births for sperm donors.

Donor conception must be conducted by medical establishments that have a permit from the Ministry of Health.[6] The law requires that such establishments create and maintain a register that shall contain:

1 data about each case of extraction, medical expert opinion, processing, labelling and storage of ova, spermatozoids and/or zygotes;
2 the forename, patronymic and family name, personal identity number, permanent address and unique identification number of the persons who have donated ova or spermatozoids;
3 the unique identification number of extracted ova, spermatozoids or zygotes, related to the number pursuant to Item 2.
4 the forename, patronymic and family name, the personal identity number, permanent address and unique identification number of the woman to whom ova, spermatozoids or zygotes have been implanted, related to the number pursuant to Item 3.[7]

Despite the above requirement for record keeping, the law prohibits any disclosure of data that may lead to identification of donors or recipients of ova or spermatozoids, unless ruled otherwise by law.[8] The data also has to be kept for only thirty years,[9] which means that unless the laws change, it is possible that such data may be destroyed within a donor-conceived person's lifetime.

Note that known donation is permitted with respect to egg donation, in that close relatives (sisters and cousins) are allowed to donate to each other.

The reasons lying behind the Bulgarian laws could not be further discerned in searches conducted by the author.[10]

The Czech Republic

The Czech Republic is seen as liberal when compared with surrounding countries, in that it permits egg, sperm and embryo donation.[11] Slepíčkova and Fučík

5 Ibid.
6 Ibid., Article 131(1).
7 Article 132(1).
8 Article 132(2).
9 Article 132(3).
10 NB: This does not mean that such reasons are not available, but rather language limitations and an inability to access Bulgarian documents limited the ability to further comment on the reasons for Bulgarian law.
11 Lenka Slepičková and Petr Fučík, 'Sociální kontext postojů k řešení neplodnosti / The Social Context of Attitudes towards Various Infertility Strategies' (2009) 45(2) *Sociologický Časopis/Czech Sociological Review* 267–290.

state that such surrounding jurisdictions are predominantly Catholic, leading their population to be more influenced by religion, and therefore less permissive in allowing or practicing donor conception. In contrast, the Czech Republic, which is predominantly atheist, allows a much wider spectrum of assisted reproductive treatment.[12]

In the Czech Republic, female partners are often most influential in deciding the option used for parenthood (be it adoption, fertility treatment with own gametes or donor conception).[13] Assisted reproduction is increasingly being accessed as a genetic link to offspring and is preferred to adopting a non-biologically related child.[14] Nevertheless, in the Czech Republic, the more religious people were in their attitudes, the less likely they were to consider donor conception or assisted reproduction.[15]

There is a large international market for assisted reproduction.

The law

There are three specific laws regulating gamete donation in the Czech Republic:

1 Law 227/2006 Coll. Act on research on human embryonic stem cells and related activities
2 Law No. 296/2008 (Czech implementation of the European Tissue and Cells Directive)
3 Law No. 373/2011 Act on specific health services

The laws regulate assisted reproduction and enshrine anonymous donation.

Only married couples affected by infertility can have access to medically assisted reproductive treatments in the Czech Republic, subject to both of them providing their written consent. With regard to donor conception, only adult women from age 18 to 35 can donate their eggs and men from age 18 to 40 can donate their sperm. Gamete donation is anonymous and known donors are strictly prohibited. The prohibition on known donors states that family members cannot donate to each other. Donors are selected by the doctors or clinics on the basis of a questionnaire filled out by the recipients. Non-identifying information about the donor such as age, blood type, interests and general appearance may be given to the recipients.

Gamete donation is altruistic, although donors are reimbursed for reasonable expenses.

12 Ibid., 269.
13 Ibid., 288–289.
14 Ibid., 269.
15 Ibid., 286.

Finally, it is important to note that one can import identity release gametes into the Czech Republic, albeit 'at great cost'.[16] However, this activity does not appear to be practiced widely.

Laws, practice and impact on those seeking information

Notably, reimbursement for reasonable expenses associated with the donation of gametes may be significantly higher than in other jurisdictions, especially in relation to egg donation. Speiers, an anthropologist who spent time in the Czech Republic studying assisted reproductive practices, states 'in a region where the average monthly salary is U.S.$1085 young women receive U.S.$800 per donation', further emphasizing that since many of the donors are students, they might otherwise work in a shop, earning closer to U.S. $250 to $300 per month. Speiers questions whether the egg then 'is a gift, a commodity, a scarce commodity or a commodity of last resort'[17] and notes that while the law states that gamete donation is altruistic, compensation for a person's time blurs the lines.[18]

Referring to interviews of employees at a clinic practicing donor conception, Speiers reports one as stating 'none of the girls talk about it being a gift, they are interested in the money'.[19]

Speiers notes that the anonymous aspects of donation in the Czech Republic can attract people from other countries who are seeking such donations, and there is a significant 'market oriented toward relatively wealthy foreign travelers'.[20] Clinics market in English, German, Italian and Russian, particularly stressing the availability of young student ova donors, with short waiting periods. The 'trade' in poorer women's anonymous ova is noted by Speiers as being a particularly lucrative aspect of the Czech Republic's multimillion-dollar medical tourism industry.[21] Another worker interviewed by Speiers is reported as stating in relation to the predominantly international clientele:

> Donor wise, women are happy that it's an anonymous donor. You don't have to worry about someone knocking on your door. They can be comfortable being in the no-tell camp, knowing that the donor does not even know if there is a birth, and the only thing she knows about them [the recipients] is that they exist. They don't know where you are from, they don't know how

16 Tabitha Freeman, Susanna Graham, Fatemeh Ebtehaj and Martin Richards, *Relatedness in Assisted Reproduction* (Cambridge University Press, 14 August 2014), p 220.

17 Amy Speier 'Reproductive Tourism' in Sarah M. Lyon and E. Christian Wells (eds), *Global Tourism: Cultural Heritage and Economic Encounters* (Rowman Altimira, Maryland, U.S. 2012), p 221.

18 Ibid., p 223.

19 Ibid., p 221.

20 Ibid., p 220.

21 Ibid. (Speiers notes that in 2006 the medical tourism industry in the Czech Republic was reported as being worth $182,000,000).

> old you are, they know you exist. There's a woman out there who wants your eggs, that's all they know, and that's all they ever know.[22]

The relevance for donor-conceived people is two-fold. First, perhaps one may assume that most of them will not be told of their method of conception. Second, for those who find out and seek more information about their donor or related donor siblings, they are unlikely to be able to access information.

For donors who wonder about the people created using their eggs, sperm or embryos, there is no avenue for them to find out information, including even the most basic information regarding whether there have been live births.

Perhaps for both parties, should they seek information, a DNA database is the only possibility of linking to genetic relatives. Placed on a global scale, however, the chances of matching at present continue to remain remote.

Estonia

The law

Relevant law in Estonia concerning assisted reproduction includes the penal code amended in 2007, the Penal Act amended in 2004 and the Assisted Fertilization and Protection of the Embryo Act[23] which was promulgated in Estonia in July 1997 and amended in 2003.

The penal code prohibits surrogacy, cloning, inheritable genetic modification techniques, social use of PGD and somatic genetic enhancements.

The Assisted Fertilization and Protection of the Embryo Act regulates artificial insemination of a woman with the sperm of a man and transfer of embryos created in vitro as well as the protection of embryos created in vitro. It includes regulations concerning the donation of sperm, ova and embryos – including that in Estonia, the donation of sperm, eggs and embryos is permitted for use by a woman and a man, or a single woman, and is anonymous.

Donors may be any adult man up to 40 years of age and any adult woman up to 35 years of age who is mentally and physically healthy and who has consented to donate his or her gametes for the purposes of artificial insemination and has entered into a corresponding written contract for that purpose.[24]

Taking into account that the Estonian population is less than 1.3 million, a single sperm donor cannot be used to create more than six children. Transfer of more than three embryos is not permitted.

Personal data relating to gamete or embryo donors may not be disclosed except in the case where an ovum donor is a relative of the woman who wishes to

22 Ibid.
23 Artificial Insemination and Embryo Protection Act, 1997 (RT I 1997, 51, 824), available at https://www.riigiteataja.ee/en/eli/530102013057/consolide, accessed 16 March 2016.
24 Ibid., § 25.

undergo artificial insemination.[25] After amendments to the act in 2003, however, the recipient(s) who have granted their consent to artificial insemination have the right to know the following information concerning the biological and social background of the donor:

- nationality
- colour (NB: this is presumably skin colour, as hair and eye colour are listed below)
- education
- marital status
- whether he or she has any children
- height
- constitution
- hair colour
- eye colour[26]

Children's right to know that they were donor conceived and access to information

A donor-conceived adult born because of artificial insemination has the right to ask information from a vital statistics office concerning his or her conception.[27] Donor-conceived people are also entitled to non-identifying information concerning the donor.[28] Thus, while Estonia is included among the countries that enshrine anonymous donation, it recognizes a right to know the method of conception, as well as some non-identifying information.

Donors – access to information

A donor does not have the right to require establishment of the identity of the mother, father or child, respectively.[29]

France

Since the establishment of sperm banks in 1973, medically assisted procreation with a third-party donor is estimated to have enabled the birth of nearly 70,000 people in France. Third-party gamete and embryo donation can only be

25 Ibid., § 15 and 28.
26 Ibid., § 27.
27 Ibid., § 28(1).
28 Ibid., § 28(2).
29 Ibid., § 26(4).

performed in France in public centres or non-profit organizations authorized by health authorities.

French law (and guidelines), like those of other nations, have always been influenced by the historical views of donor conception outlined in Chapter 1. Secrecy and anonymity were enshrined in early rules and practices throughout France.

Early French guidelines adopted by the Centre d'Etude Et De Conservation du Sperme (the Federation of Centres for the Study and Storage of Sperm) (CECOS) focused on sperm donation and were designed to create a situation where an altruistic couple helped another, to minimize the claim of adultery 'which [was] still associated with artificial insemination'.[30] The guidelines emphasized non-remuneration, anonymity and safety in relation to donor conception. The updated CECOS *Charter of Ethics*, issued in 1997, similarly included the following statement:

> The recruiting of donors shall be organized under conditions that respect their freedom, the voluntary nature of their act, and their anonymity, and shall not entail any coercion or pressure.[31]

The law

Introduced in 1994, the laws on donor conception in France were modeled on those concerning donated blood and organs. The law provides that donation is anonymous, free and voluntary. Known donation is also prohibited, so family members or friends cannot be donors to a person they know.[32]

Article 16–8 of the Civil Code provides that no information may be given to identify donors, donor-conceived people or recipients. Only in cases of therapeutic necessity may physicians access identifying information. The Criminal Code Article L.511.10 further imposes penalties of two years' imprisonment and 30,000 Euro fine for disclosing identifying information. The Code of Public Health (Article L.1211–5) further reiterates that identity is not released, and at L.1273–3 reiterates the penalty of two years' imprisonment and a 30,000 Euro

30 Guido Pennings, 'Gamete Donation from Couple to Couple in the New French Law' (1997) 16(4) *Reproduction* 795–804.

31 *International Digest of Health Law* 1997, 48 (3/4): 413.

32 Relevant laws, ordinances and regulations in France concerning gamete donation include Loi n8 94–654 of 29 July 1994; Loi n8 2004–800 of 6 August 2004; Décret no 2006–1660 du 22 décembre 2006 relatif au don de gamètes et à l'assistance médicale à la procréation et modifiant le code de la santé publique (dispositions réglementaires); Arrêté du 11 avril 2008 relatif aux règles de bonnes pratiques cliniques et biologiques d'assistance médicale à la procréation; Ordonnance no 2008–480 du 22 mai 2008 transposant en matière de don de gamètes et d'assistance médicale à la procréation la directive 2004/23/CE du Parlement européen et du Conseil du 31 mars 2004; Arrêté du 3 août 2010 modifiant l'arrêté du 11 avril 2008 relatif aux règles de bonnes pratiques cliniques et biologiques d'assistance médicale à la procréation; Loi no 2011–814 du 7 juillet 2011 relative à la bioéthique.

fine. Article L.1242–1 allows for medically non-identifying information to be provided by a doctor to the relevant authorized organization if there is a therapeutic necessity for a child conceived using donor gametes.

Searching for information

In 2004, a Dr Pauline Tiberghien, a reproductive physician, founded l'association Procréation Médicalement Anonyme (the Association of Medically Anonymous Procreation) which 'aims to educate health professionals, legislators and the general public about the harmful consequences of the complete anonymity of gamete donors, . . . enshrined in French law'.[33] The association states it is non-political and does not belong to any religious sect. It brings together donor-conceived people; donors who wish to make themselves known to any offspring; recipient parents who are searching for information for their child; couples considering using a third-party donor and who would like their child to know about his or her method of conception and information about the donor. The organization requests that all former donors be asked if they wish to remain anonymous and that future donors must agree to be identified on request by a donor-conceived adult.

Greece

The law

Despite many clinics existing in Greece, there was no legal regulation of assisted reproduction until 2002. Laws were introduced on 19 December 2002 when the Greek parliament approved the Law 3089/2002 Medical Assistance in Human Reproduction and on 18 January 2005 the Law 3305/2005 Application of the Methods of Medically Assisted Reproduction. Law 3089/2002 governs assisted reproduction, while 3305/2005 addresses practical issues including but not limited to the operation of assisted reproductive centres, gamete and embryo banks and provides for the establishment of the National Authority of Medically Assisted Reproduction (NAMAR). The NAMAR is responsible for the accreditation, designation, authorization, licensing and keeping of a registry of activity according to the directive of the European Parliament and of the Council of 31 March 2004 (2004/23/EC). However, its existence (and therefore its legislated functions) have been sporadic, troubled and almost non-existent over a number of years. This situation will be discussed in a later section.

Article 1460 of 3305/2005 imposes anonymity in donor situations. Offspring are not given any information about their donor, but may access medical information if there is a health issue. Known donors, including friends or family, are

33 Procréation Médicalement Anonyme website, available at http://pmanonyme.asso.fr/, accessed 16 March 2016.

not permitted. The identity of the child and its parents are not disclosed to the donor.

Views concerning assisted reproduction in Greece

Some authors have suggested that laws and practices concerning assisted reproduction do not sit comfortably with traditional Greek practices, family structures or belief systems.[34] There are conflicting views on the reasons regulation is necessary and what is or is not acceptable practice.

Recommendations of the Hellenic National Bioethics Commission, given at the time of the draft legislation, favored the introduction of the law stating that the 'widespread use of assisted reproduction methods reflects a reality that is beyond any doubt'.[35] They noted that irrespective of whether the law intervened, the use of assisted reproduction served a social interest in creating a family and recommended that the intervention of the law was necessary to the degree that it would guarantee certainty within the law in an 'area of complex social relations'. The commission stressed that:

> from a legal and ethical point of view, the right to reproduction and the right to found a family allow of limits, because of their connection with the rights of a third person and the interests of the child to be born.[36]

The National Commission said nothing more about donor anonymity than:

> The Commission considers necessary the provisions demanding confidentiality of personal information regarding the donors, the children to be born and their parents, in order to safeguard the privacy of all implicated parties.[37]

On the other hand, views concerning the Greek Orthodox position on the ethics of assisted reproduction disapproved of the legislation. In 2008, Dr Metropolitan Nikolaos,[38] the chairman of the Bioethics Committee of the Holy Synod of the Church of Greece, stated in relation to donor conception:

> IVF provides novel possibilities bearing ethical and social consequences that are hard to define. Thus, for the first time the idea of sperm and egg donation

34 Grigorios Leon, Angela Papetta and Chara Spilliopoulou, 'Overview of the Greek Legislation Regarding Assisted Reproduction and Comparison with the EU Legal Framework' (2011) 23(7) *Reproductive BioMedicine Online* 820–823.

35 Hellenic National Bioethics Commission, Comments on the Draft Bill on Medically Assisted Reproduction, October 22, 2002, available at http://www.bioethics.gr/index.php/en, accessed 16 March 2016.

36 Ibid., p 2.

37 Ibid., p 7.

38 Dr Nikolaus holds a BSc in Physics from the Aristotelian University of Thessaloniki, Greece, an MA in Astrophysics from Harvard University, an MSc in Mechanical Engineering from

> and the reproductive potential of surrogate mothers appear to be practically feasible. This may lead to the weakening or questioning of the relationship between parents and child; or to the unequal relationship between the two parents and the child – since one of the parents is natural while the other one is a stepmother or stepfather; or to the intervention of a surrogate mother . . . in the sacred relationship between the genetic parents and the child; or to the creation of brothers or sisters unknown to each other; or to the risk of unknown incestuous relationships, etc. Basically, every form of heterologous assisted fertilization degrades the concept of motherhood and fatherhood. Moreover, the requirement of a third person's intervention in the sacred procedure of human reproduction – and therefore in the mystery of marriage – makes it impossible for the Church to accept such a practice.[39]

In relation to the laws governing assisted reproduction, Dr Nikolaos said:

> It makes no reference to the child's rights and interests; it accepts heterologous fertilization in its various forms; it adopts single motherhood and accepts the birth of children with the deceased father's spermatozoa. Moreover, it introduces surrogate motherhood and allows embryo experimentation. Despite the publicly expressed reservations and objections of the Church, it basically undermines the institution of marriage, weakens the family bonds and alters the character of family ethics.

He further warned of confusion concerning biological identity for children born because of donated gametes or embryos. However, Dr Nikolaos added that:

> Heterologous fertilization . . . sometimes is identified with adultery; however, it is different since an extramarital relationship is not required, which is mainly the reason why adultery is characterized as a sinful and unethical act. Therefore, on the one hand, the Church ought to maintain Her reservations in regards to heterologous fertilization, but on the other hand She ought to avoid its being considered as adultery.[40]

Furthermore, in the same commentary, there were positive views expressed concerning 'homologous artificial reproduction' – assisted reproduction that

---

MIT, a PhD in Biomedical Engineering and Hemodynamics from Harvard University, a Master in Theological Studies (MTS), a Master of Theology (ThM) from Holy Cross School of Theology in Massachusetts, and a PhD in Theology from the University of Thessaloniki, Greece, on Orthodox Bioethics.

39 Dr Metropolitan Nikolaos, 'Symposium: Religion in Assisted Reproduction: The Greek Orthodox Position on the Ethics of Assisted Reproduction' (2008) 17(3) ***Reproductive BioMedicine Online*** 25–33, 29, available at www.rbmonline.com/Article/3548, accessed 16 March 2016.

40 Ibid., p 29.

does not involve gamete donation – likened as being equal to 'treatment of a common illness'.[41]

The views expressed by Dr Nikolaos are pertinent to this discussion because they outline reasons influencing the practice and its laws, given that approximately 98 per cent of the population is Greek Orthodox.

As time has moved on, discomfort with the reality of assisted reproduction has remained, but nevertheless increasingly it has been practiced in Greece.

In 2011 Leon et al. noted that while in the years since legislation was enacted the representation of the family in the media had moved from the traditional model, stories about such cases as older women using donor gametes to conceive children, and donor gametes being sold to the highest bidder in the United States, had been met with significant negative reactions from the general public. Leon et al. concluded that Greek society continues to be more protective of traditional family values that stand in contrast to the law which takes a more pragmatic approach to donor conception. That is, the law is characterized by the prevalence of benefits that can be obtained via reproductive technology and reflects of the reality of numerous assisted reproduction clinics in that jurisdiction, but sits uncomfortably with certain deeply held beliefs and views of the Greek public. Leon et al. noted:

> The specific legislation does not fit with the current picture of Greek society. On the one hand, it may lead to breakage of the traditional Greek family bond, and on the other, it attempts to impose foreign processes within Greek reality.[42]

In the context of donor conception, arguably some insight is gained into the reasons for secrecy and anonymity. Although the reality of the presence of clinics and use of assisted reproduction in Greece have meant that regulation was preferred, such practices do not fit with orthodox views and the social perception of family in Greece, allowing secrecy and anonymity to remain. In addition, such regulation was developed based on the practices at the time, with emphasis on the privacy of donors and recipient parents, with little consideration of donor-conceived people who might search for information in the future.

Concerns regarding Greek practice, regulation and oversight – implications for donor-conceived people

The practical reality of assisted reproduction in Greece remains apparent. In 2013, the Hellenic National Bioethics Committee delivered an opinion in which

41 Ibid., p 33.
42 Leon, Papetta and Spilliopoulou et al., above 23(7), p 823.

it commented on the control of medically assisted reproduction in Greece.[43] The committee noted that over time the country had developed a market for medically assisted reproduction services, with 'intense activity' –'both supply (approximately 60 centers) and demand (10,000 child acquisition attempts per year) were said to be "impressive for our population"'.[44] Major activities of centres had expanded to those who live abroad and Greece had become one of the primary host countries for reproductive tourism in Europe.

Within that setting, the committee also noted that 'despite the good intentions of the legislator' the control system that included the NAMAR had been inactive, absent of infrastructure and personnel for more than seven years. This inactivity had resulted in 'an overall lack of reliable statistics' from Greece regarding donor conception practices and a 'tolerance of a progressive deregulation of the sector'.[45] The commission considered that the situation required immediate action, as it 'threatened serious risks, especially to the health and family life of those who were accessing services'.[46] This situation was said to place those who wanted to have children in a vulnerable position for unlawful acts; to reduce the credibility of Greek units for providing high-quality services; and to expose Greece to the European Union as it (Greece) ignores obligations resulting from EU legislation 'on the proper maintenance and use of reproductive material (Presidential Decree 26/2008)'.

The commission urged the government to implement 'without delay', a system of screening provided by the law and re-activation of the independent NAMAR. The commission also emphasized the need for oversight of data units and cryopreservation banks for reproductive materials including gametes and embryos, which was lacking.

On 10 October 2014, it was reported that dozens of centers were operating in Greece without having been checked or authorized. It was announced that the NAMAR had been reactivated and its new president – Professor of Obstetrics, Aristidis Antsaklis – promised that sixty-seven units would be checked and licenses issued according to relevant Greek legislation. New software was also being prepared to connect the NAMAR with all units to record all methods of assisted reproduction and to ensure the traceability of the biological material according to community directives. The intention of oversight was to avoid 'adverse events'.[47]

43 Hellenic National Bioethics Committee, *Medically Assisted Reproduction in Greece* (2013), available at http://www.bioethics.gr/images/pdf/GNOMES/SYSTASH-ELEGXOS%20IYA.pdf, accessed 16 March 2016.

44 Ibid.

45 Ibid.

46 Ibid.

47 Panagiota Karlatira, 67 Units Practicing Assisted Reproduction in Greece without Authorization, available at http://www.protothema.gr/ugeia/article/418527/horis-adeia-oi-67-monades-upovoithoumenis-anaparagogis-sti-hora-mas/, accessed 16 March 2016.

Nevertheless, the situation remains that donation of gametes and embryos is anonymous. Lack of data keeping and control, combined with the practice of anonymous donation supported by law, clearly illustrates that it would be near impossible for anyone born because of donor conception in the past to obtain information about his or her donor(s). The situation for those conceived into the present remains much the same. DNA testing might again prove to be an avenue, but it would require knowledge of donor-conceived status, as well as some ability to trace distant genetic relatives.

Portugal

The law

The law that governs assisted reproductive technology in Portugal was enacted in 2006.[48] It applies to artificial insemination, in vitro fertilization; intracytoplasmic sperm injection; transfer of embryos, gametes and zygotes; pre-implantation genetic diagnosis; and other laboratory techniques for gametic or embryonic manipulation.[49] Only married people, or heterosexual couples living with each other in a de facto relationship for more than two years, may access assisted reproduction under the law.[50]

The law establishes the National Council for Medically Assisted Reproduction, which is responsible for oversight, guidance and advice in relation to such matters.[51]

Donor gametes and embryos

The use of donor eggs, sperm and/or embryos is permitted if other assisted reproductive techniques cannot achieve a pregnancy in the couple.[52] Those involved in providing medically assisted reproduction are to keep its use and the identity of participants confidential.[53]

Access to information

People born because of gamete or embryo donation may be given non-identifying information concerning their donor.[54] They may also apply to the National Council for Medically Assisted Procreation for information regarding whether there is a legal impediment to marriage such as consanguinity, which

48 Law No 32/2006 (Medically Assisted Procreation).
49 Ibid., Article 2.
50 Ibid., Article 6.
51 Ibid., Articles 30–32.
52 Ibid., Article 10.
53 Ibid., Article 15(1).
54 Ibid., Article 15(2), Article 19.

will nevertheless keep the identity of the donor confidential unless the donor consents otherwise.[55]

Notwithstanding the preceding conditions, a donor-conceived person may also obtain information on the identity of the donor for 'serious reasons recognized by a Court'.[56] However, it is unclear what such 'serious reasons' might be. Vera Lúcia Raposo, assistant professor at the Faculty of Law of Coimbra University, suggests events such as a medical condition requiring organ or bone marrow transplant, as well as possibly mental health issues – for example, 'severe depression caused by the uncertainty of personal identity and the loss of social belonging' – would require ceding anonymity.[57]

Anyone who violates the provisions of Article 15 (which relate to the confidentiality of donor sperm, eggs or embryos) shall be punished with imprisonment up to one year or a fine.[58]

Notification of donor-conceived status

The law provides that the birth certificate cannot under any circumstances contain the indication that a child was born because of the application of medically assisted reproductive techniques.

Constitutional challenge to donor anonymity provisions

Provisions for donor anonymity are considered to conflict with the Portuguese Constitution (CRP) which includes in its list of fundamental rights, the right to personal identity (Article 26/1CRP) and to genetic identity (Article 26/3 CRP).[59] However, the Portuguese Constitutional Court considered the issue in 2009,[60] holding the law was acceptable since it did not provide a blanket ban on accessing information, among other things. The following text considers the court's decision, as one may also glean some of the reasons or justifications that lie behind laws providing for anonymity in this jurisdiction.

In making its decision, the Portuguese Constitutional Court considered the laws of other countries, such as France and Spain, that provide for anonymity, and noted that Nordic and Anglo-Saxon jurisdictions had moved to provide for

55 Ibid., Article 15(3).
56 Ibid., Article 15(4).
57 Vera Lucia Raposo, 'Two Models of Regulation – Portugal vs Spain' (2012) 16(1) *JBRA Assisted Reproduction* 35–41, 40.
58 Law No 32/2006, Article 43.
59 J.C. Loureiro, O Direito a identidade Genetica do Ser Humano. In AA.VV. Portugal-Brasil Ano 2000 (CoimbraEditora, Coimbra, 1999); R.V. O Directo ao Conhecimento das Origens Geneticas (Coimbra Ediotra, 2008). Cited in Raposo above n 55, p 40.
60 Tribunal Constitucional Acórdão n.° 101/2009 Processo n.° 963/06 Acordam, em Plenário, no Tribunal Constitucional in *Diário da República, 2.ª série* – N.° 64–1 de Abril de 2009, available at http://www.cnpma.org.pt/Docs/Legislacao_AcordaoTC_101_2009.pdf, accessed 16 March 2016.

the release of identifying information (i.e. non-anonymous donations). It then considered the constitution of Portugal, which gave emphasis to different fundamental rights. It noted that on the one hand, there exists a fundamental right of the person born as a result of donor conception to personal identity, from which seems to follow a right to the knowledge of his or her genetic ancestry (Article 26, paragraphs 1 and 3, of the Constitution), and on the other hand, the right to found a family and the right to intimacy of private and family life (provided, respectively, in Articles 36, paragraphs 1 and 26, of the Constitution).

It also noted that Article 15 Law No. 32/2006 did not establish a definitive rule of donor anonymity, but only a prima facie rule, with exceptions expressly provided. To this end, the court viewed general statements about the existence of a right to knowledge of the genetic origins as losing relevance, because such information was available in circumstances of relative weight that deserve realization of that right.

In considering the issue of personal identity, the view was taken that such a concept is built over a lifetime in view of the relations therein and that biological ties are only one aspect of that right. The court noted that the Constitution presupposes a broader picture of the person, integrated into the reality of his or her family and social relationships and that the right to identity under the Constitution was therefore seen to cover different types of situations. The protection of the right to identity was by no means uniform and depended on context.

Emphasis was also given to family peace and affective ties linking the family. The court noted that due to the need to use this 'form of procreation' when others were not medically possible, the law was seen as a 'safeguard' to the 'peace and intimacy of family life, without third-party interference from donors that from the outset only intended to help the family formation'.[61] Here lies perhaps one of the reasons or views for choosing to maintain anonymity of the donor, except when there exist serious reasons not to.

Nevertheless, the Constitutional Court returned 'to underline' that the legal regime for non-disclosure of the identity of the donor was not closed. It noted that an application by a donor-conceived person could be made to the court, which would check the existence of serious reasons that justified the revelation, and that should such a case be brought, it must be considered in light of the right to identity and the right to development of personality found in Article 26, paragraph 1, of the Constitution, which, in these terms, may deserve prevalence in assessing the case. In addition, the Constitutional Court noted that the law provided individuals born from the use of donor conception all information relating to their genetic background except for the identity of the donor – with such latter release dependent on prior judicial authorization.

Considering that there was only a partial regime of the anonymity of donors, the Constitutional Court thus decided that the law did not deserve constitutional

61 Ibid.

censure. However, the point continues to be one of disagreement.[62] For example, Raposo, a member of the Center for Human Rights and the Center of Medical Law at Cumbria University, stated in 2012 that both provisions in the CRP act as a constitutional base for the right for everyone to know his or her personal history, including a right to know his or her genetic origin. Raposo argued that as a result, the current laws regarding donor anonymity are unconstitutional, *even when joined by the referred exceptions.*

South Africa

The law

Egg and sperm donor conception was regulated in South Africa by the Human Tissue Act of 1983 (for egg and sperm donations) and the Children's Act of 2005; enacted to govern issues related to donor-conceived and surrogate children. The Children's Act also covers parenting rights and responsibilities.[63] Donation should not be commercial, but reimbursement of costs and some 'compensation' is allowed.

Children born because of artificial fertilization or surrogacy may access medical and genetic information about the donor or the surrogate mother, but are not entitled to identifying information.[64] They may be required to undergo counselling before medical or other non-identifying information is released to them.

Known donations are permitted; however, in such circumstances, psychological evaluation and legal advice for the sperm donor, the intended mother and partner (if applicable) is recommended.[65]

Reasons for legislative position

The reasons behind the laws in South Africa concerning anonymous donation are difficult to discern, other than the historical reasons outlined in Chapter 1 of this book – including stigma about infertility (particularly male) and the secrecy that has surrounded the practice generally since its inception.

The current laws are framed within an act that emphasizes children's rights. However, in the South Africa Law Commission 2002 Report on the Review of

62 J.C. Loureiro 'O Nossa Pai e o Dador: A Questao do Anonimato dos Dadores de Gametas na Procriacao medicamente Assistida Heterologa' (2010) 7(13) *Lex Medicinae* 5–42. Raposo, above n 55, p 41.

63 Children's Act 38 of 2005, Chapter 3 Part 4 (40): Rights of child conceived by artificial fertilization.

64 Children's Act 38 of 2005, s41. (Access to biographical and medical information concerning genetic parents.)

65 Policy Committee of the SASRSS: Selection of the Sperm Donor, P4, Guidelines for gamete donation 2008.

the Child Care Act,[66] which discussed proposed changes to that act, nothing was said to explain the position taken regarding only partial release of information for donor-conceived children. Rather a statement was made as follows:

> The Commission also recommends that neither the recipient nor the child should have access to the information regarding the donor's identity. However, the Commission is convinced that children born as a result of artificial insemination procedures have a right to have access to medical and biographical information concerning their genetic parents. The Commission therefore recommends that the confidentiality provisions in the Human Tissue Act 65 of 1983 be amended to allow children born of artificial insemination access to medical and biographical information concerning their genetic parents. However, access to biographical information should be limited to children over the age of 18 years. We would like to stress that we see this as the right of the child, and not that of the donor or recipient of the gametes.

Once again, there is recognition of a right to information, but one that falls short of providing identifying information about the donors. The reasons behind this decision are unclear.

Spain

Spain historically has emphasised anonymity in relation to donors of gametes (and embryos). In 1996, Jaime Martinez, a professor of Civil Law at the University of Valencia, wrote of the numerous historical reports and commentators within Spain that had supported anonymity.[67] For example, he noted one council's comments in 1979 that considered the anonymity of the donor as 'essential' for reasons first to ensure donation of sperm did not become non-existent and second for reasons of the 'well-being' of the child.[68] Other reasons have included the practical difficulty of administering a system on the right to information of one's genetic parentage, religious beliefs condemning the practice, issues surrounding adultery and legitimacy of the child, a right to privacy of the donor, the right to personal and family privacy of the recipients and an unquestioning acceptance of the status quo.

66 South Africa Law Commission, *Report on the Review of the Child Care Act*. December 2002. (Project 110), available at http://www.justice.gov.za/salrc/reports/r_pr110_01_2002dec.pdf, accessed 16 March 2016.

67 Jaime V. Martinez 'Anonymity of the Donor in the Spanish Act on Techniques of Assisted Reproduction' in D. Evans (ed), *Creating the Child* (Kluwer Law International, 1996), pp 217–228, 220.

68 Ibid.

The law

In Spain, gamete donation (eggs and sperm) is regulated by the Law 14/2006 on Human Assisted Reproduction Techniques. In addition, there are two relevant royal decrees: 1) the Real Decreto 412/ 1996, which addresses compulsory study protocols for donors and ART users; and 2) the Real Decreto 1301/2006, which establishes rules regarding quality and safety for donation, including the collection, evaluation, processing, storage and distribution of human cells and tissues.

Donation is anonymous and confidentiality of the donors is guaranteed. The medical team not only selects the donor but also must guarantee the maximum degree of phenotypical and immunological similarity and compatibility with the recipient and her social environment.

Recipients and donor-conceived people are entitled to obtain non-identifying information about the donor, such as blood type, age and height, but are not entitled to identifying information.

Only in exceptional circumstances can other information about the donor be released. Those circumstances must be related to a danger regarding the life and health of the child (Article 5/5 law n.14/2006).

Known donation is not mentioned in the law, but it is generally presumed prohibited due to the emphasis on donor anonymity.

Notification of donor-conceived status

The law in Spain provides that origin of parentage cannot be recorded in the Civil Registry (article 7.2). Donor-conceived people conceived in Spain will not know of their status unless it is shared with them by their parents.

Criticisms of anonymity in Spain

In 1996, Professor Martinez criticized the laws enshrining anonymity in Spain, stating that 'maintaining anonymity in artificial insemination by donor was an "ad hoc" construction, contrary to defending the interests of the person most directly involved – the child'. He further criticized the laws as fulfilling the interests and eliminating the responsibilities of the other people involved in artificial insemination, thus impeding the rights and interests of the child.[69] He argued that anonymity contravened both constitutional and civil rules of law in Spain and that a child has a right to know his or her donor.

Ever since, similar arguments have been made. For example, Esther Farnós Amorós of the Universitat Pompeu Fabra notes there has recently been a change to laws regarding adoption in Catalan, emphasizing the importance of knowledge

69 Martinez, above n 67 p 222.

of a person's biological roots.[70] Since 21 July 2015, access to such information has been made available to adoptees.[71] Such laws, however, do not extend to donor conception because the Catalan Parliament does not have authority over this matter. Amorós said this situation further highlights the restricted scope (or interpretation) of another Spanish law that addresses the Rights and Opportunities of Children and Adolescents,[72] according to which children and adolescents have the right to know their genetic origin, biological parents and biological relatives, and commented that such a law is not being applied to donor-conceived people – but that it should be.

Amorós further notes that laws across regions in Spain guarantee a right to access information by adoptees and do 'not affect the parents' right to personal or family privacy, since the law protects the circumstance of the adoption from public knowledge and is subjected to restricted public access in the Civil Registry'. In addition, she argues that

> the increasing dissociation between the different spheres of parentage . . . the tendency towards a society with families based more on roles than on biology, and a distancing from the image of donor-parent are all arguments that suggest that a revision of the doctrine [that emphasizes a donors' right to privacy, amongst other things to ensure a continued supply of donor gametes,] is in order today.

In supporting her view, she states that arguments by anonymity supporters regarding 'moral damage resulting from disclosure' or 'the possible link between disclosure and a decrease in the number of donors' are not supported by evidence. Amorós then adds:

> Alternatively, disclosure of the donor's identity is consistent with the needs of donor families and with a major trend in family law supporting the right to know one's genetic origin, dissociated from biological and legal parentage.[73]

Discussion

In the jurisdictions discussed in this chapter, donating eggs, sperm or embryos is only permitted on an anonymous or confidential basis. However, the level of other information available and who may access such information again varies. Thus, even within the jurisdictions categorized as falling into the anonymity

70 Esther Farnós Amorós, 'Donor Anonymity, or the Right to Know One's Origins?' (2015) Catalan 5 Social Sciences Review, 1-10. Original source: Butlletí del Comitè de Bioètica de Catalunya, 15: 1–11 (2015) (http://canalsalut.gencat.cat/ca/home_ciutadania/actualitat/llista_butlletins/bioetica/butlleti_de_bioetica/). Translated from Catalan by Mary Black.

71 Decree 169/2015 dated the 21st of July 2015; DOGC no. 6919 dated 23rd of July 2015.

72 Law 14/2010 dated 27 May 2010, article 30.2.

73 Amoros, above n 70, p 1.

domain, the level of other information available and who may access such information differs greatly. Some jurisdictions prohibit the release of any data, while others provide explicitly for the collection and release of non-identifying information. On the other hand, some jurisdictions do not mention the collection or provision of non-identifying information at all.

When non-identifying information is collected or released, the amount of information made available again varies. Some jurisdictions allow only for the release of medical information. Others allow for basic levels of physical descriptors (such as age, hair colour and eye colour), in addition to medical information. Others allow for medical records, physical description and social information (such as interests, education and reasons for donating) or psychological data to be released.

In countries that require donors be matched phenotypically to the partner of the recipient woman (or to the woman in the couple), whether explicit provision for recording and releasing non-identifying information is mandated, the general physical characteristics of a donor may be presumed to match those of the recipients – thus, indirectly providing some information about the donor.

Finally, some jurisdictions in this chapter provide for exceptions to their rules on donor anonymity or the release of identifying and non-identifying information. First, some jurisdictions allow the release of such information in situations where there is a serious reason or exceptional circumstance – for example, a serious disease or illness that requires direct contactor interaction with the donor (e.g. a need for organ transplant) or medical information from the donor. Second, there may be provision for people to check that they are not related to another person with whom they wish to enter marital relations.

In exploring reasons for the laws and practices in the jurisdictions discussed in this chapter, some of these laws reflect past practices when secrecy was emphasized and anonymity a given for all parties involved. These laws are simply a continuance of what has been practiced for a long time. In some jurisdictions, secrecy and anonymity may continue to exist because of stigma regarding infertility or donor conception. This stigma is particularly strong concerning male infertility where sperm donation is needed, but it may also apply to female infertility which requires egg donation. In others, the reasoning relies on an intellectual separation of donation of gametes and the process of insemination as a 'medical treatment', the latter being seen as unconnected to the people involved. The privacy of donors and recipients is also often emphasized.

Religious beliefs also influence the preference for donor anonymity. The Greek Orthodox Church, for example, decrees that assisted reproductive practices devalue the sacred concept of motherhood and fatherhood by the introduction of third-party donor egg or sperm. As 98 per cent of the population are devout followers of the Greek Orthodox Church, gamete donation may remain anonymous because of the stigma surrounding the practice for those who seek assisted reproductive technologies, as well as those who donate ova or sperm. Anonymity in Spain also has a significant history in the religion and beliefs of that country.

In addition, anonymity is often found in jurisdictions where assisted reproductive clinics are a chief component of multimillion-dollar medical industries. Here, the resulting offspring is not considered, nor is their possible future quest for information on their donor because the focus is on sales and profit. This is supported by the fact that in the modern era, one of the arguments put forward for maintaining anonymity is fear that the removal of anonymity will result in a reduction of supply or demand. To this end, reasons for maintaining anonymity in the jurisdictions in this chapter also mirror those discussed in relation to jurisdictions that provide for both open-identity and anonymous donation. That is, they appear to be market based or focused on the people who seek treatment; they do not appear to be focused upon the child born as a result. The situation in the anonymity jurisdictions, and the reasoning behind their laws and practices, is thus notably similar to some jurisdictions mentioned in earlier chapters.

Criticisms have been levelled at the jurisdictions discussed in this chapter, similar to those in jurisdictions discussed in Chapter 5, regarding the denial of children's rights and interests in gaining information. Arguments appear to be building as people witness other jurisdictions recognizing such rights and interests and move toward prohibiting anonymous donations, notifying donor-conceived people of their status and providing for information release.

As with other places around the world, some people have set up organizations or support groups for those who seek information that also serve a significant role in lobbying for change. Links to DNA databases in other nations are also being made. Even within jurisdictions that have a long history of anonymous donations, things can change and are changing.

Part III of this book considers the arguments underpinning secrecy and anonymity more closely and weighs them against arguments for information release.

Part III

Anonymity or openness?

7 Examining arguments underpinning donor anonymity

Introduction

This chapter further examines some of the arguments that have been put forward in support of secrecy about donor conception and anonymous sperm, egg and embryo donation. It will be shown that none of the arguments justify the continuance of such practices. The chapter begins by considering the few arguments put forward in support of maintaining secrecy and anonymity that focus on the donor-conceived person directly before moving to consideration of the reasoning that predominantly focuses on the adults involved, or the possible effect removing anonymity may have on the fertility industry. It will highlight the flawed reasoning in many arguments put forth to convince others that anonymity should prevail. It will also show that such arguments do little more than perpetuate unhealthy stigma and shame. It is also noted again that while perceived threats to supply and demand often drive the desire to maintain an option for anonymity, open donation may not in fact 'kill' the industry. In light of this scenario, there needs to be consideration of how to support people when faced with infertility, while moving to end the secrecy, shame and anonymity that surrounds donor conception. Furthermore, the interests and needs of donor-conceived people, and not profit, need to prevail.

Arguments focused on donor-conceived people

Few of the reasons given for maintaining secrecy and anonymity relate to the children born because of donor conception. This section begins by considering those few that do. First, it examines the attempt to compare one-night stands and misattributed or unknown paternity in the general population to donor-conceived people being denied information. Second, it considers the view that as most current registers do not require active notification of donor-conceived status, true recognition of donor-conceived rights to information has not been given, and consequently, the notion of registers or information release should be dismissed. Third, it discusses the argument that Derek Parfit's 'non-identity problem', which recognizes that our choices can affect who exists in the future, supports the maintenance of donor anonymity.

The first and second arguments were seen in Chapter 5 to have been ones that underpinned the earliest guidelines in Denmark that supported donor anonymity. Clinicians sometimes still mention them today.[1] One legal scholar in the United States, Glenn Cohen, whose position is that donor anonymity should be maintained, puts forward all three arguments in support of anonymity.[2]

Although these arguments are not used by lawmakers in jurisdictions that maintain anonymity, such arguments provide for the opportunity to explore perceptions that surround donor conception and different ways of arguing for and against donor anonymity – thus, adding further rigor to the debate. That being so, although each of the arguments is used in an attempt to dismiss the call for openness, each in turn serves only to distract from the real issues faced by those seeking information. The proponents of such arguments show little knowledge, empathy or understanding of donor-conceived people's search for information or the reasons that lie behind such a search. The arguments themselves lack convincing justification to maintain laws or practices that enshrine secrecy and anonymity.

One-night stands and unknown paternity

The first argument to be considered here presents the lack of access to information by donor-conceived people about their donors as being analogous to the 2–5 per cent of children born in any given population that have misattributed or unknown genetic parentage. This situation may be due to a one-night-stand (i.e. when a woman has sexual intercourse with a person she meets who was not previously known to her, and they do not meet again) or infidelity in which a woman has an affair (usually with someone known to her, such as a friend, neighbor, brother-in-law, work colleague or other acquaintance). In rarer cases, it may result from the rape of the woman by an unknown assailant.

The argument referring to those who have misattributed or unknown genetic parentage is used in the context of donor conception to dismiss calls for information. Simply stated, it proposes that the denial of information to donor-conceived people, which leads to them not knowing their genetic parentage, should be accepted because, after all, there are other people in the population who don't know their genetic parentage. When the argument is made by fertility doctors, they are dismissing the voices of donor-conceived people born as a result of the doctors' very practices.[3] When seized on by scholars, their 'clever' arguments are an attempt to give force to what is clearly an unsatisfactory response to the call for

1 Professor Michael Chapman, IVF Specialist and Head of the Fertility Society of Australia on 'Who made me?' – Life Matters – ABC Radio National (Australian Broadcasting Corporation), 9 December 2015, producer Lindy Reine, presenter Natasha Mitchell, interview regarding information release and donor conception. Available at http://www.abc.net.au/radionational/programs/lifematters/who-made-me/7011832, accessed 16 March 2016.

2 I. Glenn Cohen, 'Response: Rethinking Sperm-Donor Anonymity: Of Changed Selves, Nonidentity, and One-Night Stands' (2012) 100 *Georgetown Law Journal* 431.

3 Chapman, above n 1.

information. That is, an argument that equates donor conception to a one-night-stand is deeply flawed and serves only to mislead. It equates differing scenarios to each other and distracts from engaging with issues relevant to donor conception, and experienced by those born as a result.[4] Consideration of the differences between the two situations (which are significant), and the arguments presented in relation to attempts to equate the two, illustrates this further.

Knowledge of the identity of the genetic parent

The first, and most obvious difference in the two cases, is that in many cases of misattributed or unknown parentage, the woman who has had sexual intercourse will in fact know the identity of the other genetic parent. The mother of a person with misattributed or unknown parentage in such circumstances may disclose the identity of the genetic parent at some point in the future.

In contrast, in cases of anonymous gamete or embryo donation, the system established by the fertility industry establishes anonymity and non-disclosure to recipients and offspring in such cases. The mother and her partner (if any) are not told the identity and are therefore not aware of whom the mother is procreating with. They are unable to disclose and have no rights to find out who the genetic parent is.

Rights to access information differs

Legal rights to access information also differ in cases where there has been sexual intercourse and genetic parentage is misattributed or unknown. In such situations, should the genetic parentage be unknown (or in doubt),[5] the woman, the woman's husband/partner, the child (usually via their representative), and/or the genetic parent, may in a number of jurisdictions seek to gain a court order to establish, or confirm, genetic parentage. A court may order DNA paternity testing of a person suspected to be the genetic parent. Where such access to DNA testing has been obstructed or delayed, the European Court of Human Rights (ECtHR) has found that a child has a right to have uncertainty as to his or her personal identity eliminated without unnecessary delay and that the state has a duty to establish alternative means to enable an independent authority to determine the paternity claim speedily.[6]

In stark contrast, in the case of donor-conceived people, in jurisdictions that maintain anonymity, the recipient parent(s) or donor-conceived person is not given the right to seek a court order for a DNA test to establish the genetic

4 One could thus refer colloquially to such an argument as a 'red herring'.

5 For example due to the woman having kept such information secret, due to the woman having been raped, due to her not knowing the man she had sexual intercourse with, or due to her being unsure of who the genetic parent may be.

6 *Mikulić v. Croatia* (European Court of Human Rights, Application No 53176/99, 7 February 2002). NB. Human rights issues are discussed further in Chapter 8.

parentage – even if he or she has a suspicion of who the genetic parent might be. Only in the most exceptional cases do some (but not all) jurisdictions that maintain anonymity allow identifying information be released. Most donor-conceived people are left with no knowledge and no means to ascertain their genetic heritage.

The need for a register of information differs

The attempt to equate one-night stands with donor conception also moves to oppose the release of information by attempting to reject arguments about the *modes* of information release. Cohen, for example, argues that as there is no register for those conceived via one-night stands, and such a register would be unacceptable, proposals for a donor conception register should also not be accepted. He refers to his argument as a 'Modest Proposal' presented in 'Swiftian tradition', presumably intended to satirize arguments for donor registers.[7] However, the attempt at a Swiftian-style argument distracts from the issues faced by donor-conceived people, recipients and donors surrounding access to information. It is also flawed and fails to convince that information concerning donor conception should not be recorded and released for the following reasons.

A register for births that result from one-night-stands already exists

A major flaw in the argument regarding a register for one-night-stands (be it presented as satirical or not) is that it fails to recognize that the law does in fact require the truthful registration of births that result from sexual intercourse. A register for children born of one-night-stands thus already exists, and is generally referred to as the 'register for births, deaths and marriages' (or some similar name) in every jurisdiction around the world. As noted earlier, in many instances a woman who has had a one-night stand will know the identity of the person with whom she has had sexual intercourse. Should she conceive and subsequently give birth, the law requires her to truthfully register the child's genetic parentage at the register for births. Such information will then appear on the birth certificate of that child. There may be penalties imposed for providing false information.

The fact that a woman may choose to lie when registering the birth of her child does not alter the existence of the law or the register for births. The law, however, also provides for situations in which untruths are told (i.e. misattributed parentage) and for circumstances in which the genetic father is truly unknown. In such

7 Note Swift's 'Modest Proposal' was a satire that mocked heartless attitudes toward the poor, as well as Irish policy in general, through the proposal that poor people might ease their economic burden by selling their children as food for the rich. In modern times, the 'Modest Proposal' is an allusion to this straight-faced form of satire. Note – attempts at mocking, ridiculing or deriding the call by donor-conceived people (or those that advocate for them) might be seen as deeply offensive and insensitive to their lived experiences, a 'clever' attempt at dismissing their search for information that is of fundamental importance to them.

instances, in many jurisdictions the law provides for court-ordered DNA paternity testing and amendment of the birth certificate should the truth of genetic parentage be revealed or confirmed. Therefore, the genetic parent can be discovered and named (i.e. identified) – as well as having legal parentage rights and responsibilities (e.g. having to pay child support).

In contrast, in many jurisdictions the law does not require truth in the registration of birth when a child was conceived because of the use of donor gametes. The law instead creates a legal fiction regarding legal parentage and permits (or enshrines) the registration of the social parent(s) (e.g. the woman who has undergone treatment and her partner) at the register of births and on the birth certificate. The law does not provide donor-conceived people (or their parents) with the right to apply for a court-ordered DNA testing of a suspected genetic parent, nor does it allow them to change the birth certificate to show the donor's name.[8] The donor thus remains anonymous.

A register for truthful information concerning donor-conceived people would simply treat them equally to others – whether operationalized via the general register of births or on a separate register that facilitates access to specific information concerning the donor conception.

Third-party involvement – for profit; and the application of public funds

In the situation of donor conception, one must also not ignore the heightened need for record keeping given the involvement of third parties in the process – including clinics that are making significant profit and governments that fund assisted reproductive treatment with public monies. In fact, the commercial nature of such practices, public funding of procedures and the reality of the large number of offspring that may result create a situation in which record keeping and traceability of donors is of utmost importance. However, in many jurisdictions that maintain the anonymity of donors, record keeping is not legally regulated. Information about how many donor-conceived people there are, whose sperm was used to conceive them and how many times such sperm was used to produce other children cannot be established. Good practice relies on faith, and little more.

Let us also not forget that donor conception is presented as a medical treatment, provided by registered medical practitioners who receive private and public funds on that basis. Record keeping concerning treatment in all other medical contexts is absolutely required, whether or not the outcome of such medical

8 Note in June 2014, Emma Cresswell, a donor-conceived female, applied successfully to Bristol County Court (UK) to remove from her birth certificate the name of the man she knew as her father (Mr Faint) and who was named on her birth certificate as such did in fact allow alteration of the birth certificate. However, this case did not place the name of the donor on the certificate, but rather replaced the social father's name with 'unknown'.

treatment proves 'successful'. In contrast, coital reproduction is not a medical treatment. It is not premised on third-party involvement from profit directly related to the creation of a child, nor is it publically funded. It is also not applied in ways that may result in hundreds of related offspring.

A register that records information about the donor, recipient, treatments and outcomes of such treatments would thus not only provide much needed information to offspring about their donors and siblings but it would also serve to heighten the likelihood of good medical practices and truth in record keeping, an ability to trace and track the use and applications of gametes and numbers of resultant offspring, and to monitor and assess the outcomes of treatments by a profitable industry that also receives, in many instances, public funds.

The recording and release of information regarding births that result from coitus is, as noted previously, already required by law.

The 'spread' and use of donor gametes

Next, consider the 'Modest Proposal' in terms of the realities of, and differences among, the number of children that may result from the respective methods of procreation being compared.

In the modern era of donor conception, gametes may be procured in one location and shipped to another, they may be cryopreserved (frozen) and the same donor's sperm may be used many times to impregnate many different women, over many years. Significant numbers of genetically related offspring may, and do, result. The situation is the same for sperm used many times in the same area, over a number of years. As we saw in Chapter 2, this practice may increase not only the risk of unwittingly engaging in a consanguineous relationship but also the fear. It may also have other psychosocial impacts on donor-conceived people (and donors) who have siblings (or offspring) that may run into the hundreds.

In comparison, one-night stands or affairs do not involve shipping gametes all over the world or maximizing profit by attempting to impregnate as many people as possible. In fact, the 'spread' of gametes in such situations is most likely very limited. It is highly unlikely that the children who are the product of an affair or a one-night stand, are going to have the same number of genetically related offspring as donor-conceived people. It would be the rare case rather than the norm (if such a case existed at all) that the same man who has a one-night stand or an affair would be having sex with five or ten[9] (or more) women at or around the same time (either locally or internationally), causing each one of them to become pregnant potentially more than once over a number of years, (potentially producing fifty or more children over a period of a few years). It would also be extremely

9 These numbers are chosen from jurisdictions that limit the application of donor sperm to five to ten families (or women). In fact, a number of jurisdictions do not impose limits within the law, and there have been reported hundreds of siblings found.

unlikely that one man would be having sexual intercourse in a manner that results in the pregnancies of tens to hundreds of women worldwide over time.

Two wrongs don't make it right

Finally, on the point of comparing misattributed or unknown parentage that results from an affair, one-night stand or even rape to donor conception, it should be acknowledged that some people born as a result of the former encounters, despite legal provision to assist them, will not be able to obtain information that they seek. Their parent(s) will continue to lie to them, or they will not be able to establish who their genetic parent is. They too may experience a variety of feelings and personal consequences associated with this situation.

However, the fact that other people in the population similarly face the challenge of seeking information about their genetic parentage, or are denied knowledge of who their genetic parent really is, does not mean that donor-conceived people should also be denied access to such information. It would be more reasonable to suggest that in all situations people should be assisted in determining as far as possible their genetic heritage, regardless of how they were conceived, rather than stating that the existence of one problem justifies the maintenance of another.

Notification of donor-conceived status

The next argument to be considered points to systems that have prohibited anonymity but have not included a mechanism that alerts people to their donor-conceived status. Therefore, some argue that the right to information has not truly been recognized and thus should be dismissed. This argument was used to support early guidelines in Denmark that provided for donor anonymity, and again by Cohen who refers to 'passive' registers and their lack of notification to people of their donor-conceived status.

Cohen correctly notes that when rights and interests are recognized regarding access to information, then some more active way of notifying donor-conceived people of their status is most likely needed. This is particularly so given that a significant number of recipients may not tell their children. However, Cohen rejects the 'active' approach because he sees it as 'frightening' and 'less desirable' than passive registers.[10] Further explanation as to why he holds such fears is not presented.

Cohen's expression of 'fear' is followed by a statement about three options that – in his mind – people have. First, he recognizes that some people may accept the active register, but Cohen simply dismisses this factor. Second, Cohen offers his preference, which is to give consideration to the active register as a way to 'help us reach reflective equilibrium on the passive registry and doubt some

10 Cohen, above n 2, p 447.

of the arguments . . . put forward in favor of it'.[11] He also offers a third option regarding only providing information to those people who know of their status and therefore may be 'harmed' by their donor conception.[12]

Notably, the latter 'option' is intertwined with consideration (and rejection) of Naomi Cahn's presentation of the call for information as one based on donor-conceived people suffering 'harm' and is also dismissed. However, I note that 'harm' to donor-conceived people is not the only reason for information release and may not always exist. Furthermore, there is an obvious underlying assumption by Cohen that those who are not told of their status must not be affected by secrecy or anonymity – something that many donor-conceived people would disagree with. Just like adoption, many people who were not told of their status early, but who did find out later, have said they always knew something was not being said or that there was a family secret or that they suspected they were not biologically related to their family. Cohen does not, it appears, have any significant understanding of the lived experiences of donor-conceived people.

Moreover, neither consideration of the *kind* of register that might be established nor rejection of the 'passive register' approach means that secrecy about conception and anonymity of donors must be maintained. The fear of actively telling children they are donor conceived may surely perpetuate the status quo but does not justify it.

In fact, consideration of the kind of registers that may be used draws attention to more complex issues of how to give true recognition to the rights and interests that donor-conceived people have to information about their status and their donor. Thus, some jurisdictions that release information have realized that not only is it important to provide access to information, but it is also important to be open and honest about the method of conception. The latter may include active notification to donor-conceived people of their status via an addendum to the birth certificate, the presence of which may serve to encourage recipients to disclose earlier.[13] Examples of these approaches detailed in Chapter 4 are found in Victoria, Australia, Ireland, Argentina and Croatia. Western Australia and the United Kingdom also have active programs to educate, facilitate and support recipient parents in telling children of their status.

Parfit's non-identity problem applied to donor anonymity

The final argument for maintaining anonymity that relates directly to the birth donor-conceived people is one that uses 'Parfit's non-identity problem'.[14] Parfit's

11 Ibid.

12 Ibid.

13 Early disclosure is said to lead to better outcomes for children. See reference.

14 The non-identity problem (also known as the 'future individual paradox') was first mentioned by T. Schwartz, 'Obligations to Posterity' in R. Sikora and B. Barry (eds), *Obligations to Future Generations* (Temple UP, Philadelphia, 1978), pp 3–14; and R. Adams, 'Existence,

non-identity problem is a philosophical argument that is 'rooted in the observation that future persons may sometimes owe their very existence and identity to choices made by present persons – choice[s] that . . . appear to make things worse for those same future persons'.[15] In such cases, however, if one chooses a different course of action, those future persons would not be born at all, but rather a different person – a 'non-identical' other – would be born.[16]

In the donor conception context, the problem is presented by focusing on future [albeit currently non-existent] children who may be born within anonymity regimes, as a result of anonymous donation. The argument is put forth that if donor anonymity is prohibited, some people who would have donated anonymously will not donate at all. Therefore, the child that would have been born using that anonymous donor's sperm, eggs or embryos will not be born at all. It is then argued that as the child cannot be said to be worse off by not having access to information about its donor than if it had never been born at all, one cannot logically reject donor anonymity on the basis of it being in 'the best interests' of the child.[17] 'Intellectual jousting' over Parfit's non-identity problem then ensues.

The application of Parfit's non-identity problem to assisted reproduction is not new. Others have written about it in the context of considering issues such as physical risks of IVF and ICSI, risks of multiple gestation, risk of transmission of genetic and/or infectious disease, risks of inadequate or incompetent child rearing, pre-implantation genetic diagnosis, sex selection, genetic manipulation, alternate family formations and more.[18] The problem has many critics, as well as critics of the critics, in turn. Some are said to 'misunderstand the argument', others are said to 'simply deny its logic' without explanation, while others are seen to 'directly engage the argument and try to identify weaknesses and counter-moves'. Others yet 'acknowledge that the problem is unavoidable under person-affecting theories of harm and search for nonperson-based theories to resolve it'.[19] I will do none of these things here.[20]

Self-Interest, and the Problem of Evil' (1979) 13(1) *Nous* 53–65; then in more detail by Kavka, 'The Paradox of Future Individuals' (1981) 11 *Philosophy & Public Affairs* 93–112, and most famously by D. Parfit, *Reasons and Persons* (Oxford UP, Oxford, 1984).

15 Melinda A. Roberts and David T. Wasserman (eds), *Harming Future Persons: Ethics, Genetics and the Nonidentity Problem* (Springer, New York, 2009), p 348.

16 Ibid.

17 Cohen, above n 2.

18 See for example, John A. Roberts, 'Procreative Liberty and Harm to Offspring in Assisted Reproduction' (2004) 30 *American Journal of Law and Medicine* 7–40.

19 Ibid., 14.

20 For examples of responses to Cohen's application of the problem to donor anonymity, see Bridget J. Crawford, 'Authentic Reproductive Regulation' (2012) 96 *Minnesota Law Review Headnotes* 31, available at http://www.minnesotalawreview.org/wp-content/uploads/2012/05/CrawfordFinal.pdf, 2; Helen M. Alvaré, 'A Response to Professor I. Glenn Cohen's Regulating Reproduction: The Problem with Best Interests' (2012) 96 *Minnesota Law Review Headnotes* 8, available at http://www.minnesotalawreview.org/wp-content/uploads/2012/05/Alv areFinal.pdf, 3; and Kimberly M. Mutcherson, 'In Defense of Future Children: A Response to Cohen's Beyond Best Interests' (2012) 96

Parfit's non-identity problem and the law surrounding donor conception

I acknowledge the application of Parfit's non-identity problem in this context as a logical philosophical thought experiment, discussed by philosophers and bioethicists with passion, and applaud the intellectual prowess and vigor with which they engage the problem. However, the bottom line is that Parfitt's non-identity problem does not ultimately resolve the issue of what the law should provide in relation to donor conception or release of information to donor-conceived people about their donors. While logically put in the context of any one issue chosen, it does not consider the multitude of other happenings or choices from large to minute that, through the same logic, may result in a different, 'non-identical' other being born at any given moment. The law is not and cannot be based on ensuring the *future* birth of any *particular* non-existent hypothetical donor-conceived child.[21]

Nor does Parfit's non-identity problem render politicians and lawmakers bound to passing or preserving a particular law, especially if the law or absence thereof on a matter leads to a practice or outcome that is determined as unacceptable. The law instead acts to order our society, and to reflect values, rules and mores by which the society lives. Because it is often responsive to practices, it changes as knowledge develops, as social and cultural views shift, or as problems are identified that need to be addressed. The law serves to 'right' wrongs, to ensure justice and equality and to recognize and uphold the rights and interests of people who exist. In the donor conception context, we have therefore seen laws passed around the world, from 1984 to the modern day, to prohibit anonymous donation based on a wide variety of factors discussed in this book. These factors include 'best interests' considerations in some circumstances; however, often they have emphasized other social values such as truth, honesty, openness and the rejection of treating people as a means to an end. They have also emphasized legal rights and the interests of those people who are actually born, including those based on equality, human rights and access to justice. In addition, much consideration has been given to the psychosocial consequences and real-life experiences of donor-conceived people, donors and recipients, the impact that secrecy and anonymity has had on them and the need to ensure access to the information they seek. No 'clever' argument can diminish this reality nor justify the continued denial of information to them.[22]

Minnesota Law Review Headnotes 46, available at http://www.minnesotalawreview.org/wpcontent/uploads/2012/05/MutchersonFinal.pdf.

21 Parfit's non-identity problem may be seen in some form in the reasoning in which wrongful life claims have been rejected in the tort of negligence in which it has been said damages were incalculable due to a requirement to compare existence to non-existence. However, in these cases, the child has already been born.

22 See further Naomi Cahn, 'Do Tell! The Rights of Donor Conceived Offspring' (2014) 42 *Hosfra Law Review* 1077.

Other jurisdictions, of course, continue to enshrine anonymity – albeit none of them based on reasoning that emphasizes or even considers Parfitt's non-identity problem. As was seen in Chapter 1 and Chapter 6, and is further discussed in this chapter, often such jurisdictions maintain secrecy and anonymity as a result of historical and/or continuing religious rejection of assisted reproductive practices, stigma and/or shame surrounding infertility, a view that donor conception equates in some way to adultery and/or economic profit evaluations driven by supply-and-demand considerations of clinics and sperm banks that believe they will make more money if anonymity is maintained. Interestingly, many of these reasons focus on the adults providing gametes or seeking treatment, or the clinics that derive significant income from current practices, ***and not on the children at all.***

Nevertheless, consideration of Parfit's non-identity problem does remind us that alternative choices, emphasis or actions can lead to alternative outcomes and futures. The choices we make regarding laws and practice must be carefully considered and justified, and as we do this, we must remember that we are not forever destined to maintain the status quo – laws can serve to address past mistakes, change today's practices and determine what tomorrow brings.

Focusing on the adults

Thus far we have seen that, mostly arguments advocating for donor anonymity have little if anything to do with those arguments considered above. Most often they have much more to do with the history of donor conception and secrecy: stigma surrounding infertility and assisted reproduction; notions of adultery that focus on adult promiscuity (and associated condemnation and shame); and in modern times the fear of losing supply or demand and thus the large profits made by the fertility industry. The discussion here will not reiterate historical reasons for secrecy and anonymity and analysis provided in Chapters 1 and 6, but will further focus on the latter three issues in more depth.

Stigma surrounding infertility and assisted reproduction

One of the major reasons for secrecy and anonymity has been the stigma[23] surrounding infertility, as well as the treatments that have been applied such as donor insemination. Stigma concerning infertility continues to exist in the present day.

23 Erving Goffman, one of the most influential sociologists of the twentieth century, defined stigma as the phenomenon whereby an individual with an attribute which is deeply discredited by his or her society is rejected as a result of the attribute. Stigma is a process by which the reaction of others spoils normal identity: Erving Goffman, *Stigma: Notes on the Management of Spoiled Identity* (Prentice-Hall, Englewood Cliffs, N.J. 1963).

It may also at times extend to donors of gametes or providers of assisted reproductive services.[24]

While in the early days of assisted reproduction and donor conception, doctors were most likely acting only with the good intent of assisting childless couples to have a family, unfortunately, rather than supporting people to openly address feelings and attitudes about infertility, doctors actively encouraged secrecy and anonymity. The legacy has been great. Although those couples did have families, the stigma for them and within society about their infertility and use of donor conception remained (and was often reinforced). Understanding what stigma is and its negative effects, however, illustrates that it is a problem associated with donor conception that needs to be addressed, rather than a reasonable justification for maintaining secrecy and anonymity.

What is stigma and what is the result?

A person may experience stigma in many ways. Stigma may be *perceived*, which refers to how people perceive others to feel about them, for example, in relation to their infertility, their intention to use donor conception and/or their lack of genetic connection to a child born as a result; *experienced*, in which a person may suffer some disadvantage or discrimination because of others' negative reactions to such things; and/or *internalized*, which refers to a stigmatized individual incorporating others' negative perceptions, beliefs or attitudes into his or her own self-assessment, resulting in reduced self-esteem or feelings of guilt or shame.

The emotional and physical effects of infertility may manifest differently in males and females, and differ across cultures.[25] These manifestations can be compounded by the presence of stigma.

In jurisdictions in which assisted reproductive treatment is permitted and available, women may undergo invasive and repeated medical procedures and suffer the physical and psychological aspects of failed treatment and of pregnancy loss. Some studies have found significantly higher reported levels of distress, strain, anxiety and depression in women related to infertility.[26] They may have perceived, experienced and or internalized stigma around not being able to achieve pregnancy easily or at all.

24 Rebecca J. Cook and Bernard M. Dickens, 'Reducing Stigma in Reproductive Health' (2014) 125(1) *International Journal of Gynecology and Obstetrics* 89–92.

25 It has been recognized that many more studies on infertile men in non-Western societies need to be conducted to understand the cultural impact on infertility. Results of studies conducted so far indicate that the emotional impact of infertility on men may be much stronger in more traditional-oriented cultures and in cultures where reproductive medicine treatment is still a social taboo. In many such cultures, the donation of sperm, eggs or embryos, and donor conception, is prohibited.

26 P. Slade, C. O'Neill, A.J. Simpson and H. Lashen, 'The Relationship Between Perceived Stigma, Disclosure Patterns, Support and Distress in New Attendees at an Infertility Clinic' (2007) 22(7) *Human Reproduction* 2309–2317, first published online, accessed 19 June 2007, doi:10.1093/humrep/dem115.

Male factor infertility is reported to be even more stigmatized than other infertility diagnoses, and males have been said to have fewer acceptable outlets for the expression of their emotional distress.[27] (Note that studies on the psychological impact of invasive reproductive treatment measures on infertile men are still missing.)[28]

For both men and women, it has been found that higher perceived stigma was related to lower perceptions of available social support, which in turn can lead to greater distress, anxiety and/or depression.[29]

Does stigma justify secrecy and anonymity?

While stigma has been, and at times continues to be, an underpinning reason that people may be secretive about donor conception, it may add to anxiety and depression, and does not in fact justify secrecy or donor anonymity. In fact, it has been suggested that taking into account patients' perceptions of stigma may help identify those at greater risk of distress, and that counselling around the issues of stigma and disclosure might be helpful.[30] One might further argue that, in a clinical context, given the research knowledge of the negative effects stigma and associated secrecy can produce, it would be negligent of practitioners to encourage secrecy and anonymity. That is, such action may add to feelings of shame and stigmatization, rather than reducing distress, and in turn have significant physical and psychological impact on those who seek assisted reproductive services.

Counselling and support

Therefore, instead of perpetuating stigma and shame, which in turn can compound feelings about infertility and donor conception as a treatment option, the provision of counselling and support must be recognized as an important part of assisted reproductive treatment. Counselling prior to, during and after treatment plays an important role in lowering rates of depression and anxiety about infertility, as well as addressing perceived, experienced and/or internalized stigma. It may also support people in understanding the importance of disclosing information to the people born as a result and educating them about it – rather than perpetuating secrecy and anonymity.

27 T. Wischmann and P. Thorn, '(Male) Infertility: What Does It Mean to Men? New Evidence from Quantitative and Qualitative Studies: Impact of Infertility on Men' (2013) 27(3) *Reproductive BioMedicine Online* 236–243.

28 Ibid.

29 P. Slade, C. O'Neill, A.J. Simpson and H. Lashen, 'The Relationship Between Perceived Stigma, Disclosure Patterns, Support and Distress in New Attendees at an Infertility Clinic' (2007) 22(7) *Human Reproduction* 2309–2317, first published online, accessed 19 June 2007, doi:10.1093/humrep/dem115.

30 Ibid.

A number of countries now recommended as a minimum that pretreatment counselling involve:

- acknowledging the past and all previous efforts of the person/couple to have a child;
- supporting the person/couple in grieving their infertility and/or the way they imagined they would have a child;
- tackling the stigma of infertility and information sharing with others;
- preparing for disclosure to the child.[31]

The initial stages of counselling may help people to deal with their feelings surrounding infertility and biological parentage, before moving to work on issues related to stigma and disclosure. All of the issues are intertwined. Strengthening the ability to accept one's infertility, cope with feelings concerning biological connection with children and to develop confidence about one's family choices may also diminish feelings of stigma and shame.

A final note for this section should emphasize that stigma and shame are not just products of the feelings of recipient parents – but rather may be perpetuated by clinicians who encourage secrecy or a society and culture that sees infertility as a failing. Education and discussion of infertility to promote understanding and openness within communities, as well as among health professionals, is therefore essential and is again preferable to continued secrecy and shame.

Betrayal and adultery

Closely related to, or perhaps an aspect of, the stigma surrounding infertility and the use of donor conception are views that donor conception is akin to adultery or a one-night stand.

As was seen in Chapter 1, the view that adult recipients and donors were somehow committing adultery by engaging with donor conception was prominent in the nineteenth century, has been emphasized within religious rejection of donor conception and is clearly still held by some proponents who support donor anonymity today. This view was illustrated by the dismissal of donor-conceived people seeking information by equating them to the 2–5 per cent of the general population that have misattributed or unknown genetic parentage (i.e. those

31 G. McCluskey and P. Gilbert, *Implications Counselling for People Considering Donor-assisted Treatment* (BICA Publications, York, 2015); P. Thorn, 'Recipient Counselling for Donor Insemination' in S.N. Covington and L.H. Burns (eds), *Infertility Counseling: A Comprehensive Handbook for Clinicians* 2nd edition (Cambridge University Press, Cambridge, New York, 2006), pp 305–318; P. Thorn and T. Wischmann, 'German Guidelines for Psychosocial Counselling in the Area of Gamete Donation' (2009) 12 *Human Fertility* 73–80; T. Wischmann and P. Thorn, '(Male) Infertility: What Does It Mean to Men? New Evidence from Quantitative and Qualitative Studies: Impact of Infertility on Men' (2013) 27(3) *Reproductive BioMedicine Online* 236–243.

born as a result of adultery or one-night stands). In relation to the application to adults who undergo treatment, and/or donors of gametes or embryos, the view also remains. For example, Clearly Cohen's views, discussed above, do not just attempt to discount the call for information release to donor-conceived offspring he implicitly and explicitly draws analogies with the act of coital adultery or one-night stands for the adults involved.

Such views are also reflected in the response by Professor Guido Pennings, a Belgian bioethicist, to findings of a government-led inquiry in Victoria, Australia, in 2012 that supported retrospective release of information to all donor-conceived people.[32] Pennings responded strongly in favour of maintaining anonymity and non-disclosure of donor details by stating (among other things) that there may be feelings of 'shame' and 'betrayal' by the partners of donors.[33] Pennings further questioned whether counselling would prevent the partner of the donor from feeling betrayed by the partner's donation. It is noted here that as with the earlier discussion about stigma and counselling for recipients of donor conception, similar counselling could, and probably would, help donors and their partners if such feelings did exist.

However, I question why advocates of donor anonymity, who argue that donor conception is acceptable, explicitly or implicitly perpetuate shame and encourage notions of adultery or betrayal.

It is an unfortunate situation (perhaps in fact an outrage) when academics, lawyers, clinicians and/or ethicists in the modern day equate donor conception to acts that are generally unaccepted and frowned on, albeit occurring, in our society – and yet insist that we continue to use such techniques while maintaining secrecy and anonymity. If there is nothing wrong with gamete or embryo donation, then why not encourage and support the adults involved – be they recipients, donors and the partners of donors – to feel proud, rather than slighted by notions of adultery, betrayal and shame. Otherwise, why allow the practice at all? Thus, while notions of adultery, betrayal and shame may underpin arguments for secrecy and anonymity, they do not justify it.

Availability of donors – effects on supply and demand

Finally, I want to address again the concern that removing donor anonymity may result in a decreased supply in donors of gametes and/or demand from those seeking donor conception anonymously (or the more sensationalist claim that removing anonymity will 'kill' donor conception).[34] Although this issue does not

32 Victorian Law Reform Committee, *Inquiry into Access by Donor Conceived People to Information about the Donors* (March 2012). The call for retrospective access to information by adult donor-conceived people is further discussed in Chapters 8 and 9.

33 Guido Pennings, 'How to Kill Gamete Donation: Retrospective Legislation and Donor Anonymity' (2012) 27(10) *Human Reproduction* 2881–2885, first published online, accessed 10 July 2012, doi:10.1093/humrep/des218.

34 Ibid.

warrant much further discussion here, it is important to reiterate that such concern is most often expressed by people who work within (or in close connection to) the fertility industry. Often it is accompanied by focus on maximizing sales and profits, and not on the people who are born as a result. As such, the argument provides no basis on which to maintain donor anonymity.

Besides this, it should be noted that supply and demand have neither decreased nor waned in countries that prohibit anonymous donation. For example, in 2007 the United Kingdom HFEA reported that '[t]he number of men registering as sperm donors rose by 6% in the year following the law removing donor anonymity'.[35] The number of donors in that country has steadily increased each year since with a slight dip in 2013. As noted in Chapter 4, in Finland, the number of donors also increased after the removal of donor anonymity. Similarly in Victoria, Australia, in 2015 the Victorian Assisted Reproductive Authority reported that 'the number of new donors registered in 2014–15 was 298, which is more than double the number in the previous financial year (120)'.[36] The fear may thus not speak to what the reality would be should donor anonymity be prohibited.

However, regardless of what the outcome would be, what is most important – and often seems forgotten in calculations of profit, fears about killing the industry, and supply and demand – are the donor-conceived people who must live with the consequences of secrecy and anonymity. It is, therefore, highly questionable that a profitable industry should decide, based on monetary calculations, to deny information about genetic heritage to an entire group of people who result from its very practices. It is even more questionable that a government would support them in doing so. The following words of Albert Franz, a donor-conceived person, resound:

> The psychological and emotional effect that [anonymity] has on many of us should not be taken for granted. . . . We have to end anonymity. . . . We have a right to know our origins. . . . There are a lot of things that need to be decided for us [as children], but I believe who we are is not one of them. Our identity should not literally be a corporate or state secret. It must be considered our birth right.[37]

35 Human Fertilisation and Embryology Authority, 'Number of Sperm Donors Up Following Anonymity Law Changes', available at http://www.hfea.gov.uk/465.html, accessed 16 March 2016.

36 Victoria Assisted Reproductive Treatment Authority, *Annual Report 2015*, p 7.

37 Albert Frantz, 'Identity Theft: How I Discovered My Secret Identity', TedX, San Francisco. Albert Frantz is a prize winning pianist and Fullbright Scholar, who grew up in a multi-racial family with a number of adopted siblings. He found out via a family friend that he was donor conceived. He discussed his views on donor anonymity a TEDx event in San Francisco using the TED conference format which was independently organized by a local community organization. It is available at https://www.youtube.com/watch?v=PligpIZzT98 published 29 December 2015, accessed 16 March 2016. (More information about Tedx events may be found at http://ted.com/tedx).

Conclusion

When those who argue for anonymity focus on donor-conceived people, they do so by dismissing the donor-conceived person's search for identifying information about his or her donor, equating a donor-conceived person's situation to others in the population born of one-night stands who may have misattributed or unknown parentage, and showing little insight into the lived experiences of people born into either position. The discussion in this chapter showed how such arguments are flawed, as are attempts to argue against donor registers.

Existential thought experiments also fail in providing any kind of foundation on which to base the law.

In fact, modern-day arguments concerning donor anonymity appear to be steeped in nineteenth- and twentieth-century views. They equate donor conception with one-night stands or adultery, perpetuate stigma surrounding infertility and do little to bring acceptance to either the practice of assisted reproduction or the process of adults conceiving children using donated gametes or embryos. While stigma is of major concern for people who face infertility, more needs to be done to support them – it is not a solution to reinforce or perpetuate their struggles, secrecy and shame.

In addition, one cannot ignore the ever present driver of the fertility industry – money. Scratch the surface of the vehement arguments to maintain anonymity and we find third-party clinics, clinicians, sperm banks and the fertility industry that may believe they will be financially served by the continuation of donor anonymity. There is a clear commercial underpinning to the belief that the wider variety of people they can get to donate, the more recipients they can cater to and the more money that can be made. For some, therefore, the concern is that if donor anonymity is removed, supply and demand will reduce and profits will fall. In fact, removing donor anonymity will not necessarily 'kill' the industry but rather will change it – as has occurred in those jurisdictions that have already moved to prohibit donor anonymity. Whatever may happen, the focus on profit is no basis on which to deny people information about their genetic heritage and their identity. Chapter 8 further explores the fundamental human right to know such information.

8 Placing the issues in a human rights framework

With the previous discussion in mind, this chapter moves to consider the issue of a right to information about genetic heritage within a human rights framework. It notes that the issue of competing interests is also often raised when considering whether a release of information should occur. That is, there is often discussion that the quest for information by donor-conceived people may compete with the interests of donors who wish to remain anonymous. Although this view does not in fact always see reality – as many donors also call for information release and sharing – this chapter considers how to balance respective interests when they do compete.

First, the human rights that may be engaged are identified.

Next, the chapter engages in a substantive human rights analysis in which the accepted approach of *balancing* rights in accordance with methodology used to resolve conflicts between competing rights holders is applied to the context of donor conception. This is done through discussion of cases heard by the European Court of Human Rights in which applicants have sought information about their genetic parentage in other contexts such as DNA testing for paternity and adoption. Principles that may be drawn from these cases are then identified. Next, with these principles in mind, a human rights analysis is applied in the abstract, to the situation of donor-conceived people searching for information and the competing right of donors to privacy – as there is clearly no actual case before the ECtHR.

The chapter examines arguments in relation to prospective removal of anonymity regimes (i.e. that anonymous donation should be prohibited for all future donations) and touches on the issue of retrospective release of information to donor-conceived people. The latter issue is further examined in Chapter 9. It is argued in this chapter that moving forward all children born as a result of donor conception should have access to information and knowledge of the circumstances surrounding their conception and birth; and that there is some support within a human rights framework also for retrospective release of information provided the approach adopted was proportionate and balanced any competing interests.

Human rights engaged for information release

There have long been arguments that place the issue of access to information by donor-conceived people about their donors within a human rights framework. For example, in 1998, Ramsey stated:

> Principles from the domain of human rights can provide an important framework for responding to one of the most pressing challenges confronting reproductive technology . . . access by donor offspring to information about their origins. . . . [P]ut at its most succinct, from a human rights perspective, one might ask the question – how can one argue against the basic human right to know one's genetic identity?[1]

Articles of the *Implementation Handbook for the Convention on the Rights of the Child* have also been used to justify laws in some European nations that prohibit anonymous donation and require information release.[2] In particular, Articles 7, 8, 3(1) and 13 have been raised as being relevant.

Article 7 of the Convention specifies that 'every child has a right to know and be cared for by their parents as far as possible'.[3] This arguably includes his or her genetic parents. The phrase 'as far as possible' exists 'as recognition of the potential that the identity of a parent may be unknown (for example due to rape) and it may simply be impossible for a child to know his or her parent(s)'.[4] It does not mean that there is a right to withhold information about a child's genetic or biological parent.[5] Tobin argues, therefore, that Article 7 'should be interpreted to create a presumption in favour of providing children with access to information about their biological parents before they turn 18 . . . if the information is available'.[6]

Further, with respect to Article 7, the *Implementation Handbook for the Convention on the Rights of the Child* states:

> [A] reasonable assumption is that, as far as the child's right to know his or her parents is concerned, the definition of "parents" includes genetic parents

1 S. Ramsey, 'Keeping Secrets and Telling Stories', opening address at Donor Issues Forum organized by the South Australian Council on Reproductive Technology, Adelaide, 30 May 1998.

2 For example, Sweden and Norway.

3 *United Nations Convention on the Rights of the Child*, opened for signature 20 November 1989, [1991] ATS 4 (entered into force 2 September 1990).

4 J. Tobin, 'Donor Conceived People and Access to Information About Their Genetic Origins: The Relevance and Role of Rights' (2012) 19(4) *Journal of Law and Medicine* 742; See also S. Allan, 'Access to Information about Donors by Donor Conceived Individuals: A Human Rights Analysis' (2013) 20 *Journal of Law and Medicine* 655., p 749.

5 Ibid.

6 Ibid., 749.

> (for medical reasons alone this knowledge is of increasing importance to the child) *and* birth parents, that is the mother who gave birth and the father who claimed paternity through partnership with the mother at the time of birth (or whatever the social definition of father is within the culture.[7]

Although such commentary is not binding, the statement nevertheless offers strong support for recognizing the claim by donor-conceived people for information about their donor(s). As early at 1994, the United Nations Committee on the Rights of the Child noted the possible contradiction between Article 7 of the Convention and the policy of some state parties 'in keeping the identity of sperm donors secret'.[8]

Similar emphasis has been placed on Article 8 of the *Implementation Handbook for the Convention on the Rights of the Child*, which provides that 'every child has a right to preserve her or his identity, including nationality, name and family relations' as recognized by law without unlawful interference. Denying donor-conceived people access to information about their genetic heritage may contravene this right by denying them access to important information that can help in the development of identity and preserve family relations. With respect to this article, the *Implementation Handbook for the Convention on the Rights of the Child* notes:

> The concept of "children's identity" has tended to focus on the child's immediate family, but it is increasingly recognized that children have a remarkable capacity to embrace multiple relationships. From the secure foundation of an established family environment, children can enjoy complex and subtle relationships with other adults and with a range of cultures, to a much larger degree than may be recognized. Thus children's best interests and senses of identity may be sustained without having to deny them knowledge of their origins, for example after reception into state care, through "secret" adoptions or anonymous egg/sperm donations and so forth.[9]

The Convention on the Rights of the Child (CRC), therefore, emphasized the need for states to maintain records critical to establishing the identity of a child, including details of a child's familial relations.[10]

Next, Article 3(1) may also be relevant. Article 3(1) provides that 'in all actions concerning children, whether undertaken by public or private social welfare institutions, courts of law, administrative authorities or legislative bodies, *the best interests of the child shall be a primary consideration*' [italics added]. The best

7 R. Hodgkin and P. Newell, *UNICEF Implementation Handbook for the Convention on the Rights of the Child* 3rd edition (United Nations, Switzerland, 2007), p 105.
8 Norway CRC/C/15/Add.23 at [10].
9 Hodgkin and Newell, above n 7, p 142.
10 See Committee on the Rights of the Child, *Concluding Observations for Norway*, CRC/C/15/Add23 at [10].

interests of the child in this context would arguably include being able to access information about his or her biological heritage, if he or she wanted.[11] In particular, their psychological health and well-being and the development of their identity may be supported by access to such information. Information release may also help them to avoid consanguineous relationships and gain knowledge of genetic relatives.

Last, Article 13 provides that the child shall have the right to freedom of expression, which includes the 'freedom to seek, receive and impart information and ideas of all kinds'. Denying donor-conceived individuals the right to seek and receive information about their genetic heritage may, therefore, contravene this right.[12]

There are clearly human rights under the CRC that may be engaged in relation to donor conception and the release of information. However, it is important to recognize that the scope of these rights remains unresolved. Interpretation and comments suggest that they support information release to donor-conceived children; however, this information release needs to be given effect by parties actually recognizing such 'rights' pursuant to the CRC. Only some countries have done so.

In addition, in considering the applicability of the CRC to this issue, there may be an obstacle for donor-conceived *adults* who are denied access to information. Arguably, a state would only be bound by the provisions of the CRC if the state was a party to it at the time of conception or throughout the donor-conceived person's childhood.[13] If the state was not a party to the CRC at that time, the person would not have cause for complaint under its provisions which do not apply retrospectively.

Therefore, it is important to consider other applicable rights that apply to all individuals and are named in other conventions.

The right to privacy for donor-conceived people

Donor-conceived people may also claim that their search for information entails the right to privacy. The right to privacy, as it appears under Article 17 of the International Covenant on Civil and Political Rights provides that:

1 No one shall be subjected to arbitrary or unlawful interference with his privacy, family, home or correspondence, nor to unlawful attacks on his honour and reputation.
2 Everyone has the right to the protection of the law against such interference or attacks.

11 The current author does not argue that all donor-conceived people will want information, but rather that, for those who do, it is in their best interests to be able to access such information.

12 The exercise of this right may be subject to certain restrictions as provided by law and are necessary (i) for respect of the rights or reputations of others; or (ii) for the protection of national security or of public order, or of public health or morals. The "right to privacy" of donors may be raised in relation to (i) and is discussed further below.

13 Tobin above n 4, fn 27.

Its equivalent may be found in Article 8 of the European Convention on Human Rights, which concerns the right with respect for private and family life. The focus of the following discussion lies in Article 8, as it has been considered in both the direct context of donor conception, as well as other contexts in which people seek to identify biological history, by various courts.

In the donor conception context, the English High Court in *Rose v. Secretary of State for Health and Human Fertilisation and Embryology Authority* [2002] EWHC 1593 (Admin) held that the right to privacy was engaged in relation to a donor-conceived person seeking information about his or her donor.[14] It recognized a 'right to obtain information about a biological parent who will inevitably have contributed to the identity of his child'. The court said in relation to Article 8:

> The bottom line . . . is that the donor provided half of each Claimant's genetic identity and it is this that creates the interest of the Claimant to seek information about him. . . . What therefore are the principles to be drawn from the authorities that are relevant to this case? They seem to me to be these:
>
> - Private and family life is a flexible and elastic concept incapable of precise definition.
> - Respect for private and family life can involve positive obligations on the state as well as protecting the individual against arbitrary interference by a public authority.
> - Respect for private and family life requires that everyone should be able to establish details of their identity as individual human beings. This includes their origins and the opportunity to understand them. It also embraces their physical and social identity and psychological integrity.
> - Respect for private and family life comprises to a certain degree the right to establish and develop relationships with other human beings.
> - The fact that there is no existing relationship beyond an unidentified biological connection does not prevent Article 8 from biting.

Rose followed the opinion expressed by the European Court of Human Rights that people "have a vital interest, protected by the Convention, in receiving the information necessary to know and to understand their childhood and early development".[15] However, it did not resolve the issue of whether information should or could be released. A substantive human rights approach requires

14 The court was only required to determine whether the right to privacy had been engaged on the facts of the case and made no determination as to whether the refusal to release identifying information would constitute a violation of this right.

15 *Gaskin v. United Kingdom* (1990) 12 EHRR 36 at [48].

balancing the rights of donor-conceived people against the right to privacy of donors in accordance with the methodology used to resolve conflicts between competing rights holders.[16] This determination is discussed next in the context of donor conception following an outline of what the donor's right to privacy entails.

The donor's right to privacy

The right to privacy also offers a counterpoint on which a donor may argue against the release of identifying information as the right to privacy includes the right to control personal information,[17] which may include information concerning a donor who donated sperm on the condition of anonymity. A donor may, therefore, argue that releasing his identifying or non-identifying information would interfere with this right.

However, although the right to privacy is given significant weight in most jurisdictions, this does not mean that the donor has an absolute right to anonymity. The right to privacy itself is not absolute. In fact, the right to privacy is a 'qualified right' that may be interfered with provided such interference is not arbitrary and is lawful.

There are many clear exceptions to the protection of private or confidential information in many areas of the law.[18] There exists statutory provision in some jurisdictions for the release of identifying information in relation to the reporting of communicable diseases;[19] suspected child abuse;[20] supply of certain drugs,

16 This methodology has become popular in human rights discourse and is increasingly being applied in international human rights courts. However, the approach has also been criticized particularly for failing to recognize (or at least masking) the moral and political questions that are essentially part of a human rights analysis: see e.g. G.C.N. Webber, 'The Cult of Constitutional Rights' Scholarship: Proportionality and Balancing' (2010) 23(1) *Canadian Journal of Law and Jurisprudence* 179; S. Tsakyrakis, 'Proportionality an Assault on Human Rights?' (2009) 7(3) *I.CON* 468.

17 S. Warren and L. Brandeis, 'The Right to Privacy' (1890) 4 *Harvard Law Review* 193.

18 L. Skene, 'Genetics and Artificial Procreation in Australia' in M-T. Meulders-Klein, R. Deech and P. Vlaardingerbroek, *Biomedicine, the Family and Human Rights* (Springer, Sydney, Australia, 2002), p 110.

19 See e.g. *Public Health and Well-Being Act 2008* (Vic), s 127; *Public and Environmental Health Act 1987* (SA), s 30; *Health Act 1911* (WA), ss 276, 300; *Public Health Act 1997* (Tas), ss 48, 49, 61 and 50(1)(c); *Public Health Act 2010* (NSW), ss 54, 55, s 56(4); *Notifiable Diseases Act 1981* (NT), s 8(1)(b); *Public Health Act 2005* (Qld), ss 70–73; *Public Health Act 1997* (ACT), s 102.

20 *Public Health Act 2005* (Qld), ss 158, 191–193; *Child Protection Act 1999* (Qld), s 148; *Commission for Children and Young People and Child Guardian Act 2000* (Qld), s 20; *Children, Youth and Families Act 2005* (Vic), ss 182, 184; *Children, Young Persons and Their Families Act 1997* (Tas), ss 13, 14; *Children's Protection Act 1993* (SA), s 11; *Family and Community Services Act 1972* (SA), s 73; *Children and Young Persons (Care and Protection) Act 1998* (NSW), ss 23, 27; *Community Welfare Act 1983* (NT), s 14(1); *Care and Protection for Children Act 2007* (NT), ss 23, 26; *Children and Young People Act 2008* (ACT), ss 356, 362; *Children and Community Services Act 2004* (WA), ss 101, 124B. In the United

or supply of drugs of addiction to registered addicts;[21] reportable deaths (to the coroner);[22] illness affecting driving ability;[23] and impairment affecting a registered health professional's ability to practice.[24] These exceptions are intended to protect others from harm, including risks to people's health and well-being. By analogy, the issues that may affect the health or well-being of donor-conceived people denied information may outweigh the need to keep information pertaining to the donor private.

Beyond the recognition of protecting the health and well-being of people, the release of identifying information to adoptees about their biological parent(s) provides another example of where the right to privacy has been lawfully 'interfered' with.[25] Such release reflects principles of equality and non-discrimination (both also human rights). For example, in Queensland, Australia, laws passed in 2010 to enable the retrospective release of information to adoptees about their birth parent(s) were explained as follows:

> [T]his retrospective removal of their rights must be balanced with the benefits that arise by allowing other parties to those adoptions access to information about their identity, family and heritage. The change in the law also ensures that parties to adoptions are treated equally, regardless of when the adoption occurred, as there is no longer any entitlement to object to the release of identifying information.[26]

The analogy between adoptees and donor-conceived people who search for information about genetic heritage is one that is clearly recognizable and was discussed in Chapter 3 and is again further discussed in Chapter 9.[27]

Assessing proposed interference: balancing competing rights

Generally, when assessing the reasonableness of a proposed or actual interference with a human right, cases that come before the courts deal with facts. For

States see e.g. USCA Title 42, Ch 67, § 5106, Federal Child Abuse Protection and Treatment Act.

21 See e.g. *Poisons Regulations 1965* (WA), reg 51FE.

22 See e.g. *Coroners Act 2003* (Qld), ss 8, 17; *Coroners Act 2008* (Vic), ss 4, 10–13; *Coroners and Justice Act 2009* (UK).

23 See e.g. *Motor Vehicle Act 1959* (SA), s 148; *Pennsylvania Code*, Ch 83. Physical and Mental Criteria, Including Vision Standards Relating to the Licensing of Drivers.

24 See e.g. *Health Professions Registration Act 2005* (Vic), s 36.

25 See e.g. *Adoption Act 1993* (ACT); *Adoption Act 2000* (NSW); *Adoption of Children Act 1994* (NT); *Adoption Act 2009* (Qld); *Adoption Act 1988* (SA); *Adoption Act 1988* (Tas); *Adoption Act 1984* (Vic); *Adoption Act 1994* (WA).

26 *Adoption Bill 2009* (Qld), Explanatory Memorandum, pp 19–20, available at http://www.legislation.qld.gov.au/Bills/53PDF/2009/AdoptionB09Exp.pdf, accessed 27 April 2012.

27 Noting that the analogy is drawn in relation to a search for *information* and not the circumstances in which adoption or donor conception takes place. Also see Chisholm, above n 2.

example, in the context of information release about biological heritage, there will be a person searching for information and either (i) a bill or enacted law that prevents the person from accessing it, or (ii) another person arguing that his or her rights will be interfered with to an unacceptable degree should such information be released. The first part of this section considers cases that have come before the European Court of Human Rights in relation to people searching for information about their biological parent. These cases, while not concerning donor conception per se, usefully illustrate the applied approach that human rights cases take, provide insight into the balancing process and provide a perspective into how the court has viewed state obligations regarding information release to people who search for genetic parents.

The second part of this section engages with the balancing of competing rights in the context of donor conception. Here, the discussion of balancing competing rights must take place in the abstract (as there is no case before the court). Nonetheless, we can assume that such a case might present itself in circumstances in which a donor-conceived person searches for information and the current law does not provide for such access, the law requires release of information to donor-conceived people and a donor challenges such release, or a donor is contacted prior to release and does not want the information to be released.

Balancing rights in other information search contexts

In *Rose v. Secretary of State for Health and Human Fertilisation and Embryology Authority*, the English High Court held that Article 8 of the *European Convention on Human Rights* was 'engaged' with respect to a donor-conceived person searching for information about his or her biological heritage. However, that case did not illustrate the balancing process necessary to weigh competing rights. A number of cases considered by the European Court of Human Rights have applied the balancing process in relation to Article 8 in other contexts in which people have sought information about a biological parent.[28]

In *Gaskin v. United Kingdom*,[29] the applicant who had been placed in public care in the United Kingdom as a baby, where he stayed until he reached his majority, had requested access to the records kept on him by social services but was given only partial access. The European Court of Human Rights decided that Gaskin's Article 8 right to have his private and family life respected by the state had been breached by the British government because there had been no independent appeal body to which he could have taken his case. The court also decided that people in Gaskin's position, who had been in public care as children, should not in principle be obstructed from accessing their care records – these

28 The focus from here on is on Article 8 of the European Convention on Human Rights as this is the right that has been considered in cases concerning the search for information. However, the same analysis could arguably be applied using any of the rights considered throughout this article.

29 European Court of Human Rights, Application No 10454/83, 1989.

records acted as the memories of parents, to which most individuals had access but to which people in Gaskin's position did not.[30] It has been noted that the emerging principle from *Gaskin* is that Article 8 creates a 'right to deeply personal data', Steyn and Slarks noting that 'the data will not be personal enough if it simply relates to the claimant. [However] . . . a positive obligation [will] arise under Art 8, [if] the data [is] necessary for the claimant to establish the details of his or her own identity'.[31]

In the 2002 case of *Mikulić v. Croatia*,[32] the applicant, a 5-year-old girl, complained about the length of a paternity suit that she had brought with her mother. She also complained about the lack of procedural means available under Croatian law to enable the courts to compel the alleged father to comply with a court order for DNA tests to be carried out. The European Court of Human Rights weighed the vital interest of a person in receiving the information necessary to uncover the truth about an important aspect of her or his personal identity against the interest of third parties in refusing to be compelled to undergo medical testing. The court held that the procedure available did not strike a fair balance between the right of the applicant to have her uncertainty as to her personal identity eliminated without unnecessary delay and that of her supposed father not to undergo DNA tests. It found that the state had a duty to establish alternative means to enable an independent authority to determine the paternity claim speedily, and there had been a breach of the proportionality principle regarding the interests of the applicant, who had been left in a state of prolonged uncertainty about her personal identity.

In *Odièvre v. France*[33] the European Court of Human Rights considered Article 8 was also applicable in the case of an adopted person searching for information about her biological mother. The court reiterated that Article 8 protected, among other interests, the right to personal development which included a vital interest in obtaining information necessary to discover the truth concerning important aspects of one's personal identity, such as the identity of one's parents. The court held that birth, and in particular the circumstances in which a child was born, formed part of a child's – and subsequently the adult's – private life guaranteed by Article 8. Furthermore, individuals were entitled, in the name of biological truth, to know their personal history and any inability to gain access to this information that is imputable to the state interfered with Article 8. *Odièvre*, however, did not find in favour of releasing identifying information about the biological birth mother in this circumstance. The applicant had been given access

30 See also *MG v. United Kingdom* (European Court of Human Rights, Application No 39393/98, 24 September 2002) at [27].

31 K. Steyn and H. Slarks, 'Positive Obligations to Provide Access to Information under the European Convention on Human Rights' (2012) 17(4) *Judicial Review* 308, 310–311. Steyn and Slarks further note that the Strasbourg court has not ruled out Article 8 giving rise to a broader positive obligation for the state to provide access to personal data that goes beyond that necessary for development of one's identity.

32 European Court of Human Rights, Application No 53176/99, 7 February 2002.

33 European Court of Human Rights, Application No 42326/98, 13 February 2003.

to non-identifying information about her mother and natural family that had enabled her to trace some of her roots. The relevant French legislation, while preserving the principle that mothers were entitled to give birth anonymously, facilitated searches for information about a person's biological origins by setting up a National Council on Access to Information about Personal Origins. The applicant could use the legislation to request disclosure of her mother's identity, subject to the latter's consent being obtained. Therefore, the court held that competing interests had been appropriately balanced.

However, the dissenting judgement in *Odievre* is also important to note. It found that the requirement for consent from the mother completely sidestepped the right-to-know information:

> The mother thus has a discretionary right to bring a suffering child into the world and to condemn it to lifelong ignorance. This, therefore, is not a multilateral system that ensures any balance between the competing rights. The effect of the mother's absolute "right of veto" is that the rights of the child, which are recognized in the general scheme of the Convention (*Johansen v. Norway*, 7 August 1996; *Kützner v. Germany*, 26 February 2002), are entirely neglected and forgotten.[34]

The dissenting view, therefore, was that the French law, by giving absolute priority to the right of the mother, who retains the right to decide whether her information would be released, precluded any balancing of the interests at stake and was thus unacceptable.

In the subsequent case of *Jäggi v. Switzerland*,[35] which concerned the retrieval of DNA to establish paternity, the importance of balancing *all* of the rights without any absolute priority being given to any of them was adopted. The European Court of Human Rights also emphasized the state's role in *actively* supporting respect for private life:

> [W]hile the essential object of Article 8 is to protect the individual against arbitrary interference by the public authorities it does not merely compel the State to abstain from such interference: in addition to this negative undertaking, there may be positive obligations inherent in effective respect for private or family life.

The court further noted that the preservation of legal certainty cannot suffice in itself as grounds for depriving an applicant of the right to ascertain her or his parentage.

34 *Odièvre v. France* (European Court of Human Rights, Application No 42326/98, 13 February 2003), joint dissenting opinion of Wildhaber, Bratza, Bonello, Loucaides, Cabral Barreto, Tulkens and Pellonpää JJ (at [7]).

35 European Court of Human Rights, Application No 58757/00, 2006.

Finally, in *Godelli v. Italy* the right of an adopted child to know her biological mother was considered. The applicant was abandoned at birth, and the mother refused to be named on the birth certificate. The applicant was later adopted, but she wanted to know who her biological mother was. In 2006, she applied to have her birth certificate rectified, but her application was denied on the basis that she was prohibited from gaining access to the information concerning her origins because her mother, at the time of the birth, had not agreed to have her identity disclosed. The ECtHR held that such a denial did not strike a fair balance in weighing the competing rights and interests at stake. It stated that an individual's interest in discovering his or her parentage did not disappear with age, quite the reverse. However, the applicant's request for access to information to enable her to trace some of her roots while ensuring the protection of third-party interests was met with a blanket and final refusal without any possibility of appeal – the mother's rights and interests in preserving her anonymity were automatically given preference. The ECtHR thus held that the Italian legislation provided no means for a child who was adopted and had not been formally recognized at birth to request access to non-identifying information on his or her origins or the release of the identity of the mother. This decision was considered to overstep the country's margin of appreciation and constituted a violation of Article 8.

Deriving relevant principles

All of these decisions of the European Court of Human Rights agree that having information about one's genetic parentage is vital to a person's identity and that Article 8 of the European Convention on Human Rights is engaged in relation to this stance. The court has further emphasized that balancing the rights of *all* people is necessary. In the European context, while the court recognizes a margin of appreciation in terms of what a state may do in facilitating access, all of the previously described decisions reflect the position that there are *positive* obligations to support people seeking information, including facilitating them in their search. In the DNA paternity testing cases, it was seen as a state obligation to have some method of identifying the parent, for example, if there was refusal to undergo a paternity DNA test. In the adoption cases, the positive effects of permitting a mother to give birth anonymously – thus protecting her health and well-being at the time – was recognized; however, this did not justify a system that precluded the resultant child from finding out about his or her genetic heritage. Again, it was seen that a balance needed to be struck, and when one wasn't (usually as a consequence of a blanket denial of information) this constituted a violation of Article 8.

Balancing the rights of donor-conceived people and donors

We may now consider how these principles apply in the context of donor conception. In evaluating whether a donor-conceived person's right to information would interfere with a donor's right to privacy in an arbitrary or unlawful way, there are two broad considerations:

1 Will the interference pursue a *legitimate aim*?
2 Are the measures used to achieve that aim *proportionate* and, if so, *justified*?[36]

Again, this requires a balancing of claimed rights and a consideration of the measures that might be taken to support competing rights when such competing rights exist.

Legitimate aim?

Lawful interference with a donor's right to privacy must fulfil a legitimate aim: to meet the rights of donor-conceived people to have information about their genetic parentage. Is this legitimate? A consideration of the numerous arguments set out in prior chapters, including the search for identity, access to health information, the risk and fear of consanguineous relationships and a fight for equality and truth clearly support that there is a legitimate aim to the release of information.

Furthermore, in the human rights context, it has been shown that the search for one's identity is relevant to Articles 7 and 8 of the Convention on the Rights of the Child, Article 17 of the International Covenant on Civil and Political Rights, and Article 8 of the European Convention on Human Rights – with the last-mentioned having been considered by the United Kingdom High Court and the European Court of Human Rights. The emerging principle from these courts has been that Article 8 creates a right to deeply personal data needed to establish one's own identity, and that the state has a *positive obligation* to support people seeking such information.

In addition, pursing health information, both for an individual and for the purposes of protecting the public's health, are clearly legitimate aims. Notably, the health implications of denying access to information may also engage the 'right to health' espoused in Article 25 of the Universal Declaration of Human Rights and required by Article 12 in the International Covenant on Economic, Cultural and Social Rights. The right to health includes entitlements such as the prevention, treatment and control of diseases and access to health information.[37]

Finally, the law in a number of jurisdictions does, in fact, require the recording and release of identifying and non-identifying information to donor-conceived individuals.[38] However, it depends on where and when a donor-conceived indi-

36 *Odièvre v. France* (European Court of Human Rights, Application No 42326/98, 13 February 2003).

37 Office of the United Nations High Commissioner for Human Rights and the World Health Organization, *The Right to Health: Fact Sheet 31* (2008), pp 3–4.

38 See Chapter 4.

vidual was conceived as to whether the person can access information about his or her genetic heritage. Such laws were noted in Chapter 4. On the other hand, many jurisdictions continue to provide for anonymous donation and secrecy concerning the method of conception. For example, in many jurisdictions that have laws providing for non-anonymous donation, such laws do so only prospectively (from the date of their enactment). The reality is that a large number of donor-conceived people, even within those jurisdictions, are left without information. From the perspective of international human rights law, differential treatment based on where and when a donor-conceived child was born may represent an interference with the right to equality before the law under Article 26 of the International Covenant on Civil and Political Rights and Article 14 of the European Convention on Human Rights.

Each of these factors, independently and in combination, provides a legitimate basis for granting access to information for donor-conceived people. However, the existence of a legitimate aim for the release of confidential donor information is a *necessary* but not a *sufficient* condition to justify an interference with the donor's right to privacy. The release of information must also be justified and proportionate for achieving the aim.

Justified?

The question of whether the release of information to donor-conceived people about their donors is justified may be divided into considerations of the prospective release of information and the release of information from past donations. That is, whether all future donations should be non-anonymous and whether donor-conceived people already in existence should be given access to information even in instances where the donor was told that his donation would be anonymous.

Prospective release

Given this discussion, it is strongly arguable that under international law, pursuant to rights under the Convention on the Rights of the Child, the International Covenant on Civil and Political Rights and Article 8 of the European Convention on Human Rights, all donor-conceived people should be given access to information about their genetic origins. In fact, a prospective regime that requires disclosure of all identifying information would effectively avoid *any interference* with a donor's right to privacy, simply because those who do not wish to be identified may choose not to donate their gametes or embryos. A prospective regime would therefore be justified.

Professor Tobin, a human rights expert, in discussing the prospective release of information, agrees that a state has a positive obligation to support the realization of these rights.[39] In practice, if a state permits assisted reproductive treatment ser-

39 Tobin above n 4.

vices within its jurisdiction, the regulation of these services must ensure access to information that will allow donor-conceived individuals to realize their identity rights.[40] Tobin further states that '[a] failure to ensure this access would represent an inference with the rights of donor-conceived people for which there is no reasonable justification'.[41]

Release of information to those already born

The question of opening records of the past, where a donor may have been told he or she would remain anonymous is not easily answered because of potential competing rights and interests. If a donor consented to the release of information, there would not be any issue, and thus one 'solution' that some people suggest is asking the donor and only releasing information with consent. However, this would leave some donor-conceived people absent of information and therefore create inequity dependent on individual consents. The question becomes whether it would be justified to release information *without the consent of a donor* if he or she was previously told his or her donation would be anonymous.[42] The answer to such questions are open to debate and disagreement.

One view is that allowing for access to past donor identifying information would run 'counter to the requirement under international human rights law that any inference with the right to privacy must not only be prescribed by law, but that the law in question must be accessible and sufficiently foreseeable'.[43]

However, in the alternative, it may be argued that laws would be accessible provided there were long lead times, education and support programs prior to the introduction of a regime that fosters the release of information. Concerning 'foreseeability', it may be argued that laws permitting information release have always been 'sufficiently foreseeable'. That is, donors might never have *reasonably* expected to remain anonymous – clearly, the children created were going to grow up and there was a significant likelihood that they would seek information.

Moreover, if we are truly to engage in balancing, then we cannot take the position that the core content of the right to privacy cannot be interfered with under any circumstance. To do so means that we 'have left behind the idea that the right at stake can be weighed against competing public interests'.[44] For example, if the starting position is that a 'guarantee' of anonymity at any time in the past means that laws can never be introduced to change this position, then the balancing exercise is made redundant.[45] That is, the donor's right is given absolute priority and hence assessment of the donor-conceived person's rights is impossible.

40 Ibid.
41 Ibid., p 753.
42 Ibid.
43 Ibid., p 742 (emphasis added).
44 Tsakyrakis, above n 16 at 492.
45 The 'guarantee' itself is also questionable as there is little evidence of such guarantees other than some consent forms (not contracts) that stated recipient parents would not be told the

It is important to return to the proposition that the right to privacy may be interfered with for the protection of health or morals, or for the protection of the rights and freedoms of others – in this instance, the health, morals, rights and freedoms of donor-conceived people. The argument that legislation, which would provide access to records of the past, is not acceptable because it will alter the position donors might arguably have believed to be true – that is, anonymity in perpetuity – may not be enough of a justification to deny access to information by donor-conceived people.

As described in Chapter 5, examples of such laws may be found in Switzerland, where laws enacted in 2001 provided for the release of identifying information to those conceived via donor sperm used after the act and those conceived in the past. The laws created a register where people conceived with sperm used after the enactment of the law could access identifying information, and provided that in all past cases, physicians who have used assisted reproductive techniques using donated reproductive cells must provide information to donor-conceived people on request.

In Victoria, Australia, laws were passed in 2016 to grant access to information for all donor-conceived people regardless of when they were born, subject to the person about whom information shall be released being able to lodge a contact preference form. Breach of the preference would result in a significant fine (of approximately $7,000). In recommending the contact veto/preference model that had been proposed, the Victorian Law Reform Committee inquiry in 2012 into access to information by donor-conceived people in Australia recommended the release of information to all donor-conceived people stating:

> While the release of identifying information to donor conceived people may *potentially* cause discomfort and distress to donors (although this will not always be the case), it is certain that donor conceived people are *actually* suffering from their lack of knowledge about donors. Although debates about the consequences of releasing identifying information often focus on the suffering that donors may experience, the fact is that many donor conceived people are already suffering, in some cases quite profoundly, from not having access to this information.[46]

The balance, as presented, arguably weighs in favour of the release of information being justified on such grounds, regardless of whether the donor was 'guaranteed' anonymity by the medical professionals involved in the conception (noting that in some jurisdictions they may never really have been in the position to make

identity of the donor, and the donor would not be told the identity of the recipient parents or offspring. Many do not mention the donor-conceived person at all. In addition, in many jurisdictions there has never been a legislative guarantee of anonymity.

46 Victorian Law Reform Committee, *Inquiry into Access by Donor Conceived People to Information about the Donors*, March 2012, p 73 (emphasis added).

such a promise). Again, this does not end the balancing exercise. It still requires a consideration of any proposed method for the release of information and whether such a method would be proportionate.

Proportionality

The principle of proportionality requires that there be a reasonable relationship between a particular objective to be achieved and the means used to achieve that objective. Here the question is whether laws requiring the release of information to donor-conceived people about their donors would be a reasonable means of satisfying their rights in relation to any interference with the donor's right to privacy, or whether there is a more minimal approach that would satisfy this aim. A decision made regarding what would be a suitable method (i.e. law or other action) for the release of information needs to take into account that proportionality principles dictate that the method should impair as little as possible the right in question, be carefully designed to meet the objectives in question, and not be arbitrary, unfair or based on irrational considerations.

To this end, one may return to the suggestion that an alternative to a blanket legal requirement for retrospective release of identifying information would be to require the release of non-identifying information, and then to seek the consent of the donor regarding identifying information.[47] This method would not interfere with the right to privacy because it relies on consent and mirrors the system considered in *Odièvre*, described earlier. In effect, it would require active facilitation of searches for information about a person's biological origins but ultimately require consent to release identifying information. This method may help to meet positive obligations to support donor-conceived people born in the era of secrecy in accessing information.

However, a 'consent first' approach could leave donor-conceived people in the same position they are currently in should the donor refuse consent: that is, absent of information. Such an approach gives the donor's right absolute priority and is neither justifiable nor proportionate. In addition, it appears unacceptable that in order to contact the donor to seek his or her permission to release identifying information, a third party – be it the clinic or a regulatory authority – would be given information that pertains to the donor, while the donor-conceived person may continue to be denied such information.

Therefore, the alternative is to provide for information release subject to a contact veto or expression of contact preference.[48] The contact veto/preference system operates to protect people from unwanted contact by another person,

47 Tobin above n 4, notes it may be difficult to draw the line between identifying and non-identifying information. See also *Rose v. Secretary of State for Health and Human Fertilisation and Embryology Authority* [2002] EWHC 1593 (Admin) at [39] (Baker J).

48 S. Allan, 'Psychosocial, Ethical and Legal Arguments for and Against the Retrospective Release of Information about Donors to Donor Conceived Individuals in Australia' (2011) 19(1) *Journal of Law and Medicine* 354.

while still allowing the release of information. This system was implemented in some states of Australia (e.g. New South Wales), the United Kingdom, and some states in the United States, when release of information about past adoptions occurred.[49] In the donor conception context, it would mean that prior to information release a donor or a donor-conceived person could lodge a statement expressing the extent to which, if any, he or she would be willing to have contact with the other party. The person seeking information would have to agree not to make contact with the person who has lodged the statement, or only to engage in the type of contact preferred (e.g. email, letter or phone call). There may be penalties imposed if a veto is breached. In this sense the donor's privacy is protected by preventing interference with the intimate sphere of the person's daily life, as noted by Lord Mustell in *R v. Broadcasting Standards Commission; Ex parte British Broadcasting Corp* [2001] QB 885 at [48]:

> [T]he privacy of a human being denotes at the same time the personal "space" in which the individual is free to be itself, and also the carapace, or shell, or umbrella, or whatever other metaphor is preferred, which protects that space from intrusion.

Simultaneously, the donor-conceived person's right to privacy is respected by allowing access to information necessary to uncover the truth about an important aspect of his or her personal identity. However, donor-conceived people, under the contact veto/preference system, must also make a compromise if the donor refuses contact, as then their rights do not go so far as to be able to 'establish and to develop relationships with the donor for the development and fulfilment of their own personality'.[50] As such, the contact veto option is not arbitrary or unfair, and is based on rational considerations of how best to *balance* interests.

To ensure that donors' rights and freedoms are also protected, long lead times to the introduction of such laws, and the provision of intermediary and education services, would ensure that individual donors and donor-conceived people are supported. The contact veto/preference system would enable people to regulate their conduct in accordance with such laws to ensure that they continue to have control over the extent to which their right to privacy might be infringed.[51]

49 See further Chapter 9.

50 This right was recognized in the early decision of *X v. Iceland (Application 6825/74)* (1976) 5 DR 86 at 87 to be part of the concept of 'respect for private life' now protected by Article 8 of the European Convention on Human Rights.

51 In its recent report, the Victorian Law Reform Committee (n 46) accepted both the contact veto and counselling options as valid ways to implement a system of retrospective disclosure while also meeting the needs of donor-conceived people.

Conclusion

Clearly, there is scope for different interpretations and arguments when considering the applicability of a human rights framework to calls for information release to donor-conceived people about their donors. This chapter has argued that from a human rights perspective, there is support for such release within the Convention on the Rights of the Child, the International Covenant on Civil and Political Rights and the European Convention on Human Rights. However, the right to privacy of the donor who does not wish his or her privacy to be interfered with must also be considered.

For prospective release of information, laws that require consent to release of information prior to donating would not interfere with a donor's right to privacy because he or she could simply choose not to donate gametes. Given the rights of the child to identity, name, knowledge of parents, privacy, health and information, it is imperative that moving forward all donor-conceived people be given access to information about their biological parents and heritage.

Concerning donations made in the past, where the donor(s) may have been promised anonymity, a substantive human rights analysis also shows that legal action to release information would be legitimate and justifiable. To ensure that the system implemented to do so would be proportionate, it is suggested that the contact veto/preference system be used. This system would enable the donor to prevent unwanted contact and protect the intimate sphere of the donor's daily life, while still allowing donor-conceived people to have the information they seek. This system would be a proportionate way to *balance* the rights of those donors who wish to protect their privacy with the rights of the donor-conceived person. This approach has recently been adopted in Victoria, Australia. However, given the contentious nature of the issues surrounding retrospective release of information about donors, the matter is further explored in Chapter 9.

9 Information for all? Opening records from the past

Introduction

The previous chapters have presented arguments for and against secrecy and anonymity, and have suggested that openness about infertility, donor conception and access to information by those who seek it should be preferred. These discussions included analysis in Chapter 8 of the issues raised by information release within a human rights framework. The framework clearly supports prospective release of information – meaning a ban on donor-anonymity moving forward. In jurisdictions that currently practice anonymity, this in itself would be a big step forward. Chapter 8 also raised the issue, and included discussion, of opening records of the past.

This chapter considers the release of information to *all* donor-conceived people in light of the fact that calls for information are made by those already in existence. Discussion moves beyond the application of a human rights framework analysis to consider whether legislation that addresses acts that have already passed may be enacted, and if so, when. The release of information in the context of adoption is then considered as a way to illustrate the implementation of a contact veto/preference system and how fears did not turn into realities. Arguments that have been raised in protest of opening records from the past in relation to donor conception are also considered and responded to. Alternatives to full retrospective release of information are noted. Finally, the chapter moves to discuss what else is and would be needed, both to preserve records and in relation to the kinds of support services that might be provided.

Opening records of the past

In general, laws in all jurisdictions operate from the day they were enacted onward – that is, prospectively. This is particularly important in criminal law contexts because it would be unjust to make something criminal after the fact, exposing people to criminal sanctions and penalties for behavior already committed when it was not illegal. Many jurisdictions have provisions in their constitutions or law that prohibit 'ex post facto' criminal laws or laws that carry sanctions or penalties.[1]

Occasionally, although not commonly done, laws are acceptably passed that relate to actions undertaken in the past, where no law existed at the time, or the prior law is seen to give rise to an injustice that needs to be corrected.[2] This occurs even if such laws 'might be considered to work some injustice to one party, but are clearly required to rectify a manifest injustice to others'.[3] In Australia, for example, there has been judicial recognition of the power to pass 'retrospective' legislation,[4] the only qualification on such power being that where retrospective legislation deprives someone of a property right it must do so on just terms.[5] A number of retrospective acts have also been passed in the United Kingdom, which does so on the basis of parliamentary sovereignty.[6]

Perhaps the most analogous situation relevant to donor conception and the call for records from the past to be open, however, is that of adoption.

Analogy with adoption: opening past records

Throughout much of the twentieth century, many Western countries had legislation intended to prevent adoptees and adoptive families from knowing the identities of birth parents and vice versa. After a decline in the social stigma surrounding adoption over the past thirty years, a number of Western jurisdictions changed their laws to allow for the release of formerly sealed birth records – subject to some limitations, such as contact or information vetoes or preference forms. Examples of Australia, the United Kingdom and the United States, are discussed next to illustrate the systems put in place.

1 See for example, Brazilian Constitution, Art 5 Sect XL; Canadian Charter of Rights and Freedoms, s11(g); French Penal Code, Art 112–1; Constitution of Ireland, Art. 15.5.1; Wetboek van Strafrecht (Criminal Law) (Netherlands), Art 1; Portuguese Constitution, Art 29.

2 D.C. Pearce and R.S. Geddes, *Statutory Interpretation in Australia* 6th edition (Butterworths, Sydney, 2006), p 314.

3 *Doro v. Victorian Railways Commissioners* [1960] VR 84, Adam J at 86.

4 See *R v. Kidman* (1915) 20 CLR 425 per Isaacs, Higgins, Gavan Duffy, Powers and Rich JJ (Griffith CJ dissenting); *Millner v. Raith* (1942) 66 CLR 1; *Polyukhovich v. Commonwealth* (1991) 172 CLR 501; and *Tuitupou v. Minister for Immigration and Multicultural Affairs* (2000) 60 ALD 361.

5 *Georgiadis v. Australian and Overseas Telecommunications Corp* (1994) 179 CLR 297; *Australian Constitution Act 1901* (Cth), s 51(xxxi).

6 See for example, *Statutory Instruments (Production and Sale) Act 1996*; *Caravans (Standard Community Charge and Rating) Act 1991*; *Domestic Rates Etc. (Scotland) Act 1987*; *The Scotland Act 2012; The Wireless Telegraphy (Validation of Charges) Act 1954*. For discussion see Oonagh Gay, Retrospective Legislation Standard Note: SN/PC/06454 Last updated: 14 June 2013 (Section Parliament and Constitution Centre).

Australia

In Australia, all states and territories have legislation that sets out the rights that adopted people have to information about their birth parents, and all state and territory legislation provides adopted people with the right to identifying information about their biological parents, including their original birth certificate. All such laws were passed with retrospective effect, with the possibility of contact or identifying information vetoes being implemented in the first instance in a number of states. Over time, the veto system, which allowed relinquishing parents or adopted children to opt out of the retrospective system, has slowly been removed from those jurisdictions that had implemented it, with the option of an information veto now remaining only in South Australia.

In Queensland, Australia, identifying information and contact vetoes applied only to adoptions that occurred prior to 1991. However, in 2010 Queensland enacted the Adoption Act 2009 (Qld), which retrospectively removed the option of placing a veto on identifying information. The acting Child Safety Minister, Karen Struthers, said at the time:

> No longer will we have the most restrictive adoption laws in the country. . . . Under the new Act, which will come into force on February 1, 2010, adopted people and birth parents will have the right to identifying information regardless of when the adoption took place. The new laws balance people's right to information about their birth parents or son or daughter who was adopted, with the right of others to maintain their privacy. Currently more than 3000 Queenslanders affected by an adoption that occurred before 1991 are prevented from obtaining identifying information about their birth parents or son or daughter who was adopted. The new Act will give these people the right to access information about their own identity or that of a son or daughter for the first time. The new laws will make it possible for people to access identifying information about themselves and their birth parents but still requires them to respect another person's privacy if they do not wish to be contacted.[7]

The explanatory memorandum of the Queensland act details that people's privacy would be protected by contact vetoes and placing fines for breach of such vetoes. The act states 'this retrospective removal of their rights must be balanced with the benefits that arise by allowing other parties to those adoptions access to information about their identity, family and heritage. The change in the law also ensures that parties to adoptions are treated equally, regardless of when the

7 Queensland Government, Department of Child Safety statement reported at http://www.mysunshinecoast.com.au/articles/article-display/new-adoption-laws-for-queensland,16035, accessed 16 March 2016.

adoption occurred, as there is no longer any entitlement to object to the release of identifying information'.[8]

Similarly, Western Australia previously allowed for both contact and information vetoes; however, information vetoes were removed. In this jurisdiction, a person who wishes to gain access to information that was previously restricted by an information veto, and where a contact veto is in place, is required to be interviewed by an approved counsellor and to sign an undertaking not to contact the vetoer. Breach of the undertaking imposes penalties of $10,000 and twelve months in prison. The purpose of counselling in these instances is to ensure that the rights of all involved parties are fully understood and that people are made aware of some of the issues that may arise in the search and reunion process.[9]

In 1992, the NSW Law Reform Commission detailed the reasoning for retrospective release of information about adoptees in that state. In relation to the retrospective enactment of legislation, they reiterated that there is no legal principle preventing legislation from having retrospective operation.[10] They recognized that the law relating to information about adoption needed to deal fairly with many different people and situations and that a further complication existed, in that:

> [T]he law has to deal with the consequences of adoptions that took place over a long period of time – from the 1920s to the mid-1970s – and over that period there were major changes in adoption law and practice. The degree of secrecy that prevailed at the time of the adoption, the amount of information supplied to the parties, and the information available from existing records, all vary considerably according to the period in which the adoption took place, the agency which arranged the adoption, and other factors. It is a difficult task to design a law that will deal appropriately with all the people and situations involved in this complex picture.[11]

The NSW Law Reform Commission concluded that in passing retrospective laws in NSW that allowed identifying information release to adoptees, there had been a weighing of the competing interests of different groups of people affected by adoption, namely adopted people, birth parents, adoptive parents and other relatives.

> [T]he view that prevailed was that the law should enable adopted persons and birth parents to have the right to information, even though this did mean a

8 Adoption Bill 2009 (Qld), Explanatory Memorandum, pp 19–20, available at http://www.legislation.qld.gov.au/Bills/53PDF/2009/AdoptionB09Exp.pdf, accessed 16 March 2016.

9 The Australian Institute of Health and Welfare, *Adoptions Australia 2006–2007* (2008).

10 New South Wales Law Reform Commission, Review of the Adoption Information Act 1990, Issues Paper 7 (1992), Chapter 3, [3.14].

11 Ibid., Chapter 3.

> change from the position as it was when the adoption order was made. The interests of those who felt threatened by the new law were acknowledged by a number of measures, notably the contact veto system.[12]

The Victorian Adoption Network for Information and Self-Help Inc. (VANISH) noted that despite the initial anxiety surrounding the retrospective release of information regarding adoption, it is now well accepted as normal for adopted people to want information about their birth parents.[13]

That some jurisdictions provide the option for vetoes pertaining to contact to be placed does not take away the force of arguments that advocate for information release. The Australian Institute of Health and Welfare (AIHW) reported in 2008 that in 2006–2007 there were 2,851 applications made in relation to adoptions, 83 per cent of which were for identifying information. In that year, there were eighty contact vetoes lodged. The vast majority of information applications (both identifying and non-identifying) were made by the adopted person, at 73 per cent. Fifteen per cent were lodged by birth parents and 7 per cent by other relatives. Nine in ten adopted persons seeking identifying information were age 25 years and over, and over two-thirds were age 35 years and over.[14] The AIHW also notes that over the years, the number of applications for information far exceeded the number of vetoes lodged against contact or the release of identifying information.[15]

United Kingdom

In the United Kingdom, there have been various laws and systems implemented to allow access to identifying information about biological parents by adoptees.

Since 1930 under the Scottish Adoption Act, adopted persons age 17 and older have had the right to full access to their adoption records and original birth records.

In England and Wales, a variety of laws were adopted over a period of more than forty years, which provided for access to information and a variety of systems related to disclosure and contact. The first set of laws, passed in 1975, had followed a report in 1973 that emphasized the negative effects that secrecy and the failure to share family information had on the adopted person's identity, feelings of self-esteem and overall mental health.[16] Subsequent parliamentary debate

12 Ibid.

13 Commonwealth, Senate Committee Hansard, 3 November 2010, 65–70, Mr Cole (from VANISH).

14 The Australian Institute of Health and Welfare, *Adoptions Australia 2006–2007* (2008), p 27.

15 Ibid., p 30.

16 E.W. Carp, 'Does Opening Adoption Records Have an Adverse Social Impact? Some Lessons from the U.S., Great Britain, and Australia, 1953–2007' (2007) 10(10) *Adoption Quarterly* 3–4, 29–52, doi: 10.1080/10926750802163188.

supported access to records, but heard from opponents who worried that opening records would violate promises to birth mothers that children would not be able to trace them, lead to unwanted contact or people full of resentment 'landing' on the mother's doorstep. Such fear had led to a requirement for compulsory counselling to be required prior to being able to access birth records.

In 1989, the Children Act established a voluntary register for adopted adults and their birth relatives, which although having numerous registrants, saw little success.[17]

This act was followed in 2002 by the Adoption and Children Act, which came into effect in 2005, and gave birth relatives the right to ask an adoption support agency (ASA) to provide intermediary services. Carp explains that the ASA, on receiving an application from a birth relative, would establish the identity of the adopted person, search for him or her and, if he or she consented, disclose his or her identity to the birth relative and facilitate contact. The act also provided for contact vetoes aimed at balancing and safeguarding the rights of all members of the adoption triad (i.e. adoptees, relinquishing parent(s) and adoptive parents).[18]

In relation to the laws in the United Kingdom, Carp notes the following:

> In the 80 years since records have been open in Scotland and more than a quarter century in England and Wales, 55 per cent of the 550,000 people adopted in Scotland, England, and Wales have sought genealogical information from their records and/or established contact with a birth relative, usually the mother. . . . No cases have been reported so far of either blackmail or vindictiveness being displayed on the part of adopted people. . . . Studies have demonstrated that searches for birth family members by adopted adults have been highly successful. . . . 97 per cent of the searchers state that meeting their birth relatives made no difference in their feelings for their adoptive parents.[19]

In total, there have been more than 225,000 information and/or contact exchanges, and the sky didn't cave in.

United States

In the early 1980s in the United States, voluntary mutual consent adoption registries and intermediary services were established in a number of states to assist adoptees searching for information or contact. However, complaints that such registries and intermediaries were 'cumbersome, expensive and ineffective' led to

17 Carp notes 38,525 registrations had been received by 1991, 71 per cent (27,346) were from adopted adults and 29 per cent (11,179) were from birth relatives; however, the success rate was dismal. In England and Wales during this period, only 2.4 per cent or 912 successful matches were recorded.

18 Carp, above n 16.

19 Ibid., p 43.

calls that adoptees deserved equal rights to information. In 1998, Oregon passed laws that enabled access to information, which was amended to include a contact preference form.[20] The contact preference form permitted a birth parent a choice of one of the following three options:

1 "I would like to be contacted"
2 "I would prefer to be contacted only through an intermediary"
3 "I prefer not to be contacted at this time"

The Oregon Legislature viewed the contact preference form as a solution to the problem of how to balance the privacy rights of birth mothers against adopted adults' civil right to access their original birth records.

Carp notes that within a day after the law in Oregon went into effect,

> nearly 2,400 adoptees had applied to the Oregon Health Division's Center for Health Statistics for their original birth certificates; and by the end of June this number climbed to 3,655 and by November to 4,962 . . . of those 4,962 birth records that had been issued, 325 contact preference forms had been received, of which 214 birth mothers wanted direct contact, 21 wanted contact through an intermediary and 77 wanted no contact.[21]

He further reports that five years after the Oregon law was enacted, 8,190 adopted adults received a copy of their original birth certificates, during which time only 503 birth parents filed contact preference forms. By 2006, there were 9,129 birth certificates issued, with only 83 birth parents attaching requests for 'no contact' to the birth certificates.[22]

Current reported figures show that 9,672 birth certificates have been issued, with no adverse events.[23]

In 2000, the state of Alabama followed in the use of contact preference forms. Other states that have also adopted this approach include:

- Alaska – original birth certificate (OBC) provided, no contact vetoes/ preferences;
- Colorado – access to records and birth certificates has been available for some time but with different rules applying depending on when people were born. Amendments to the law were introduced in 2014 to eliminate different standards of access based on the date of adoption. The law also removed prior ability to place a contact preference since it was no longer seen as

20 Carp, above n 16.
21 Ibid., p 37.
22 Ibid., p 38.
23 American Adoption Congress, State Legislation Website, available at http://www.americanadoptioncongress.org/state.php#OR, accessed 16 March 2016.

necessary. Since May 2014, over 1,800 requests for original birth certificates have been processed by the State Registrar's Office;

- Maine – access legislation was enacted on January 1, 2009, allowing adults, age 18 and older, to get their OBC. Since that date, more than 1,280 OBCs have been released to adoptees. Of the limited number of birth parents completing contact preference forms, only eight have requested no contact;
- New Hampshire – since June 2005, OBCs have been available to adoptees age 18 and older. As of January 2012, over 1,572 OBCs were released. Only twelve birth parents have indicated they do not want contact. No harm has been reported.
- Rhode Island – since 1 July 2011 adult adoptees 25 years of age or older born in Rhode Island may obtain a non-certified copy of their original birth certificate. Since July 2, 2012, 759 adoptees have received their OBCs with ten birth mothers indicating on the contact preference form that they do not want contact.

Note also that in Kansas, adoption records were never sealed, and adoptees could always access information once they turned 18.

More important, where the open access subject to contact preference approach has been adopted, birth mothers' lives have not been destroyed or their privacy invaded, as had been repeatedly predicted. In the following years, there have been no reports of privacy violations or the break-up of families as a consequence of unwanted contact. Very few people placed 'no contact' preferences on their form.

The analogy to donor-conceived people

The analogy between adoptees and donor-conceived people can be drawn in relation to their search for information about their biological heritage.[24] In particular, it has been shown that donor-conceived and adopted people may share common feelings concerning being denied information about their status, being denied access to information about their biological parent(s) and or siblings, and about the secrecy that has shrouded both practices.[25] Thus, while there may also be differences concerning the circumstances of conception or birth, the search for information about genetic heritage and the reasons that underpin such a search, are shared.

Worldwide, we are seeing an increased call for identifying and non-identifying information as donor-conceived individuals reach their late twenties and onward.

24 R. Chisholm, 'Information Rights and Donor Conception: Lessons from Adoption?' (2012) 19(4) *Journal of Law and Medicine* 722.

25 A. Turner and A. Coyle, 'What Does It Mean to Be Donor Offspring? The Identity Experience of Adults Conceived by Donor Insemination and the Implications for Counselling and Therapy' (2000) 15(9) *Human Reproduction* 2041.

These donor-conceived individuals were conceived in the 1970s and 1980s. They call for a similar system as was implemented for adoption in which records have been opened and the option for a contact veto/preference is open to the biological parent. There are also many individuals who have yet to reach adulthood, or are yet to be conceived in those jurisdictions that do not have legislation that requires information recording and release, who may in the future call for information about their donors.

In an Australian Senate Committee Inquiry in 2010, Mr Egan of Family Voice Australia commented:

> if legislation establishing a national register was retrospective, contact vetoes could be put in place the way they are in adoption cases [n]o-one wants to force themselves on someone else, but they do have a right to know where they come from, who they are, who their relatives are and so on. That should include the ability to track donor siblings so you know who your brothers and sisters are. That seems to me a fundamental human right. That is the 'right to know' stuff.[26]

The author of this book has also advocated that contact vetoes or preference forms may be a way to balance competing interests when they exist, while allowing for the release of information to all donor-conceived people who seek it.[27]

Criticism and fear

Of course, similar criticism and fear has been expressed as was expressed many decades ago in relation to opening adoption records. To illustrate such criticism, I refer to a paper published by Professor Guido Pennings,[28] voicing his concerns about Victoria's recommendations to allow for access to information by all donor-conceived people, subject to a contact veto and respond to some of the points he raised.[29]

26 Commonwealth, Senate Committee Hansard, 29 October 2010, pp 19–20, Mr Egan (Family Voice Australia).

27 See for example, S. Allan, 'Psychosocial, Ethical and Legal Arguments for and Against the Retrospective Release of Information about Donors to Donor-Conceived Individuals in Australia' (2011) 19(1) *Journal of Law and Medicine* 354.

28 Guido Pennings, 'How to Kill Gamete Donation: Retrospective Legislation and Donor Anonymity' (2012) 27(10) Human Reproduction 2881–2885, first published online, accessed 10 July 2012, doi:10.1093/humrep/des218.

29 For the full response made by the author to Professor Pennings see S. Allan, 'Donor Identification 'Kills Gamete Donation'? A Response' (2012) 27(12) *Human Reproduction* 3380–3384, first published online, 2 October 2012, doi:10.1093/humrep/des351.

Professor Pennings asserts that the legislative regime suggested (and now adopted) in Victoria may be:

a *'unfair; [in that] the government comes back on a previous agreement, unilaterally. This decision can be seen as abuse of power'.*[30] However, the exact purpose of introducing legislation to allow access to information by all donor-conceived people, subject to a contact veto/preference, was to rectify a previous injustice and to balance interests of *all* those involved and affected. The purpose is to ensure that the law is in fact fair, and that injustices suffered by people are addressed via the law. There is no abuse of power when a government acts to do such a thing. The method adopted reflects the weighing and balancing of respective rights, and comes up with a solution that respects each party.

b *'ungrateful . . .[and] in a way [donors] have been cheated into donating'.*[31] Stating that releasing information is 'ungrateful' only serves as an attempt to silence the people who are calling for information. Such statements are insensitive to the interests, needs and rights of donor-conceived people, who are not ungrateful to their donors, but rather, desire information.

We are reminded, as per the discussion throughout this book, that for some, the search for information is a question of identity – having a sense of self, knowing about their heritage. There is also the desire to know familial medical history, particularly where there may be a serious heritable illness. Some discuss the risk or fear of partnering with a half-sibling or donor. Others just want to know their donor's name, or thank them, or know why the donor donated. Cutting through all of the arguments is that we should not be perpetuating a system that actively deceives people about their origins or denies them information most other people have. Openness and honesty and a right to choose for themselves. Nothing in this suggests a tenet of 'ungratefulness'.

Furthermore, if perhaps the donors were 'cheated' into donating as Professor Pennings suggests, it was by the unsustainable promise for anonymity made by clinicians or through the lack of choice given to them in the first place. Addressing this situation does not represent a lack of gratitude it represents the recognition that something has to be done to rectify what has occurred.[32]

c *'inconsistent'.*[33] Professor Pennings asserts that 'donors are counselled so as to enable them to make a well-informed decision'. He then states that the problem with retrospective legislation is that the conditions on which their decision was made will be changed. He states: '[T]he retrospective changes

30 Pennings, above n 28, p 1.
31 Ibid., p 2.
32 Allan (2012), above n 29
33 Pennings, above n 28, p 2.

inherently deny the donor's autonomy, because he (or she) has not given informed consent within the amended situation'.[34]

There are a number of problems with this argument. First, it fails to recognize the submission of donors that have reported that they do not feel that they were counselled adequately about the consequences of their donation, nor that they gave truly 'informed consent'. For example, we may refer back to the quote from the donor cited in Chapter 2 who said he didn't understand what he was doing; didn't think he had given truly informed consent; didn't believe he had a contract with anyone; just wanted to help people; and that it wasn't until he had his own children that it dawned on him that he had helped to conceive seven other children that are 'out there somewhere', that might not know, and that he had 'so many questions and fear[s he] will never know, they will never know'.[35]

Studies similarly show that donors' thoughts on the matter may change over time.[36] Some studies also indicate that the majority of donors agree to the release of medical records;[37] however, there is yet to be a system put into place that ensures these records are updated and that vital information is disseminated to offspring and recipient parents. What is certain is that there is not a blanket refusal, as such, to share information.

Professor Pennings' assertion that 'inconsistency' exists between the promise for anonymity at the time of donation and a move to now share information with donor-conceived people is therefore again not in itself reason to deny change. The purpose of engaging in the current analysis is to recognize that in the present day donors, donor-conceived people and recipient parents do in fact want to share information – be it moving forward, or in relation to information relating to past donations. However, it also recognizes the concerns of those who do not want their lives 'interfered' with, and as such explores how to *balance* competing interests and injustices in such circumstances. There are no inconsistencies involved in such a process.

d *'disrespectful'*. Professor Pennings states that 'retrospective changes imply that the donor is used solely as a means to serve someone else's interests.'[38]

34 Pennings, above n 28, p 2.
35 Donor, Victorian Assisted Reproductive Treatment Authority, 'Time to Tell Seminar', public communications by donor, parents and donor-conceived individuals (7 May 2011).
36 M.A. Crawshaw, E.D. Blyth and K.D. Daniels, 'Past Semen Donors' Views about the Use of a Voluntary Contact Register' (2007) 14(4) *Reproductive Biomedicine Online* 411; K. Daniels, E. Blyth, M. Crawshaw and R. Curson, 'Short Communication: Previous Semen Donors and Their Views Regarding the Sharing of Information with Offspring' (2005) 20(6) *Human Reproduction* 1670.
37 J.N. Robinson, R.G. Forman, A.M. Clark, D.M. Egan, M.G. Chapman and D.H. Barlow, 'Attitudes of Donors and Recipients to Gamete Donation' (1991) 6(2) *Human Reproduction* 307; P.P. Mahlstedt and K.A. Probasco, 'Sperm Donors: Their Attitudes Toward Providing Medical and Psychosocial Information for Recipient Couples and Donor Offspring' (1991) 56(4) *Fertility and Sterility* 747.
38 Pennings, above n 28, p 2.

This is somewhat of an ironic statement in that it fails to recognize that similarly one can argue that donor-conceived people are being conceived to serve someone else's interests in procreating – be that the recipient parents, the donor, or both. Professor Richard Chisholm, former Australian family law judge and commissioner of the NSW Law Reform Committee states:

> From Kant we have the maxim (sometimes called the "principle of humanity") that we should treat human beings "never merely as a means, but always at the same time as an end". . . . Historically, donor conception has been little regulated, perhaps because it was seen within a medical paradigm: as a service for the intended parents, a "treatment", so to speak, for their infertility. Although, of course, the parents will love their much-desired child intensely, we might hesitate to describe the process as designed for the benefit of the individual created by it. Arguably, donor conception in circumstances of secrecy involves the creation of human beings in circumstances where they will be misled about the truth of their genetic origins. It seems strongly arguable that such a practice violates the Kantian principle.'[39]

Perhaps, therefore, it is disrespectful not to *also* consider the children who have been created because of the use of donor gametes.

The donors

This is not to say that the rights and interests of donors should not be considered. We saw in Chapter 3 that in fact many donors actually wonder about the people they helped to conceive and also search for information. Chapter 4 revealed that some jurisdictions provide for retrospective release of information, and donors are offered support and intermediary services. In fact, in jurisdictions where support is offered, it is the general experience that donors are willing to share information.

In Chapter 8, it was also seen how respect for, and protection of, a donor's right to privacy may be given via allowing people to place contact preference statements that can limit contact to various forms (such as email, letters, etc.) or to no contact at all. This means that information can be shared, but that the intimate sphere of a person's life and relationships are controlled by that person. There is no forced contact and no forced relationship. In this sense, a balancing of needs can occur and multiple people's interests and rights met.

Any jurisdiction that moves to release information about donors from the past might also consider long lead times, consultation, education and support services to ensure that any such system is not one that is feared.

39 R. Chisholm, 'Information Rights and Donor Conception: Lessons from Adoption?' (2012) 19(4) *Journal of Law and Medicine* 722.

Alternatives to retrospective legislation requiring donor identity to be released

Nevertheless, while the arguments are strong for the release of identifying and non-identifying information to donor-conceived people who seek such information (subject to a contact preference statement if that was deemed required), it is also important to note that there are alternate positions that could be taken should such a stance be rejected. This is important as something more than the status quo – which is often no information – is needed. Two further possibilities include the release of non-identifying information to donor-conceived people born because of anonymous donation, or to contact all donors and ask them whether they consent to the release of identifying information.[40] These possibilities are explored next, noting also their shortcomings.

Release non-identifying information

An alternative to releasing identifying information to all donor-conceived people regardless of when they were born would be to provide non-identifying information to the donor-conceived person conceived with anonymous gametes in the past. Such an approach may be seen as a significant compromise; however, clearly there would be no breach of donor privacy.

That said, there are significant problems presented by this approach. First, there may be concern over what information would be deemed non-identifying. There is the risk that such a position would lead to little or no information at all, leaving people in the same position that they were in before.

In the alternative, such an approach could be seen as almost the same as releasing identifying information. For example, consider the non-identifying information available about anonymous donors in the United States in which parents are provided a long list of physical characteristics, educational background, interests, medical and family history, ethnicity, silhouettes and sometimes childhood photographs, voice recordings and explanations about why the donor donated. (Compare this to non-identifying information released elsewhere that is limited to hair colour, eye colour and other minimal descriptive factors.)

If, therefore, it was decided that *only* non-identifying information should be released for those born before a certain date, then clearly a list of what information would be available is important.

Such an approach may also suffer because it inherently precludes further contact and leaves it unknown whether such contact may be desired. As a consequence, it also precludes the possibility of a more comprehensive personal exchange of information when little information is on record.

40 Sonia Allan, Submission to the Senate Committee Inquiry into Donor conception, Access to Genetic Information and Donor Identification (2010).

Consent first approach

A second alternative to releasing identifying information to all donor-conceived people with full retrospectivity is to contact each donor and ask for his or her consent. As we saw in Chapter 4, this approach was adopted in the Netherlands for pre-2004 donors and is being considered in New South Wales, Australia.

The argument is that this approach would not interfere with the donor's right to privacy or previous assumptions about anonymity because it relies on consent. Although this is true to some extent (as it would still require *contacting* the donor), we must recognize that this approach would leave some donor-conceived people without information should the donor refuse consent. It ultimately leaves the decision in the hands of one party – who may effectively veto information sharing – and can leave the other party without any information at all.

The consent first approach is supported by the fertility industry to a greater degree than full retrospective release of information. Some doctors within the industry feel that this would be a better way for them to uphold their strong practice of confidentiality and protection of patient privacy.

Recording keeping

Whichever approach is ultimately decided on, it is of absolute importance that in the meantime all records of donor conception are preserved.

Mr Richard Egan of FamilyVoice Australia in his submission to an Australian Senate Committee inquiry said:

> You need to collect the data before clinics go out of business. Some of it will be very patchy going back to the 1970s and so on, but we need to get that information into a central registry before it is too late. Some people may not start looking for their donor father until they are 30 or 40, so these things come up at different times in people's lives. [There is] an absolute right to know.[41]

In some instances, records have been destroyed or tampered with, so there is a call for governments to protect what is left. To this end, it is important to note that different jurisdictions have taken different approaches in answering the question of how information is recorded and tracked, and where it is ultimately stored. The most effective systems seen around the world are those that require clinics or sperm banks to transfer to a central register details of all donations, details of any treatments (including recipient details) and details of a birth. This system truly allows tracking of a donation through to birth. In some nations, birth will be presumed if follow-up is not provided. Such tracking is important

41 Commonwealth, Senate Committee Hansard, 29 October 2010, 19–20, Mr Richard Egan of Family Voice Australia.

because without data recording and protection, people born as a result of donor conception may never know they are donor conceived or may find it difficult to trace information.

In relation to past records, some jurisdictions (e.g. Victoria, the Netherlands), have also moved to require the centralization of all records to ensure their ongoing existence and ability to access them.

Laws should also be introduced that prohibit the destruction or tampering with records currently in existence.

Support services

The recording and release of information relating to donor conception is not a simple matter. Gamete and embryo donors may be used by several families, which means that a donor may have multiple offspring who wish to seek information, or about whom they wish to seek information. Siblings may also wish to share and exchange information. Simply recording a donor's information in a file or on a register, and releasing it on request, may not be adequate in all situations. Some people may need support at different stages of the process, while others may feel that they do not. This final section discusses when support services may be necessary, who would provide them and who would pay for them.

When might support services be necessary?

Support services might be necessary or desirable at the point of donation (to donors), at the point of treatment (to recipients), after treatment (to recipients regarding disclosing to children) and at the point of information retrieval and exchange (to donors, recipients and to donor-conceived people). Alternatively, they may be important for some people, at some stages of donor conception or information exchange, and not at others.

Donor-conceived people may wish to have information about their donor, their conception and their siblings (if any) and may need support or intermediary services to understand the system or to make contact. There may or may not be the need for further counselling or support on the matter. Where contact vetoes/preference statements are implemented, donor-conceived people may be required to undergo some form of mandatory counselling or an information session to ensure they understand what the veto/preference statement means, so that they can make any required undertakings in law regarding such a statement.

Donors may require counselling, information or support services at the stage of donation to ensure that they understand the implications of being a donor, including that their gametes will be used in the attempt to conceive a child (or many children) and that any person born because of the donation may wish to seek information about the donor. Subsequent to gametes being used, some donors may seek counselling, information or support services when they find out that live births have occurred – this is usually sought independently. When a request for information is made by a donor-conceived person or a recipient, donors may need support in understanding how the information release system works, including, for example, what information will be released and when, and how any prior contact veto/preference would operate. However, individual donors may or may not feel that they need 'counselling' about the information release per se, or future contact. Intermediary and support services may be differentiated in this regard from counselling because they may provide a service (if required) to link or inform people, while not creating a counselling scenario.

Recipients may also require counselling, information or support services at the point of engaging in donor conception treatment, including the importance of disclosure to offspring about their status and the longer-term possibility that the offspring may wish to seek information about their donor. Ongoing education and support services in relation to how to discuss donor conception with their child, and how to support their child if they decide to seek further information, might also be provided. Similarly, if recipients wish to seek information about the donor or siblings early, support or intermediary services (in the case of parties agreeing to contact) may be necessary depending on the individuals involved. Again, they may or may not need or seek other forms of counselling to discuss their emotions or other relevant factors surrounding information sharing.

In addition, the linking that may need to occur should donors and donor-conceived people or donor-conceived siblings wish to contact each other may be complex and may, at times, also call for the provision of intermediary services (i.e. services that use an intermediary person to navigate initial contact). This may be true for all situations in which information is released – be it prospectively or retrospectively – or for individual people who require such services.

In relation to retrospective release of information, it may be important to ensure support services are available, such as:

1 mandatory or voluntary counselling (e.g. for all parties in relation to any contact veto/preference statements; or in relation to the giving/denial of consent [depending on the system that is implemented])
2 intermediary services as required (e.g. where donors and donor-conceived people wish to move to contacting each other, but require support)
3 A combination of both (1) and (2).

Discussion of what the parties expect if they are releasing or receiving information, or moving toward contact, may also be important. For example, some people may want only information and may not want to meet; others may want information and only a limited form of other contact (e.g. letter exchange, or to meet once or twice); while others may wish to form a longer lasting relationship. Helping people negotiate and discuss what their respective expectations are may be useful.

Note, the provision of such counselling, an intermediary, education or support services should not be underpinned by a view that donor conception leads to unhealthy outcomes or negative consequences for all. For many people, as discussed throughout this book, the search for information and contact is part of a healthy development of self and relationships.

Who would provide counselling, an intermediary or support services? Who would pay for them?

It is important in thinking about counselling, an intermediary and support services to consider who would provide these services, and of course, who would pay for them. To this end, Chapter 3 discussed that different jurisdictions that provide for the recording and release of information have taken different approaches to the provision of counselling and intermediary services.

Counselling at the point of donation or treatment for recipients and donors

Counselling or support at the point of donation or treatment usually occurs in the clinic or sperm bank at which the donation or treatment is taking place. Follow-up counselling, if needed, might also take place in a clinic, or might occur via an independent counsellor, social worker or psychologist (e.g. with expertise related to fertility, cancer or whatever the needs may be). The recipients usually bear the cost of such counselling, either directly, or through the fees they pay the sperm banks or clinics.

Support services at the point of seeking information

At the point of seeking information, the provider of information may differ from the provider(s) of counselling or intermediary support services. For example, information may be held on the Births, Deaths and Marriages Register but counselling or an intermediary or support services may be provided by an external registered psychologist, social worker or other experienced provider (e.g. after-adoption services or a counsellor experienced with donor conception). Who pays for such services may also differ.

In Chapter 3, we saw examples of a variety of approaches that have been adopted across those jurisdictions that provide for information release. These included approaches in which:

1 a register is operated within the state health department; no mandatory counselling or intermediary services are required; public funding pays for the register (although application fees for information may apply). (e.g. NSW, Australia, Finland);
2 a stand-alone body is responsible for the register and also for mandatory counselling, and intermediary and support services. The body also provides public education services. Public funding pays for all services (although application fees for information may apply). (e.g. the system to be implemented in Victoria, Australia);

3 a central register holds and releases information; people are referred to approved counsellors for mandatory counselling. The register is publicly funded (although application fees for information may apply). People seeking information must pay for their own counselling despite it being mandated. (e.g. Western Australia);
4 a central register holds and releases information; people may choose to undergo counselling. The register and or oversight of clinics is funded via levees placed on the industry (via registration and per cycle fees) as well as public funding. (e.g. United Kingdom HFEA);
5 a central register holds information about donors, intermediary services are outsourced to a unit experienced in providing such services. (e.g. the Netherlands);
6 a DNA register is operated by a designated service that also provides intermediary services. A fee is paid for DNA testing. Public funding supports operation of intermediary services. (e.g. UK pre-1991 register; the Netherlands);
7 a clinic/hospital may keep information on file, manages its release, and may also provide counselling or support services on their premises if required.

   a Retrieval of information and counselling of the person seeking such information may be provided for free (at least in the clinic that the author visited) (e.g. Austria); or
   b Clinic may charge a fee for both retrieving the information and any counselling services provided.

8 a clinic/hospital may keep information on file and manage its release, but do not provide counselling or intermediary support services at all. There may or may not be a fee to access information.

Anecdotally, the existence of a centralized register, with optional rather than mandatory intermediary or support services to meet the needs of the particular parties involved is the preferred approach chosen by those seeking information. Such a system is seen to be best suited to providing consistency and equity to all, and providing points of contact and support as needed. Elaborate systems that *mandate* counselling of adults who willingly want to know about each other may prove costly and unnecessary. Clinic-based control of records and release proves inconsistent across clinics and can prove burdensome and costly for those searching for information with mixed outcomes.

Because people have an interest in having information about each other, it is essential to have good systems in place to ensure ease of access to such information, support services as necessary and as little financial burden on those seeking information as possible.

Discussion

There is no evidence that donor-conceived people pose a substantive risk to their donors or their siblings. There is value in openness and honesty, and in facilitating their search for information. The desire to conduct genealogical research, the development of identity, the need for medical history and all the other reasons people search for information about their heritage is well understood and accepted in our society. It appears contradictory that such understanding is not equally applied to donor-conceived people.

On the other hand, because of the complexities that surround donor conception and promises made to donors in the past about anonymity, it may be desirable (or necessary) to enact laws that facilitate and control information release – in the sense that it might happen in a supported and guided way. For past donations, where the donation had taken place under conditions of anonymity, such an approach could be coupled with the implementation of a contact veto or contact preference system similar to that used in relation to release of information regarding adoption in some jurisdictions. Such an approach would recognize the needs of the person who is searching for information, but protect the intimate sphere of people's daily lives who do not want to have contact. It may reflect an abundance of caution, as it is unlikely that unwanted contact would take place, but it would serve to quell fears surrounding the search for information by donor-conceived people about their donors and donor-siblings (and vice versa).

No matter what approach is taken, it is important to continue to question whether, and if so to what extent, donor-conceived people as a sub-group within the population should be treated differently – and why. That is, denying them access to information about their genetic heritage appears grossly inequitable and unfair in a day and age in which access to such information is taken for granted by most people. It is also of fundamental importance to act to preserve records and to provide support services for people who search to the extent that any person who is searching requires them.

Part IV

Conclusion

10 Conclusion

The focus of this book has been to explore the history of donor conception, the secrecy and anonymity that has surrounded it, and the call for access to information by donor-conceived people about their donors and siblings. The primary questions asked have been whether 1) donor-conceived people have the right to access information about their donor and, if so, 2) whether such a right should be upheld for all donor-conceived people even if the donor was assured that he would remain anonymous. To delve deeply into such questions, the book has explored what underpins the call for information, including the psychosocial impacts of donor conception on donor-conceived people; a quest for honesty, openness and truth; calls for equity and equality; recognition of the importance of genetic heritage to many people; identity reasons; health reasons; and more. It has also detailed the experiences in searching of some donor-conceived people, recipient parents and donors. The stories of people throughout have made the quest for information more understandable and pronounced.

The consideration of the laws and practices of jurisdictions around the world provided detailed discussion of, and insight into, those jurisdictions that have recognized the right to information and that facilitate access in various forms. Examination of jurisdictions with dual-track systems, or that continue to enshrine secrecy and anonymity, enabled further consideration of what underpins the thinking about the issues raised by donor conception. Detailed examination of what has led to the respective jurisdiction's laws exposed differing emphasis. The growing number of countries that recognize a right to information do so by focusing on the person who is born because of such practices and the impact denial of information can have on his or her life. In contrast, some countries maintain secrecy and anonymity, perpetuate stigma and shame and are at times focused on supply and demand, sales and profit. I have argued throughout the book that this situation is unacceptable and needs to be resolved.

It was also seen that there are a variety of approaches to information release. Issues surrounding whether information should be held on a central register, how access should occur, whether support systems are put into place or mandated and the age at which access should occur were illustrated through consideration of systems around the world. The notification of donor-conceived people of their status was also explored, and it was again seen that there are a small but growing number of nations that have taken the step of legislating to alert people of their status.

It is appropriate to consider measures that will give people who will be born in the future access to information about their biological heritage and kin. Changes to laws would ensure that the interests of future children are paramount.

It is also important to consider what to do about those people who already exist. Many donor-conceived people who are already in existence are unable to obtain information about their donors and experience considerable distress and anguish. Others, while not feeling that they have suffered harm, still search for information. Most important, there is a clear injustice in denying them information that is seen as fundamental to their identity and that is a right that most others take for granted. Donor-conceived people's ability to access information is constrained because of decisions made before they were conceived by adults involved in the practice, including their parents, the donor and those that work within the fertility industry.

However, it is important to consider donors who may have been acting altruistically in making their donations and were promised anonymity. Many now empathize with donor-conceived people and recognize their need to know the identity of their donor. Some search themselves for information, having realized after their donation that they too longed to know more about the people they helped to create. Nevertheless, other donors may oppose information release, may be concerned about how their family relationships would be affected or may fear unwanted contact.

I have argued that one can balance interests regarding a desire to access information with a desire to protect the private sphere of one's life, by adopting the contact preference system that was used in relation to release of information in the adoption context. This system has now been made law in Victoria, Australia. The emphasis has been on ensuring that there will be no unreasonable interference in donors' lives should donor-conceived people have access to identifying information, but not to deny people their right to know more about themselves, how they came about and to whom they are related. Significant support systems have also been put into place for donors, recipients and donor-conceived people. A donor would still be contacted before information release and would have control over the extent to which contact may occur after such release, including stating the type of contact permitted, or that no contact is to occur.

Alternative systems that may lead to information release include contacting donors to ask for their consent to such release, or the release of non-identifying information. Although these systems are not preferred, they would do something more than maintaining the status quo in which donor-conceived people are denied access to any information they seek.

Whichever system might be adopted in nations moving forward, it is of fundamental importance to recognize that it is vital to preserve information. As society changes, stigma and shame may subside, different family formations may be embraced and people may become more comfortable sharing the truth. To do so, it is vital that information is not lost or destroyed.

As we look to the future, it is certain that more work needs to be done in supporting and encouraging parents to tell their children about the method of their conception, and in reducing secrecy and shame. Programs that educate and support them are very important. Similarly, donors should be counselled and supported, and programs established that help clinicians to also understand the importance of information release and to recognize that their practice moves well beyond the treatment of people seeking to have children. If such technologies are used to build families, and are seen as an acceptable means to do so, acknowledgement and care for the people who result, who have rights and interests in knowing who they are and where they came from, is essential.

Recognition that human relationships and human development will both be served by the cultivation of openness, honesty, compassion and responsiveness to donors, donor-conceived people, half-siblings and their extended families would serve everyone well. One cannot ignore that healthy human development and identity formation often include (among other things) questioning genetic origins, kinship and connections throughout the life cycle. Young children ask how they were made; as they grow up, they consider their sense of belonging within their immediate and extended family, and the world beyond them; adolescents move to construct their adult identity; questions of kinship across multiple generations arise again as people move to date, marry and parent children of their own; and as we age, we may think of the generations that have come before us and those that will follow. Our connectedness is important to us as people, in all sorts of ways. The lived experiences of donor-conceived people all over the world show us how they are denied of what most of us simply take for granted.

This book has presented arguments to not only show that there should be an end to anonymity, secrecy and shame but has also detailed different legal systems and practices that can support the process of recording and release of information, enabling people to contact each other if wanted, and truly recognizing and supporting different family formations and kinship ties. Such a move will surely benefit not only the donor-conceived people that live today, and those who will be born in the future, but also their extended families, donors, recipients and generations to come.

Index

For Product Safety Concerns and Information please contact our EU
representative GPSR@taylorandfrancis.com
Taylor & Francis Verlag GmbH, Kaufingerstraße 24, 80331 München, Germany

www.ingramcontent.com/pod-product-compliance
Ingram Content Group UK Ltd.
Pitfield, Milton Keynes, MK11 3LW, UK
UKHW020012200926
475702UK00014B/1850
9781138363496